Media Law in Australia

Media Law in Australia

Third Edition

Lesley Hitchens AM

This book was originally published as a monograph in the International Encyclopaedia of Laws/Media Law.

Founding Editor: Roger Blanpain
General Editor: Frank Hendrickx
Volume Editors: Peggy Valcke & Eva Lievens

Wolters Kluwer

Published by:
Kluwer Law International B.V.
PO Box 316
2400 AH Alphen aan den Rijn
The Netherlands
E-mail: lrs-sales@wolterskluwer.com
Website: www.wolterskluwer.com/en/solutions/kluwerlawinternational

Sold and distributed by:
Wolters Kluwer Legal & Regulatory U.S.
920 Links Avenue
Landisville, PA 17538
United States of America
E-mail: customer.service@wolterskluwer.com

ISBN 978-94-035-1449-9

e-Book: ISBN 978-94-035-1459-8
web-PDF: ISBN 978-94-035-1469-7

The Author

Lesley Hitchens AM is an Emerita Professor at the University of Technology Sydney (Australia) having been Dean of the Faculty of Law from October 2021 Acting Provost until retirement. She commenced her academic career in the United Kingdom working at the universities of Leicester and Warwick. Upon returning to Australia, Lesley took up an academic position with the University of Melbourne and later with the University of New South Wales. She has also held visiting positions at universities in the UK including the University of Manchester and Birkbeck College.

Prior to commencing her academic career, Lesley practised as a commercial lawyer for seven years, first in Sydney with Allens and later with Herbert Smith (now Herbert Smith Freehills) in London.

Her main research area is communications regulation, and she has focused on broadcasting and electronic media regulation. A particular focus of her work has been ownership and control and diversity regulation, and in 2006 she published *Broadcasting Pluralism and Diversity*, a comparative study of policy and regulation covering the United States, the United Kingdom, and Australia. She is also the co-author of a text examining English media laws, *Media Law: Text, Cases and Materials.* Her research has also focused on content regulation, especially ethical standards and the place of commercial content, and regulatory responses to the media broadband environment. Lesley has been involved in a number of Europe-based projects.

The Author

Table of Contents

List of Abbreviations

AANA	Australian Association of National Advertisers
ABA	Australian Broadcasting Authority
ABC	Australian Broadcasting Corporation
ABC Act	Australian Broadcasting Corporation Act 1983 (Cth)
ACCC	Australian Competition and Consumer Commission
ACMA	Australian Communications and Media Authority
ACT	Australian Capital Territory
ALRC	Australian Law Reform Commission
APC	Australian Press Council
BSA	Broadcasting Services Act 1992 (Cth)
BVOD	Free-to-air catch up services
CA	Communications Alliance
CA(UK)	Court of Appeal (United Kingdom)
CB	Community Broadcasting
CCA	Competition and Consumer Act 2010 (Cth)
CRB	Commercial Radio Broadcasting
CTB	Commercial Television Broadcasting
Cth	Commonwealth of Australia
DIGI	Digital Industry Group Inc.
Espionage Act	National Security Legislation Amendment (Espionage and Foreign Interference) Act 2018 (Cth)
FCA	Federal Court of Australia
FOI (CTH)	Freedom of Information Act 1982 (Cth)
HCA	High Court of Australia
HL(UK)	House of Lords (United Kingdom)
Information Code	Australian Code of Practice for Disinformation and Misinformation
MEAA	Media, Entertainment and Arts Alliance
NBN	National Broadband Network
NITV	National Indigenous Television Service

List of Abbreviations

NSW	New South Wales
NSWCA	New South Wales Court of Appeal
NSWIRC	NSW Industrial Relations Commission
NSWSC	New South Wales Supreme Court
NT	Northern Territory
OAIC	Office of the Australian Information Commissioner
OSA 2021	Online Safety Act 2021 (Cth)
PAS Act	Communications Legislation Amendment (Prominence and Anti-siphoning) Act 2024
QLD	Queensland
SA	South Australia
SASC	South Australia Supreme Court
SBS	Special Broadcasting Service
SBS Act	Special Broadcasting Service Act 1991 (Cth)
SCAG	Standing Council of Attorney's-General
STB	Subscription television broadcasting
SVOD	Subscription video on demand
TAS	Tasmania
VCC	Victorian County Court
VSC	Victorian Supreme Court
VSCA	Victorian Supreme Court of Appeal
VIC	Victoria
WA	Western Australia
WASC	Western Australia Supreme Court

Broadcasting Codes of Practice

ABC, Code of Practice (January 2024)	Australian Broadcasting Corporation, Code of Practice (1 January 2024), https://live-production.wcms.abc-cdn.net.au/ef432a28208d110deef1feec3ec5ee61 (accessed 23 July 2024.
ACTA, Community Television Broadcasting Codes of Practice (June 2011)	Australian Community Television Alliance, Community Television Broadcasting Codes of Practice (9 June 2011), https://www.acma.gov.au/sites/default/files/2019-10/Community%20Television%20Broadcasting%20Codes%20of%20Practice%20%28ACTA%29.pdf (accessed 23 July 2024).

ANRA, Open Narrowcast Radio Codes of Practice (2011)	Australian Narrowcast Radio Association, Open Narrowcast Radio Codes of Practice (2011), https://www.acma.gov.au/publications/2019-10/rules/anra-codes-practice-open-narrowcast-radio (accessed 23 July 2024).
ASTRA, Subscription Broadcast Television Codes of Practice (2013)	Australian Subscription Television and Radio Association, Subscription Broadcast Television Codes of Practice (2013), http://www.astra.org.au/pdf/news/ASTRA_Subscription_Broadcast_Television_Codes_of_Practice_2013_with_new_Appendix_A.pdf (accessed 23 July 2024).
ASTRA, Subscription Narrowcast Television Codes of Practice (2013)	Australian Subscription Television and Radio Association, Subscription Narrowcast Television Codes of Practice (2013), http://www.astra.org.au/pdf/news/ASTRA_Subscription_Narrowcast_Television_Codes_of_Practice_2013_with_new_Appendix_A.pdf (accessed 23 July 2024).
ASTRA, Subscription Narrowcast Radio Codes of Practice (2013)	Australian Subscription Television and Radio Association, Subscription Narrowcast Radio Codes of Practice (2013), http://www.astra.org.au/pdf/news/ASTRA_Subscription_Narrowcast_Radio_Codes_of_Practice_2013_with_new_Appendix_A.pdf (accessed 23 July 2024).
ASTRA, Open Narrowcast Television Codes of Practice (2009)	Australian Subscription Television and Radio Association, Open Narrowcast Television Codes of Practice (2009), https://www.acma.gov.au/sites/default/files/2019-10/ASTRA%20Open%20Narrowcast%20Television%20Codes%20of%20Practice%202009.PDF (accessed 23 July 2024).

List of Abbreviations

CRA, Commercial Radio Code of Practice (March 2017)	Commercial Radio Australia, Commercial Radio Code of Practice (15 March 2017, incorporating changes from March 2018), https://www.commercialradio.com.au/CR/media/CommercialRadio/Commercial-Radio-Code-of-Practice.pdf (accessed 23 July 2024).
CBAA, Community Radio Broadcasting Codes of Practice (October 2008)	Community Broadcasting Association of Australia, Community Radio Broadcasting Codes of Practice (23 October 2008), https://www.cbaa.org.au/sites/default/files/media/Community%20Radio%20Broadcasting%20Codes%20of%20Practice%20-%20Print%20Friendly%20PDF_w_appendices.pdf (accessed 23 July 2024).
FTV, Commercial Television Industry Code of Practice (2015)	Free TV Australia, Commercial Industry Code of Practice (1 December 2015, amended 2018), https://www.freetv.com.au/wp-content/uploads/2019/07/Free_TV_Commercial_Television_Industry_Code_of_Practice_2018.pdf (accessed 23 July 2024).
SBS, Code of Practice (July 2021)	Special Broadcasting Service, Code of Practice (July 2021, amended 4 April 2022), https://www.sbs.com.au/aboutus/wp-content/uploads/2023/04/sbs_code_of_practice_2021_amended_2022.pdf (accessed 23 July 2024).

General Introduction

§1. General Background of the Country

I. Political and Legal System of the Country

1. Australia is a constitutional monarchy and a federal nation. King Charles III (the King of the United Kingdom) is the head of state, but this is primarily a formal and ceremonial role. The King's powers are delegated to the Governor-General, her representative in Australia. Formally known as the Commonwealth of Australia, the federation was formed in 1901 and comprises six states (formerly British colonies). The Australian Constitution establishes the national parliament, the Australian Parliament, and sets out the specific heads of power of the Australian Government (also known as the Federal Government).[1] Each state has a state constitution and its own government, which like the Federal Government, has three arms: legislature, executive, and the judiciary. The state governments are allowed to pass laws on any matter provided that it is not one of the Australian Government's specific heads of power. Australia is a common law system.

2. The Australian Constitution specifically reserves to the Australian Government the power to make laws over 'postal, telegraphic, telephonic, and other like services'.[2] The High Court of Australia (HCA) has held that this power permits the Federal Government to make laws for radio and television broadcasting, and it has continued to be used by the Federal Government to regulate online content.[3] The Australian Constitution does not provide for any direct legislative power over the print media.

3. At the Federal level, there are three levels of the court exercising federal jurisdiction and determining matters under Commonwealth legislation:

- The High Court of Australia (HCA).
- The Federal Court of Australia.
- The Federal Circuit and Family Court of Australia.

---

1. Australian Constitution, s. 51, http://www.aph.gov.au/About_Parliament/Senate/Powers_practice_n_procedures/Constitution. Legislation that is passed by the Parliament of Australia is referred to as Commonwealth legislation. Therefore, Commonwealth legislation is identified by the abbreviation, 'Cth'.
2. Australian Constitution, s. 51(v).
3. *See R v. Brislan; ex parte Williams* (1935) 54 CLR 262 (HCA) and *The Herald and Weekly Times and anor v. The Commonwealth of Australia* (1966) 115 CLR 418 (HCA).

4. The HCA is the highest court in Australia, and it also deals with constitutional matters and some appeals from the Federal court, and states and territories courts. There are also specialist tribunals. With some exceptions, most states and territories have three levels of courts:

- Supreme Court.
- District or County Court.
- Local Court.

II. Geography and Population

5. Australia's physical and demographic features pose challenges for media and communications policy and delivery. Australia's population is estimated to be 26,966,789 as of 31 December 2023.[4] Geographically, Australia is a very large island continent – the world's sixth-largest country – but it is also a very dry continent, and this has led to the population mostly settling in coastal areas.[5] Relative to the size of the country, the population is small so the media market is also small. Over half of the population is located in three capital cities on the east coast of Australia – Sydney, Brisbane, and Melbourne. The delivery of media and communication services across Australia is difficult because, outside capital cities, the country is quite sparsely populated.

III. Social and Cultural Values

6. There is no dominant or identifying social or cultural identity, although the concepts of equality, respect, and freedom are central to Australian values whilst belief in a 'fair go' and a sense of mateship are seen as Australian characteristics.[6] Australia is shaped by its Indigenous and British colonial history. Indigenous Australians are one of the oldest continuing living cultures in the world, although reconciliation with First Nations peoples remains unresolved. The nation has actively encouraged immigration from a broad range of countries with around 30% of the population born overseas. This has had a strong influence on the cultural diversity of Australia. Australia has a commitment to a multicultural Australia which values cultural and linguistic diversity within the law and in keeping with the maintenance

4. Australian Bureau of Statistics, https://www.abs.gov.au/statistics/people/population/national-state-and-territory-population/dec-2023 (accessed 13 Jul. 2024).
5. Australian Government, *About Australia*, http://australia.gov.au/about-australia/our-country (accessed 27 Apr. 2012).
6. Australian Government, *Australia in Brief* (2021), chrome-extension://efaidnbmnnnibpcajpcglclefindmkaj/https://www.dfat.gov.au/sites/default/files/australia-in-brief-2021.pdf (accessed 19 Dec. 2022). *See also Australian Values Statement*, https://immi.homeaffairs.gov.au/help-support/meeting-our-requirements/australian-values (accessed 19 Dec. 2022).

of democratic values.[7] The recognition of the cultural diversity of Australia is also reflected in the organization of media, and radio and television services are available which provide multilingual programming.

§2. The Media Landscape

I. Overview of Media Markets and Main Actors

7. The Australian media market is heavily concentrated.[8] In the early part of the nineteenth century, the newspaper market was notable for the number of newspaper titles and the diversity of ownership, but over time, the number of titles has reduced considerably, as well as the number of owners, although online publishing has seen the entry of some international titles. There are currently only two national English language daily newspapers, *The Australian* and the *Australian Financial Review,* owned by News Corp Australia and Nine Entertainment[9] respectively, and Sydney and Melbourne are the only two cities to have competing local titles, whilst the remaining capital cities have only one daily title, each with an online presence. Overall, there are only ten newspaper titles (in addition to the national titles) covering metropolitan and state-wide markets.[10] Ownership of these titles rests with only three owners: Nine, News Corp Australia (part of the Murdoch family's global corporate group), and Seven West Media. Seven West Media owns two titles, both based in Western Australia (WA). There are a number of regional newspaper titles '… of varying size and quality, but with little impact or newsgathering capacity beyond their own area'.[11] Four companies essentially control the newspaper market: News Corp Australia controls 54.4% market share; Nine controls 16.1%; Seven West Media 5.6%; and Australian Community Media 8.2%.[12]

7. Australian Government, *Multicultural Australia: Australia's multicultural statement* (2017), chrome-extension://efaidnbmnnnibpcajpcglclefindmkaj/https://www.homeaffairs.gov.au/mca/Statements/english-multicultural-statement.pdf (accessed 19 Dec. 2022).
8. Australian Government, *Convergence Review, Discussion Paper: Media Diversity, Competition and Market Structure*, (2011), 12. *See also* IbisWorld, *Newspaper Publishing in Australia* (March 2022), 22, IbisWorld, *Radio Broadcasting in Australia* (August 2022), 21 and IbisWorld, *Free-to-Air Television Broadcasting in Australia* (August 2022), 22.
9. The newspapers now controlled by Nine Entertainment Co (Nine) were owned by Fairfax Media until December 2018 when the two companies merged. Fairfax Media had been publishing newspapers for 177 years. As a result of the merger, the name no longer exists. The merger was made possible by the relaxation of cross-media rules in 2017 (*see* Part IV, s. 3).
10. IbisWorld, *Newspaper Publishing in Australia* (July 2024), 29.
11. Australian Government, *Report of the Independent Inquiry into the Media and Media Regulation*, https://webarchive.nla.gov.au/awa/20120320233242/http://pandora.nla.gov.au/pan/132662/20120321-1002/www.dbcde.gov.au/digital_economy/independent_media_inquiry.html (accessed 22 Dec. 2022), para. 3.10. *See also* IbisWorld, *Newspaper Publishing in Australia* (March 2022), 22.
12. In mid-2019, Nine Entertainment sold the Fairfax rural and regional newspapers, around 140 titles, to Australian Community Media. Since 2018, Australian Community Media has sold or ceased publication of around 60 titles: IbisWorld, *Newspaper Publishing in Australia* (July 2024), 55-6.

8. There are two public broadcasters who provide free-to-air television, radio and digital services: the Australian Broadcasting Corporation (ABC) and the Special Broadcasting Service (SBS). The ABC fulfils a more traditional public service broadcasting role, whilst the SBS offers a more specialized service providing multilingual and multicultural programmes, including the National Indigenous Television (NITV) service. Both broadcasters provide a national service, and the ABC also provides local and regional radio services. Both services operate steaming, catch-up, and podcasting services.

9. Commercial radio and television services dominate broadcasting provision. Three networks – the Seven, Nine, and Ten Networks – provide commercial television broadcasting services in the metropolitan markets. Through affiliation agreements with regional licensees, they also provide the bulk of the programming to the regions. Although broadcasting licences are organized on a regional basis, with control over metropolitan markets and affiliation agreements with regional licensees, most services are essentially national in their programming output. Commercial free-to-air television services attract 73.2% market share as compared with 12.6% for ABC); and, 5.5% for SBS, and the balance is held by regional broadcasters.[13] Prior to digital services becoming available, the mainland capital cities and some regional areas had access to three commercial television stations, whilst most other areas had access to two. Although digital transmission has meant that the number of channels available has increased, the commercial digital channels do not tend to offer new content.

10. As of June 2021, there were 276 Commercial Radio Broadcasting (CRB) services operating across Australia, although almost all services are part of a network.[14] Four groups control around 60% of the market share, the ABC 20.7%, and the balance held by small companies.[15] The commercial radio industry, through their industry body, Commercial Radio Australia, has developed a Radio App that enables around 350 commercial radio stations (including ABC and SBS services) to be streamed.

11. Subscription broadcasting services did not begin in Australia until 1995, and they still occupy a relatively small share of the market, although that is changing with the arrival of subscription video on demand (SVOD) and IPTV services. Like other parts of the media sector, subscription services is also a highly concentrated segment. Foxtel, the main subscription service provider, is owned by News Corporation (65% interest) and Telstra Corporation Limited, the main telecommunications provider in Australia (35%). Over the past five years, the market for SVOD services such as Netflix, Stan, and Disney+ has grown significantly. Whilst Foxtel is the largest provider of subscription services in the sector, competition from the

13. IbisWorld, *Free-to-Air Television Broadcasting in Australia* (June 2024), 53.
14. Australian Communications and Media Authority, *Annual Report 2020-21*, 40.
15. IbisWorld, *Radio Broadcasting in Australia* (June 2024), 52.

SVOD services has challenged its traditional dominance and market share, forcing it to revise prices and offerings.[16] Netflix entered the Australian market in March 2015, and Disney+ in November 2019. In January 2015, Stan, an Australian SVOD, commenced services. Initially, it was owned jointly by Fairfax Media and Nine, but following their merger, it is now wholly-owned by Nine. Foxtel has a market share of 43.5%. Foxtel, along with Netflix (17.7%), Stan (7.1%), and Disney+ (5.7%) dominate this market, although, over the past ten years, Foxtel's market share has halved because of the new competition.[17]

12. Community broadcasting services are non-profit-making services intended to meet community needs, whether a local community or some community interest. As of June 2021, there were 360 community radio licences, 68 of which were remote Indigenous broadcasting services. The main type of service offering tends to be local community services (51%), followed by Aboriginal and Torres Strait Islander community interests (25%), whilst the balance is mainly spread between religious, special interest, ethnic, and music community interests. There are five community television services.[18]

II. Infrastructure

13. The main television and radio delivery platform remains the free-to-air wireless platform, although free-to-air viewing is in decline.[19] The switch from analogue to digital television services across Australia was completed in December 2013. Radio services continue to be available in analogue form with extensive digital simulcasting and additional radio services provided by digital transmission. There are no plans in place for the switching off of analogue radio. In relation to radio services, digital is seen as a supplementary technology. Most free-to-air services also provide streaming and catch-up services.

14. The main delivery platform for subscription services is a cable with satellite used where cable infrastructure is not available or practical. Subscription services are also delivered via broadband and mobile technology, and this sector, SVOD and free-to-air catch-up services (BVOD), is now growing quickly. Three-quarters of Australians now live in households with at least one SVOD service whilst around 50% have access to two or more services.[20]

16. IbisWorld, *Pay Television and Internet Protocol Television Services in Australia* (June 2024), 12.
17. IbisWorld, *Pay Television and Internet Protocol Television Services in Australia* (June 2024), 54-5.
18. Australian Communications and Media Authority, *Communications and Media in Australia: Supply and use of services, 2019-2020* (April 2021), Appendix C.
19. Australian Communications and Media Authority, *Communications and Media in Australia: Supply and use of services, 2019-2020* (April 2021).
20. Australian Communications and Media Authority, *Communications and Media in Australia: Supply and use of services, 2019-2020* (April 2021), 23–24.

15. Free-to-air television is no longer the dominant source for viewing. In 2021, SVOD services attracted more viewing by adult Australians (58%) whilst free-to-air fell to 50%. BVOD viewing also increased to 37%.[21] Radio listening remains reasonably steady, although with some decline. In June 2021, 77% of Australian adults listened, although there is increasing use of music streaming services (67%).[22] Accessing the Internet is now almost universal and around 84% of users access the internet multiple times a day, especially via a mobile phone.[23]

III. Technological and Economic Developments in the Media Markets

16. Broadband development was slow in Australia. In response to concerns about speed and lack of provision in the rural and regional areas, the Australian Government, in 2009, commenced the development of the National Broadband Network (NBN) which was intended to provide a fibre-to-the-premises wholesale broadband network to 90% of premises. The remaining 10% (representing the more remote areas) would be provided with broadband delivered via wireless and satellite. The construction of the network was to take place over an eight-year period. Following a change of government in 2013 a new Statement of Expectations was delivered to NBN Co (the Government-owned company responsible for the construction of the NBN) which required the NBN to use a mix of technologies in the most cost-effective manner for the network development which meant not all households would receive a fibre-to-the-premises network, whilst download speed expectations were reduced.[24] A further change in Government in mid-2022 resulted in a new Statement of Expectations aligning more closely with the original purpose of the NBN.[25] NBN Co will stay in public ownership for the foreseeable future and whilst the company is expected to be economically efficient, this should not be at the expense of its fundamental purpose to provide fast, reliable, and affordable access to broadband. As a result of the Statement of Expectations, and increased government investment, customers will be able to access significantly faster download speeds.[26] There will also be a renewed focus on improving regional and remote

---

21. Australian Communications and Media Authority, *Communications and media in Australia: How we watch and listen to content* (June 2022), https://app.powerbi.com/view?r=eyJrIjoiOWEzMzY1ZDktNzhiYi00ZWY0LTk1MTAtNmY https://www.acma.gov.au/publications/2022-06/report/communications-and-media-australia-how-we-watch-and-listen-content (accessed 23 Dec. 2022).
22. Australian Communications and Media Authority, *Communications and media in Australia: How we watch and listen to content* (June 2022), https://www.acma.gov.au/publications/2022-06/report/communications-and-media-australia-how-we-watch-and-listen-content (accessed 23 Dec. 2022).
23. Australian Communications and Media Authority, *Communications and media in Australia: How we use the internet* (December 2022), *https://www.acma.gov.au/publications/2022-12/report/communications-and-media-australia-how-we-use-internet*, (accessed 23 Dec. 2022).
24. NBN Co Ltd, *Statement of Expectations* (24 Aug. 2016), https://www2.nbnco.com.au/content/dam/nbnco2/2018/documents/Policies/soe-shareholder-minister-letter.pdf (accessed 23 Jan. 2019).
25. NBN Co Ltd, *Statement of Expectations* (19 Dec. 2022), https://www.nbnco.com.au/content/dam/nbn/documents/about-nbn/policies/statement-of-expectations-2022.pdf (accessed 4 Jan. 2023).
26. NBN Co Ltd, *NBN Corporate Plan 2023*, 13, https://www.nbnco.com.au/content/dam/nbnco2/documents/NBN-Co-Corporate-Plan-2023.pdf (accessed 4 Jan. 2023).

access and speeds. As of December 2022, 8.5 million premises (residential and business) were connected to the network whilst the number of premises ready to connect was 12.1 million in June 2022.[27]

17. The Australian media industry, like other countries, is experiencing challenges as the business model for media changes. The print media faces declining circulation and advertising, as well as the impact of increased online advertising, the reluctance of readers to pay for access to content online, and increased use of social media platforms to access news.[28] The latter's impact has been diminished to an extent by the News Media Bargaining Code, introduced in 2021 (*see* Part IV, section 5 *infra*). The commercial broadcasting industry is also facing the challenge of declining advertising revenue and competition from the growth of online and subscription media services.[29] Radio listening has suffered less due to the habit of listening to the radio in the car.[30] Print, radio, and television media no longer account for the majority of advertising expenditure in Australia. Online advertising expenditure increased from less than AUD 1 billion in 2005 to AUD 8.8 billion in 2018, accounting for 53% of advertising in 2018. Print media advertising declined from 55% in 2003 to 11% in 2018.[31] Free-to-air television broadcasters have been able to recover some of their declining advertising revenue through the operation of BVOD services which carry advertising, however, this is not sufficient to recoup the lost revenue from traditional television advertising.[32]

18. Despite the impact of changing media markets and technological developments, there has been little interest demonstrated by successive governments to respond holistically to these policy and regulatory challenges. Between 2010 and 2012 two government reviews were undertaken: the Convergence Review and an Independent Inquiry into Australian media. The Review and Inquiry both delivered their final reports in April 2012. There was some overlap between the Review and the Inquiry, although the latter was more focused on the effectiveness of media codes of practice and the role of the Australian Press Council (APC). Apart from one half-hearted attempt to introduce legislation responding to the recommendations, which failed, the recommendations of the Review and Inquiry have laid dormant.

---

27. NBN Co Ltd, *NBN Corporate Plan 2023*, 8, https://www.nbnco.com.au/content/dam/nbnco2/documents/NBN-Co-Corporate-Plan-2023.pdf (accessed 4 Jan. 2023).
28. IbisWorld, *Newspaper Publishing in Australia* (March 2022), 11–13.
29. IbisWorld, *Free-to-Air Television Broadcasting in Australia Industry Report* (August 2022), 11–12 and IbisWorld, *Radio Broadcasting in Australia Industry Report* (August 2022), 11–12.
30. IbisWorld, *Radio Broadcasting in Australia Industry Report* (August 2022), 12.
31. Australian Competition and Consumer Commission, *Digital Platform Inquiry Final Report* (2019), https://www.accc.gov.au/focus-areas/inquiries-finalised/digital-platforms-inquiry-0 (accessed 6 Jan. 2023), 121.
32. Australian Government, *Prominence Framework for connected TV devices Proposal Paper* (December 2022), 23.

19. Media ownership and control is one area where there has been reform. In 2017, the Federal Government relaxed the rules, including the removal of cross-media ownership rules.[33] However, in order to gain support from Parliament for the media ownership rule changes, the Government agreed to institute an inquiry into the impact of digital search engines, social media platforms, and other digital content aggregation on competition in media and advertising services markets. The inquiry was also to focus particularly on the supply of news and journalistic content, and the implications for media content creators, advertisers, and consumers.

20. The Australian Competition and Consumer Commission (ACCC) was charged with the inquiry in December 2017 and produced its final report in July 2019.[34] The report focused on the digital platforms operated by Facebook and Google because the amount of time Australians spent on these platforms dwarfed all other websites or apps. Both platforms were essentially able to act as gatekeepers.[35] Amongst its recommendations, the ACCC proposed a voluntary code of practice to be developed by the digital platforms to govern business relations with news media companies (*see* Part IV, section 5 *infra*) and a code to regulate misinformation and disinformation (*see* Part III, Chapter 3, section 8 II *infra*).

§3. Sources of Media Law

21. As a common law jurisdiction, the sources of law for media will be found in both statute and case law. Industry regulation also plays a special role in the broadcasting sector. Whilst the regulation of radio and television services, and now online services, is primarily a matter of federal law, the Australian Constitution does not confer any direct legislative power on the Australian Government for the print media. Regulation of the print media is primarily a matter for state and territory governments. The print media are not in general subject to any specific laws, although some general laws, such as those dealing with defamation and contempt, will have particular relevance to the print media, and also, to the broadcast media. Some states, such as New South Wales (NSW), require newspapers to provide identification details of the title's printer and publisher.[36] The Copyright Act 1968 (Cth), section 195CD requires one copy of all newspapers to be deposited with the National Library of Australia, whilst a number of state governments also require deposits with their state libraries.[37]

33. *See* Part IV.
34. Australian Competition and Consumer Commission, *Digital Platforms Inquiry Final Report* (July 2019), https://www.accc.gov.au/focus-areas/inquiries-finalised/digital-platforms-inquiry-0 (accessed 6 Jan. 2023).
35. Australian Competition and Consumer Commission, *Digital Platforms Inquiry Final Report* (July 2019), https://www.accc.gov.au/focus-areas/inquiries-finalised/digital-platforms-inquiry-0 (accessed 6 Jan. 2023), 6.
36. Printing and Newspapers Act 1973 (NSW), s. 4.
37. *See*, for example, Library Act 1939 (NSW), Pt 3A, now includes electronic publication.

22. The main legislative instrument governing the broadcasting sector is the Broadcasting Services Act 1992 (Cth) (BSA). The BSA provides the main source of regulation for all broadcasting services, including technical spectrum planning, licensing, ownership and control, and content regulation. It also contains provisions regulating online content. The Enhancing Online Safety Act 2015 (Cth) established the Office of the eSafety Commissioner, introduced a complaints process for cyber-bullying material aimed at an Australian child, a complaints system for the non-consensual sharing of intimate images, and transferred the administration of the online content scheme under the BSA from the Australian Communications and Media Authority (ACMA) to the eSafety Commissioner. The Online Safety Act 2021 (Cth) (OSA 2021) put in place greater protections and standards and increased the Commissioner's investigative and enforcement powers. Although the BSA has relevance to the public broadcasters, there are also specific statutes governing their operations. The Australian Broadcasting Corporation Act 1983 (Cth) (ABC Act) governs the ABC and the Special Broadcasting Service Act 1991 (Cth) (SBS Act) governs the SBS.

23. Other communications-specific Federal legislation will also have an impact on the broadcasting sector:

- The Radiocommunications Act 1992 (Cth) regulates technical planning, and allocation of the radio frequency spectrum. This includes broadcasting, although some aspects of this are also covered in the BSA. The BSA is responsible for spectrum planning in what is termed the 'broadcasting services bands'. For broadcasting services delivered outside the 'broadcasting services bands', the Radiocommunications Act will be relevant.
- The Telecommunications Act 1997 (Cth) deals with facilities and services which carry telecommunications, and this legislation will be relevant to some of the delivery platforms used to carry broadcasting services.

24. Although the BSA incorporates an ownership and control regulatory scheme for broadcasting, the Competition and Consumer Act 2010 (Cth) (CCA), the general competition and merger statute, will also apply to the broadcast and print media industries.

25. Under the Foreign Acquisitions and Takeovers Act 1975 (Cth), the media sector (newspapers, radio and television, and their associated online sites) is regarded as a sensitive sector and so foreign investment in the media sector will be affected by this legislation (*see* Part IV, section 4 *infra*).

26. Industry regulation also plays a part in both the print media and broadcast media sectors and so the codes developed through these industry schemes will be relevant also. A self-regulatory scheme in relation to print media (and their online sites) is administered through the APC and complaints are determined in accordance with the Council's Standards of Practice (*see* Part II, Chapter 6, section 1 *infra*). The Media Entertainment and Arts Alliance (MEAA), the body representing journalists and those employed in the media industry, also operates a complaints scheme in relation to member journalists (*see* Part II, Chapter 6, section 2 *infra*). The Alliance's Journalist Code of Ethics applies only to members of the Alliance.

27. A co-regulatory scheme, established under the BSA, operates in relation to the broadcasting sector. This means that the industry bodies representing each category of broadcasting service develop a code of practice. The codes deal mainly with content regulation (and are considered further in Part III, Chapter 3 *infra*). The codes will be relevant to the determination by broadcasters of complaints and will also be applied by the statutory regulatory body, the Australian Communications and Media Authority (ACMA) if a matter falls for its determination. The codes are registered by the ACMA. A co-regulatory scheme applies to the regulation of online content established under the OSA 2021. The Communications Alliance (CA) has responsibility for the codes of practice against which complaints are determined (*see* Part III, Chapter 3, section 8 *infra*).

Part I. Freedom of Speech

§1. Introduction

28. Australia, as a liberal democracy, is unusual in not having an express guarantee of free speech. Despite its written constitution, there is no charter of human rights. It follows that there are no special guarantees of media freedom. This does not mean, however, that there is no recognition of free speech. Australia has ratified the International Covenant on Civil and Political Rights.[38] Whilst, this creates no enforceable rights under Australian law, courts will be mindful of Australia's international obligations when determining a relevant matter.[39] The common law recognizes general freedom of speech. It is in effect residual freedom: a freedom that exists to the extent that the existing law allows.[40]

§2. Implied Freedom of Political Communication

29. Despite the lack of an express free speech guarantee, the HCA has held that an implied freedom of political communication can be derived from the Australian Constitution.[41] The implied freedom was first recognized in 1992 through two HCA decisions, delivered by the Court together: *Australian Capital Television Pty Ltd v. The Commonwealth of Australia (No 2)* [42] and *Nationwide News Pty Ltd v. Wills.* [43] The High Court held that if the system of representative government established under the Constitution was to be effective, it was necessary for the public to be free to discuss matters concerning government. The implied freedom, however, was not considered absolute freedom: '[t]he guarantee does not postulate that the freedom must always and necessarily prevail over the competing interests of the public'.[44] Perversely, perhaps, the legislation struck down in *Australian Capital Television* had sought to regulate the broadcasting of political advertising during federal election

38. Australia ratified the covenant in 1980.
39. *Minister of State for Immigration and Ethnic Affairs v. Teoh* (1995) 183 CLR 273.
40. *See* E. Barendt, 'Free Speech in Australia: A Comparative Perspective', *Sydney Law Review* 16 (1994): 149, 149–150.
41. The High Court of Australia is the highest authority on Australian constitutional law.
42. (1992) 108 ALR 577.
43. (1992) 108 ALR 681. The issue in *Nationwide* was whether federal legislation that made it an offence, either in writing or orally, to bring members of the Industrial Relations Commission into disrepute was valid. The legislation did not provide any defences such as fair comment.
44. *Australian Capital Television Pty Ltd v. The Commonwealth of Australia (No 2)* (1992) 108 ALR 577, 597, per Mason CJ.

periods so that access to broadcasting would not be the preserve of the best-resourced political parties and candidates. The legislation would have prohibited paid political advertising and established a system allocating free airtime.[45]

30. Following these two decisions, later decisions of the High Court seemed to widen the scope of the implied freedom of political communication.[46] In *Theophanous v. Herald & Weekly Times*, the majority appeared to broaden what might be contemplated by 'political communication': suggesting that it was not confined to political publications and addresses but encompassed all speech referable to the development of public opinion on a range of issues,[47] and to be open to the idea that the implied freedom could create positive rights.[48] *Theophanous* held that the implied freedom could be used as a defence in defamation proceedings.

31. However, in 1997, in a unanimous decision, the High Court contained these more expansive interpretations of the implied freedom for political communication. In *Lange v. Australian Broadcasting Corporation*, the former Prime Minister of New Zealand, David Lange, sued the ABC for defamation in relation to a current affairs programme dealing with the manner in which Lange had made decisions whilst prime minister.[49] The ABC pleaded the implied freedom of political communication as a defence. The High Court held that the constitutional basis for the freedom was to be derived from the text and structure of the Constitution rather than broader notions, as advanced in the earlier cases, of representative democracy or government.[50] Similarly, the concept of 'political communication' was confined to what was necessary to enable the Australian people to exercise an informed choice as electors.[51] The High Court also confirmed that the implied freedom did not confer any personal rights, rather the freedom operated as a constraint on the exercise of legislative and executive powers.[52]

32. The High Court developed a new test to determine the validity of law whereby a law that burdened the freedom of political communication would be invalid unless it was '… reasonably appropriate and adapted to serve a legitimate end'.[53] Although the Court rejected the *Theophanous* constitutional defence, it expanded the common law defamation defence of qualified privilege to ensure the freedom of political communication (*see* Part II, Chapter 3, section 2, IX, D *infra*).

45. For the current rules on political broadcasting and advertising, *see* Part III, Ch. 4.
46. *See Theophanous v. Herald & Weekly Times* (1994) 182 CLR 104; *Stephens v. West Australian Newspapers* (1994) 182 CLR 211; and, *Cunliffe v. Commonwealth* (1994) 182 CLR 272.
47. (1994) 182 CLR 104, 124 per Mason CJ., Toohey and Gaudron JJ.
48. (1994) 182 CLR 104, 125–126 per Mason CJ., Toohey and Gaudron JJ.
49. (1997) 189 CLR 520.
50. A. Stone, 'Freedom of Political Communication, the Constitution and the Common Law' *Federal Law Review* 26 (1998): 219, 251–252.
51. (1997) 189 CLR 520, 560.
52. (1997) 189 CLR 520, 560.
53. (1997) 189 CLR 520, 567–568.

§3. State Guarantees of Free Speech

33. The lack of a human rights charter at the Federal level has led three Australian jurisdictions, Victoria, Queensland, and the Australian Capital Territory (ACT) to adopt their own charters.[54] In such cases, the charter will only have jurisdiction over state or territory matters, as relevant. The ACT was the first to enact human rights protection with the Human Rights Act 2004 (ACT). In 2006, Victoria enacted a Charter of Human Rights and Responsibilities and in 2019 Queensland enacted the Human Rights Act. In each instance, the State or Territory Government and public authorities are required to act consistently with the recognized rights. Freedom of expression is recognized expressly in each statute.

§4. Specific Free Speech Protection in the Media Context

34. Freedom of speech may also be protected or promoted through specific legislation. This is especially relevant to the media context, and aspects of broadcasting legislation illustrate this. For example, laws relating to ownership and control of media or content regulation, ensuring fairness and balance are intended to promote the communication of information and ideas. But, of course, in the absence of constitutional protection of free speech, such instances of free speech promotion will be vulnerable to legislative change.

35. Even where laws are designed to protect other interests, they may seek to balance those rights with the right of freedom of expression. An example of this can be seen in the Racial Discrimination Act 1975 (Cth).[55] Part IIA of the Racial Discrimination Act addresses acts done in public places that amount to racial vilification. Section 18C states:

> It is unlawful for a person to do an act, otherwise than in private, if:
>
> (a) the act is reasonably likely, in all the circumstances, to offend, insult, humiliate or intimidate another person or a group of people; and
> (b) the act is done because of the race, colour or national or ethnic origin of the other person or of some or all of the people in the group.

---

54. Another state, Tasmania, abandoned plans in 2012 to introduce a charter of human rights, citing budgetary concerns.
55. The state and territory jurisdictions, with the exception of the Northern Territory, have racial discrimination legislation: Anti-Discrimination Act 1977 (NSW); Anti-Discrimination Act 1991 (QLD); Racial Vilification Act 1996 (SA); Anti-Discrimination Act 1998 (TAS); Racial and Religious Tolerance Act 2001 (VIC); Criminal Code Act Compilation Act 1913 (WA), Appendix B (WA); and, Discrimination Act 1991 (ACT). The Northern Territory considered introducing racial vilification laws, but no further progress has been made: Department of Attorney-General and Justice, *Discussion Paper: Modernisation of the Anti-Discrimination Act* (September 2017), https://justice.nt.gov.au/__data/assets/pdf_file/0006/445281/anti-discrimination-act-discussion-paper-september-2017.pdf (accessed 8 Jan. 2018).

36. An act is something which '… causes words, sounds, images or writing to be communicated to the public'.[56] However, there is an exemption, from liability that seeks to protect legitimate expression, provided by section 18D:

> Section 18C does not render unlawful anything said or done reasonably and in good faith:
>
> (a) in the performance, exhibition or distribution of an artistic work; or
> (b) in the course of any statement, publication, discussion or debate made or held for any genuine academic, artistic or scientific purpose or any other genuine purpose in the public interest; or
> (c) in making or publishing:
> – a fair and accurate report of any event or matter of public interest; or
> – a fair comment on any event or matter of public interest if the comment is an expression of a genuine belief held by the person making the comment.

37. Despite the presence of section 18D, the racial vilification provisions have been controversial in recent years with suggestions that they unduly restrict freedom of speech, particularly following a decision of the Federal Court concerning articles written by a journalist, Andrew Bolt.[57] In 2009, Bolt wrote two articles which were published in print and online editions of a Victorian-based newspaper, the *Herald Sun*. Mr Bolt also wrote two blog articles which were published on the *Herald Sun* website. The subject matter of the articles and posts was fair-skinned Aboriginal people, in relation to whom it was suggested were not genuinely Aboriginal and were claiming to be Aboriginal, merely to access benefits available to Aboriginal people. In the articles and posts, Bolt named a number of fair-skinned Aboriginal people who were prominent in the community, including academics and activists.

38. The applicant brought proceedings against Bolt and the publisher of the *Herald Sun*, on her own behalf and on behalf of other fair-skinned Aboriginal people claiming that the publications were a breach of section 18C. Bolt and the publishers, the Herald and Weekly Times Pty Ltd, argued that the writings were not in breach of section 18C, but that if they were, they were exempt under section 18D. The Court found that there was a breach of section 18C and that the offensive acts were not exempted under section 18D. The section 18D defence did not apply because, in the view of the trial judge, the articles included significant errors of fact and distortions of truth, and were written using inflammatory and provocative language, containing gratuitous references. The trial judge concluded that the mockery and inflammatory language went beyond what was necessary to make the journalist's point. Because of these factors, the judge determined that the comment could not be described as fair comment and that the nature of the articles indicated a lack

56. Racial Discrimination Act 1975 (Cth), s. 18C(2)(a).
57. *Eatock v. Bolt* [2011] FCA 1103 (28 Sep. 2011), www.austlii.edu.au.

of reasonableness and good faith. The judge emphasized the basis of his findings, and that his judgment did not exclude discussion of difficult subjects, such as race, in Australia:

> It is important that nothing in the orders I make should suggest that it is unlawful for a publication to deal with racial identification including challenging the genuineness of the identification of a group of people. I have not found Mr Bolt and HWT to have contravened s 18C simply because the newspaper articles dealt with subject matter of that kind. I have found a contravention because of the manner in which the subject matter was dealt with.[58]

39. Despite the judge's caution about the basis of his judgment, there were suggestions that the outcome meant that freedom of expression had been unduly constrained.[59] This was the view also of the then Federal Government which has proposed to amend the Racial Discrimination Act 1975 (Cth).[60] The proposed amendments would have replaced sections 18C and 18D with a new provision to:

- Narrow the grounds for an act in a public place to constitute racial vilification. Under the exposure draft, an act would only be unlawful if it vilified or intimidated another person or group of persons. 'Vilify' is defined to mean to incite hatred and 'intimidate' to cause fear of physical harm.
- Broaden the exemption for protection of freedom of expression. There would be an exemption for words, sounds, images or writing spoken, broadcast, published or otherwise communicated in the course of participating in the public discussion of any political, social, cultural, religious, artistic, academic or scientific matter. The exemption would not have included any requirement for reasonableness or good faith.

The Government subsequently abandoned plans to amend the Racial Discrimination Act. However, two subsequent section 18C cases revived criticism. In the first, three students were sued by an Aboriginal woman for posting comments on Facebook following her request to them to leave a campus computer lab reserved for Indigenous students. The case was dismissed on the basis that it would not constitute a breach of section 18C.[61] In the second, an Aboriginal woman complained to the Australian Human Rights Commission that a cartoon published in one of the

58. *Eatock v. Bolt* [2011] FCA 1103, para. 461 (28 Sep. 2011).
59. *See*, e.g., A. Dodd, 'The Bolt decision will have implications for us all', *The Drum,* 28 Sep. 2011, http://www.abc.net.au/unleashed/3026182.html (accessed 20 Apr. 2014) and T. Wilson, 'Foundation must be principles, not worthy aspirations', *Institute of Public Affairs,* 20 Dec. 2013, https://ipa.org.au/news/3023/foundation-must-be-principles-not-worthy-aspirations (accessed 20 Apr. 2014).
60. Australian Government, Exposure Draft: Freedom of Speech (Repeal of s. 18C) Bill 2014, 25 Mar. 2014, http://www.ag.gov.au/Consultations/Documents/Attachment%20A.pdf (accessed 20 Apr. 2014).
61. *Prior v. Queensland University of Technology & Ors (No 2)* [2016] FCCA 2853 (4 Nov. 2016), www.austlii.edu.au.

major newspapers was a breach of section 18C.[62] The complaint was later withdrawn.[63] Although these two claims were unsuccessful, there were again calls for reform or repeal of the racial vilification provisions, leading the Federal Government to establish a parliamentary inquiry into the Racial Discrimination Act to consider whether the legislation imposed unreasonable free speech constraints and recommendations for changes.[64] In 2017, the Government introduced the Human Rights Legislation Amendment Bill 2017, which proposed to replace the words 'offend, insult, humiliate … ' in section 18C with 'harass'. The Government was unsuccessful in passing the amendment through Parliament, although it did make amendments in the handling of complaints by the Human Rights Commission.

40. The debate about the relationship between freedom of expression and the racial discrimination laws could be said to be indicative of the lack of a properly articulated consensus as to the basis for free speech protection in Australia. The absence of an express guarantee of freedom of expression arguably contributes to this lacuna.

62. Australian Broadcasting Corporation, Triple J HACK (16 Nov. 2016), https://www.abc.net.au/triplej/programs/hack/why-i-took-bill-leak-cartoon-to-the-human-rights-commission/8030268.
63. Australian Human Rights Commission, *Complaint by Ms Dinnison against The Australian and Mr Leak Chronology*, https://www.humanrights.gov.au/news/stories/commission-reveals-details-18c-complaints.
64. Parliamentary Joint Committee on Human Rights, *Inquiry Report: Freedom of Speech in Australia* (28 Feb. 2017), https://www.aph.gov.au/Parliamentary_Business/Committees/Joint/Human_Rights_inquiries/FreedomspeechAustralia/Report.

Part II. Regulation of Print Media

Chapter 1. The Journalists' Profession

41. To practise as a journalist in Australia, it is not necessary to attain any specific qualifications. This applies to journalists in the print and electronic media. Some journalists may undertake specific journalism training, but this is not a prerequisite, or even seen as necessary, to the practice of journalism. In the same way, journalists do not have any special status under the law. Journalists may choose to belong to the Media, Entertainment and Arts Alliance (MEAA). The MEAA is a trade union organization, although journalist members of the Alliance agree to be bound by the MEAA Journalists' Code of Ethics (*see* further Chapter 6, section 2 *infra*).[65] Unless specifically mentioned, the law applies to print and electronic media journalists in the same manner. What is meant by a 'journalist' is challenged by the changing modes of news and information delivery and ways of working and this Part provides an indication of the lack of clarity as legislation embeds different definitions affecting journalists' protection and liability.

65. http://www.alliance.org.au/code-of-ethics.html (accessed 10 Feb. 2014).

Chapter 2. Journalists' Rights

§1. Role of Journalists as Watchdogs of Society

42. Although the law, in general, gives no special status to journalists, the important role they play has been acknowledged by the HCA, although it is clear that the exercise of that role will be tempered by the recognition of other interests:

> No doubt the free flow of information is a vital ingredient in the investigative journalism which is such an important feature of our society. Information is more readily supplied to journalists when they undertake to preserve confidentiality in relation to their sources of information. It stands to reason that the free flow of information would be reinforced, to some extent at least, if the courts were to confer absolute protection on that confidentiality. But this would set such a high value on a free press and on freedom of information as to leave the individual without an effective remedy in respect of defamatory imputations published in the media.
>
> That is why the courts have refused to accord absolute protection on the confidentiality of the journalist's source of information, whilst at the same time imposing some restraints on the entitlement of a litigant to compel disclosure of the identity of the source. In effect, the courts have acted according to the principle that disclosure of the source will not be required unless it is necessary in the interests of justice. […]
>
> The liability of the media and of journalists to disclose their sources of information in the interests of justice is itself a valuable sanction which will encourage the media to exercise with due responsibility its great powers which are capable of being abused to the detriment of the individual. The recognition of immunity from the disclosure of sources of information would enable irresponsible persons to shelter behind anonymous, or even fictitious, sources.[66]

§2. Journalists' Independence

43. In keeping with the lack of legal special status for journalists, journalists do not enjoy any special recognition of independence. Save for journalists who may be self-employed, journalists will be subject to the usual constraints of employment and the priorities – commercial and otherwise – of the organization for which they work.

§3. Protection of Journalistic Sources

I. Shield Laws

44. Journalists who become members of the MEAA adhere to a Code of Ethics,[67] which includes the following obligation:

66. *John Fairfax & Sons Limited v. Cojuangco* (1988) 165 CLR 346, 354–355 (HCA).
67. http://www.alliance.org.au/code-of-ethics.html.

> Aim to attribute information to its source. Where a source seeks anonymity, do not agree without first considering the source's motives and any alternative attributable source. Where confidences are accepted, respect them in all circumstances.
>
> However, despite this ethical obligation, at common law, journalists are obliged to answer questions and produce documents even if this would mean disclosing the journalists' sources.

45. Arguments about the importance of being able to protect sources in order to uncover the truth and report on matters in the public interest have not found favour, and the courts have consistently upheld the importance of journalists answering questions so that all relevant evidence is before the courts.[68] Whilst this remains a firm rule, some judges may be willing to exercise a discretion whereby journalists are not required to disclose their sources if justice can be achieved without the disclosure.[69] The common law has also recognized two other situations in which journalists might not be required to disclose their sources:

- During the interlocutory stage of defamation proceedings in which a news organization is a defendant, the defendant will not be forced to disclose its source during the discovery process, unless the plaintiff can establish that it is in the interests of justice.[70] The rule is referred to as the 'newspaper rule', but it has been held to apply to broadcasting.[71] There will be no obligation to disclose the source if the matter settles before trial.
- In circumstances where a person has suffered wrongdoing from an unknown wrongdoer, the victim can apply for pre-trial discovery in order to obtain the identity of the wrongdoer from a third party, who has been involved, perhaps innocently, in the wrongdoing.[72] It has been held that for an order to be made, the applicant must establish that it is necessary in the interests of justice: that the making of the order is necessary to provide the applicant with an effective remedy.[73] If the applicant has a defamatory action available against a news organization, the court will not make the order for preliminary discovery because it would seem that the applicant has an effective remedy available.[74]

46. The absence of a journalist's privilege has not been a dormant matter. In the mid-2000s, two journalists, Gerard McManus and Michael Harvey, were charged with contempt for their refusal to disclose to the court the source of information

68. *McGuinness v. Attorney-General (Vic)* (1940) 63 CLR 73 (HCA).
69. *John Fairfax & Sons Ltd v. Cojuangco* (1988) 165 CLR 346 (HCA).
70. Considered in *John Fairfax & Sons Limited v. Cojuangco* (1988) 165 CLR 346 (HCA). The newspaper rule might not be able to be invoked if the journalists in question had gone against the wishes of the sources: *Liu v. The Age Company Limited* [2012] NSWSC 12, para. 204 (NSWSC).
71. *Wran v. Australian Broadcasting Commission* [1984] 3 NSWLR 241 (NSWSC).
72. *See*, for example, Uniform Civil Procedure Rules 2005 (NSW), Pt 5 r. 5.2.
73. *John Fairfax & Sons Limited v. Cojuangco* (1988) 165 CLR 346, 357 (HCA).
74. *Ibid.* If the news organization pleads qualified privilege as a defence, then the court may exercise its discretion in favour of the order unless the news organization surrenders the defence: *ibid. See also Liu v. The Age Company Limited* [2012] NSWSC 12 (NSWSC).

about government plans to reduce war veteran benefits. They were each found guilty of contempt of court and, although not imprisoned, were fined AUD 7,000.[75]

47. The prosecution of McManus and Harvey led to the introduction of statutory protection in the form of shield laws. The Australian Government was the first to do this (2011), and since then the states have followed.[76] The result is a patchwork of shield laws, with no uniform approach.[77] The Evidence Act 1995 (Cth) provides protection as follows:

(1) If a journalist has promised an informant not to disclose the informant's identity, neither the journalist nor his or her employer is compellable to answer any question or produce any document that would disclose the identity of the informant or enable that identity to be ascertained.
(2) The court may, on the application of a party, order that subsection (1) is not to apply if it is satisfied that, having regard to the issues to be determined in that proceeding, the public interest in the disclosure of evidence of the identity of the informant outweighs:
  (a) any likely adverse effect of the disclosure on the informant or any other person; and
  (b) the public interest in the communication of facts and opinion to the public by the news media and, accordingly also, in the ability of the news media to access sources of facts.
(3) An order under subsection (2) may be made subject to such terms and conditions (if any) as the court thinks fit.[78]

48. In the digital environment, the definition of 'journalist' will be especially important, and the definition of 'journalist' in the Evidence Act 1995 (Cth) seems to embrace a broader notion than one who is employed as a journalist: 'a person who is engaged and active in the publication of news and who may be given information by an informant in the expectation that the information may be published in a news medium'.[79] A news medium is also broadly defined as 'any medium for the dissemination to the public or a section of the public of news and observations on news'.[80] However, the definition of 'informant' may have the effect of narrowing the broader definition of journalist since it seems to confine journalist to one whose

75. *R v. Gerard Thomas McManus and Michael Harvey* [2007] VCC 619 (VCC).
76. The Northern Territory and South Australia introduced shield laws in 2018: Evidence (National Uniform Legislation) Amendment (Journalist Privilege) Act 2018 (NT), s. 10A, and Evidence Act 1929 (SA), Pt 8A, respectively. Queensland only introduced shield laws in 2022: Evidence Act 1977, Div. 2B.
77. A plan for uniform evidence laws has led to some common approaches across the jurisdiction but there has not been complete harmonization. A further commitment to harmonising shield laws was made in late 2022. A working group was established but no further progress has been indicated: Australian Government, *Standing Council of Attorneys-General Communiqué* (5 Jul. 2022).
78. Evidence Act 1995 (Cth), s. 126K. The protection will not apply if the identity of the informant is already known or can be ascertained: *Ashby v. Commonwealth of Australia (No 2)* [2012] FCA 766 (13 Jul. 2012) (FCA).
79. Evidence Act 1995 (Cth), s. 126J.
80. Evidence Act 1995 (Cth), s. 126J.

work is that of a journalist: 'a person who gives information to a journalist in the normal course of the journalist's work in the expectation that the information may be published in a news medium'.[81]

49. The ACT has adopted a shield law that is in similar terms to the Evidence Act 1995 (Cth).[82] New South Wales[83] and Victoria[84] have also adopted laws that are similar to the Evidence Act 1995 (Cth), although, crucially, they do not include the broader definition of a journalist. Hence, the NSW definition of 'journalist' is confined to the more traditional notion of a journalist who may be employed as such: 'a person engaged in the profession or occupation of journalism in connection with the publication of information in a news medium'.[85] South Australia has adopted the NSW definition of a journalist.[86] The Victorian shield laws adopt a similar definition to NSW but provide further elaboration:

> For the purpose of the definition of a journalist, in determining if a person is engaged in the profession or occupation of journalism, regard must be had to the following factors:
>
> (a) whether a significant proportion of the person's professional activity involves:
>   – the practice of collecting and preparing information having the character of news or current affairs; or
>   – commenting or providing opinion on or analysis of news or current affairs – for dissemination in a news medium.
>
> (b) whether information, having the character of news or current affairs, collected and prepared by the person is regularly published in a news medium;
>
> (c) whether the person's comments or opinion on or analysis of news or current affairs is regularly published in a news medium;
>
> (d) whether in respect of the publication of:
>   – any information collected or prepared by the person; or
>   – any comment or opinion on or analysis of news or current affairs by the person.
>
> the person or the publisher of the information, comment, opinion or analysis is accountable to comply (through a complaints process) with recognised journalistic or media professional standards or codes of practice.[87]

81. Evidence Act 1995 (Cth), s. 126J.
82. Evidence Act 2011 (ACT), ss 126J & 126K.
83. Evidence Act 1995 (NSW), s. 126K.
84. Evidence Act 2008 (VIC), s. 126K.
85. Evidence Act 1995 (NSW), s. 126J.
86. Evidence Act 1929 (SA), s. 72.
87. Evidence Act 2008 (VIC), s. 126J.

The Northern Territory, whilst drawing on some aspects of the Commonwealth model, has adopted broader definitions, in part, so that, on the face of it, a journalist is not necessarily someone engaged in the profession or occupation of journalism.[88]

50. Tasmania provides protection against disclosure of the identity of the source of protected confidence, but the provisions make no reference to journalists.[89] The shield laws in WA have also adopted a narrow definition of journalist that is in similar terms to the NSW definition.[90]

II. Whistle-Blower Protection

51. Legislation providing protection to whistle-blowers can be found at the state and territory level, as well as at the Federal Government level, and offers a fragmented framework of protection. In general, the focus of the legislation is on the whistle-blower, and the provisions do not assist in situations where journalists may be involved or have received information. However, in February 2019, the Australian Government passed a new whistle-blower protection, the Treasury Laws Amendment (Enhancing Whistle-Blower Protections) Act 2018, designed to improve protections for those who make disclosures in the private sector and harmonize the framework with public sector protection. The Act primarily amends existing whistle-blower protection in the corporate and financial sectors and introduces a protection scheme in the tax sector. Significantly, for the first time, a journalist may receive a disclosure in certain circumstances (although not in the taxation protection scheme).[91] The circumstances are modelled on the Federal public interest disclosure regime. The Public Interest Disclosure Act 2013 (Cth) provides protection from liability for Australian Government public service employees who report suspected wrongdoing. In general, the protection only applies if the disclosure is made to the relevant officer, appointed to receive such disclosures or to the whistle-blower's supervisor. External disclosure is only permitted in limited circumstances:

- Provided it is in the public interest, an external disclosure can be made if an internal disclosure has been made and the investigation has not been completed within the specified time limits, or the whistle-blower reasonably believes the investigation or outcome was inadequate.

---

88. Evidence (National Uniform Legislation) Act 2011 (NT), s. 127A(6).
89. Evidence Act 2001 (TAS), s. 126B.
90. Evidence Act 1906 (WA), s. 20G. The operative shield law provision is s. 20I, whilst s. 20J addresses the discretionary factors to be considered. The shield laws are in similar terms to the Cth and NSW legislation. The Evidence Act 1906 (WA) also contains protected confidence provisions (s. 20C) that apply to journalists: s. 20A. In *Hancock Prospecting Pty Ltd v. Hancock* [2013] WASC 290 (6 Aug. 2013) (WASC), the court observed that the application of shield laws was a factual issue and would always vary according to the facts: para. 176. In this instance, the court refused to order the production of documents since such an order would be oppressive and an abuse of process and undermine the protection under s. 20I: para. 168.
91. Treasury Laws Amendment (Enhancing Whistle-Blower Protections) Act 2018 (Cth), Sch. 1, Pt 1, s. 137AAD.

– An external disclosure can be made in an emergency if the whistle-blower believes there is an imminent and substantial danger to health and safety or the environment.[92]

Under the Public Interest Disclosure Act, if the circumstances arise whereby an external disclosure can be made, such a disclosure could be made to a journalist, although journalists are not expressly named in the legislation. Legislation to improve protections under the Public Interest Disclosure Act commenced in July 2023, although these reforms did not make express provision for journalists.[93] However, the Treasury Laws Amendment (Enhancing Whistle-Blower Protections) Act 2018 makes express mention of journalists. The definition of a journalist is intentionally narrow in order to avoid disclosure on social media or self-defined journalists being covered by the protection.[94] Thus, a 'journalist':

> means a person who is working in a professional capacity as a journalist for any of the following:
>
> (a) a newspaper or magazine;
> (b) a radio or television broadcasting service;
> (c) an electronic service (including a service provided through the internet) that:
>   i. is operated on a commercial basis, or operated by a body that provides a national broadcasting service (within the meaning of the Broadcasting Services Act 1992); and
>   ii. is similar to a newspaper, magazine or radio or television broadcast.[95]

52. A similar model applies in some states, with specific mention of disclosure to a journalist.[96] In NSW, the Public Interest Disclosures Act 2022 (NSW) specifically permits a protected disclosure to a journalist but only if certain criteria are met, including where disclosure has been made in the proper manner, the disclosure is substantially true, the disclosure was not made anonymously, and the maker of the disclosure has been notified that the agency would not investigate or refer the disclosure, would cease investigating, or has not received notification at the end of the investigation period (section 28).

92. Public Interest Disclosure Act 2013 (Cth), s. 26.
93. Public Interest Disclosure Amendment (Review) Act 2023 (Cth). The Federal Government has also led a consultation on further reforms to the public disclosure legislation: https://consultations.ag.gov.au/integrity/pswr-stage2/#:~:text=The%20second%20stage%20of%20reforms%20is%20an%20opportunity%20to%20improve,supports%20for%20whistleblowers%20are%20needed (accessed 22 Jul. 2024).
94. Revised Explanatory Memorandum, Treasury Laws Amendment (Enhancing Whistle-Blower Protections) Bill 2018 (Cth), para. 2.70.
95. Treasury Laws Amendment (Enhancing Whistle-Blower Protections) Act 2018 (Cth), Sch. 1, Pt 1, s. 1377AAD(3).
96. No disclosure to a third party is provided in the Public Interest Disclosures Act 2002 (TAS); the Protected Disclosures Act 2012 (VIC); or, the Independent Commissioner Against Corruption Act 2017 (NT).

53. Disclosure to a journalist is specifically provided for in the following states:

- Public Interest Disclosure Act 2012 (ACT), section 27.
- Public Interest Disclosure Act 2010 (QLD), section 20.
- Public Interest Disclosure Act 2018 (SA), section 6.
- Public Interest Disclosure Act 2003 (WA), section 7A.

In each case, the disclosure to a journalist can only be made in circumstances similar to the NSW model, although there are variations in the way a journalist is defined.

54. The Public Interest Disclosures Act 2022 (NSW) is intended to simplify procedures for those making disclosures, impose clearer responsibilities to deal with disclosures and improve protections. A journalist is defined as 'a person engaged in the profession or occupation of journalism in connection with the publication of information in a news medium'.[97]

III. Official Secrets

55. In 2018, the Australian Government introduced new laws dealing with official secrecy, espionage, foreign interference, sabotage, treason, and so forth. The National Security Legislation Amendment (Espionage and Foreign Interference) Act 2018 (Cth) (Espionage Act) was considered necessary for national security protection. The Espionage Act is part of a tranche of laws focusing on security protection (*see also* Part II, Chapter 3, section 3, III). It repealed long-standing official secrecy laws[98] and introduced laws with a reach that is not confined to classified information. The Espionage Act introduces Part 5.6 and Division 122 into the Criminal Code 1995 (Cth) (Criminal Code). Part 5.6 covers a range of secrecy offences applying to Commonwealth officers and persons who are not Commonwealth officers, although the offences relating to non-Commonwealth officers are narrower. The offences cover information that is 'inherently harmful' (such as classified information) and information that would otherwise 'cause harm to Australia's interests'.[99] The definition of the latter is drafted very widely. Pursuant to section 122.4A of the Criminal Code, a non-Commonwealth person can be liable for communicating or dealing with information that is classified or is otherwise harmful or prejudicial according to sections 122.4A(1)(d) and (2)(d). A very wide definition of 'deal' applies and includes: receives it, possesses it, conceals it, copies it, and, makes a record of it (section 90.1). The draft legislation caused particular consternation for journalists who could find themselves in receipt of documents in breach of the legislation. Towards the end of the passage of the legislation, the Australian Government agreed to introduce a defence for journalists. Section 122.5(6) provides a defence if the journalist communicated, removed, or dealt with the information in

97. The legislation uses the definition from the Evidence Act 1995 (NSW), Part 3.10, Div. 1C.
98. Official Secrets Act 1979 (Cth), s. 79 and Criminal Code 1995 (Cth), s. 91.1.
99. Criminal Code 1995 (Cth), s. 121.1.

his/her capacity as a journalist reasonably believed at the time that engaging in that conduct was in the public interest. The defence applies to a '... person engaged in the business of reporting news, presenting current affairs, or expressing editorial or other content in news media'. There are also protections for editorial and administrative staff who may be acting under direction. Whilst the defence will offer some comfort for the media, the effectiveness of the defence will turn on establishing several important elements, especially, what constitutes the 'public interest'. Press freedom remains a significant concern, highlighted by the execution of two search warrants in June 2019 on the home of a News Corporation journalist[100] and the second on the Sydney offices of ABC.[101] In both cases, the raids related to publications based on leaked classified documentation. Although the legal basis for the warrants was on the now-repealed section 79 which provided no defence for journalists, the raids were of such a nature that they prompted a parliamentary inquiry with reference to freedom of the press.[102] The Committee recommended, *inter alia*, that the Government should review secrecy provisions and offences and consider whether public interest journalism is adequately protected. In December 2022, the Government established a review of the secrecy provisions contained in Commonwealth laws to consider whether there are secrecy offences that are no longer required, and amendments necessary to protect public interest journalism. A final report was published in November 2023 making a number of recommendations, including greater protections for public interest journalism.[103]

100. *See Smethurst v. Commissioner of Police* (2020) 376 ALR 575 (HCA).
101. *See Australian Broadcasting Corporation v. Kane (No 2)* [2020] FCA 133 (FCA).
102. Parliamentary Joint Committee on Intelligence and Security, *Inquiry into the impact of the exercise of law enforcement and intelligence powers on the freedom of the press* (August 2020, Canberra), https://parlinfo.aph.gov.au/parlInfo/download/committees/reportjnt/024411/toc_pdf/Inquiryintotheimpactoftheexerciseoflawenforcementandintelligencepowersonthefreedomofthepress.pdf;fileType=application%2Fpdf (accessed 3 Apr. 2023).
103. Attorney-General's Department, *Review of Secrecy Provisions: Final Report* (November 2024), https://www.ag.gov.au/sites/default/files/2023-11/secrecy-provisions-review-final-report.pdf (accessed 22 Jul. 2024).

Chapter 3. Journalists' Liability

§1. General Position

56. No specific liability regime operates for journalists. Liability will arise as part of the general law, and journalists will be treated in the same manner as citizens in general who may face criminal or civil liability. In criminal law, liability must be proved beyond a reasonable doubt by the prosecution. In civil law, the plaintiff must prove on the balance of probabilities the liability of the defendant.

57. In criminal or civil actions, liability may not fall solely on the journalist who has been responsible for the wrongdoing. Depending upon the nature of the media in question, publishers, editors, producers, distributors, licensees, and proprietors may face liability jointly with the journalist.

§2. Defamation

I. Introduction

58. Under the tort of defamation, liability will arise for the publication of material that may damage a person's reputation unless a defence can be established. To establish defamation, there must be a defamatory matter referring to the plaintiff, and the matter must have been published to a third party. Defamation is primarily a matter of civil liability, although criminal liability can also arise (*see* XI *infra*).

59. In 2006, Australia adopted uniform laws of defamation. Prior to this, there were eight defamation laws, with substantial differences between them, covering the states (six) and territories (two) of Australia, originally drawn from the English law of defamation. The former position created considerable complexity, especially in relation to nationally published media, and, increasingly so, as online communications developed, with forum shopping common. However, it took more than twenty years to reach an agreement. Under the Australian Constitution, the Australian Government does not have the power to make a national law of defamation, and so defamation was a matter for each state and territory. After a long period, the Standing Committee of Attorneys-General (now known as the Standing Council of Attorneys-General (SCAG)) agreed upon a model law. Each state and territory proceeded to enact a statute based on the model law. The uniform approach to law-making does not prevent a legislature from enacting different laws or, over time, amending the uniform law and diverging from the uniform model. Amendments to the uniform legislation took effect in July 2021. These amendments arise out of the Stage One review of the uniform legislation which took place between 2019-2020.[104] Although all states and territories agreed to the draft amendments, two jurisdictions – Western Australia and the Northern Territory - have not introduced the amendments into

104. Council of Attorneys-General, *Review of Model Defamation Provisions: Discussion Paper* (February 2019).

their local law, and it is not clear if they will. The Stage One amendments largely dealt with identified issues of the then current uniform defamation laws, which will be highlighted in the following paragraphs. The Stage Two review reforms were settled by SCAG in 2023, with agreement to have legislation in place by July 2024. However, South Australia is giving further consideration to the reforms, and it is not clear whether Western Australia and the Northern Territory will adopt them. NSW, Victoria and the ACT have incorporated the Stage Two reforms into their legislation. Part A of Stage Two clarifies the liability of digital intermediaries in situations where third parties publish material via the intermediary. These reforms are partly a response to a decision of the HCA which held that media companies were liable as publishers of comments posted by members of the public on the media companies' Facebook pages. [105]A statutory exemption from liability for third-party content will apply to caching services, conduit services, or storage services, provided such intermediary did not take an active part in publication.[106] Search engine providers will also be exempt from liability if their role was limited to providing an automated process for the user of the search engine.[107] A new defence for publications involving digital intermediaries has also been introduced, designed to clarify when a digital intermediary might be considered to have editorial control.[108] Part B of the reforms extends absolute privilege to communications made to an official of a police force whilst acting in that capacity.[109] The intention is not to deter a person making a complaint to police, if there is a threat of defamation proceedings, especially in cases of reporting of sexual assault. The laws adopted by the states and territories in connection with the uniform scheme are as follows:

- NSW – Defamation Act 2005.
- Queensland – Defamation Act 2005.
- SA – Defamation Act 2005.
- Tasmania – Defamation Act 2005.
- Victoria – Defamation Act 2005.
- WA – Defamation Act 2005.
- ACT – Civil Laws (Wrongs) Act 2002.
- NT – Defamation Act 2006.

60. Despite some differences between the jurisdictions, in general, the adoption of uniform legislation has provided greater clarity. In the following review of defamation law reference will be made to the Defamation Act 2005 (NSW), although where there is significant divergence from the uniform laws in a state or territory, such differences will be noted. With regard to reference to the Stage One review amendments in the following paragraphs, it should be recalled that these as yet do not apply to Western Australia or the Northern Territory. Whilst the uniform defamation laws are the primary source of the laws on defamation, they are not a code,

105. *Fairfax Media Publications Pty Ltd v. Voller* (2021) 273 CLR 346 (HCA).
106. Defamation Act 2005 (NSW), s. 10C.
107. Defamation Act 2005 (NSW), s. 10D.
108. Defamation Act 2005 (NSW), s. 31A.
109. Defamation Act 2005 (NSW), s. 27(2)(b1).

nor do they replace the common law. The common law continues to play an important role in defamation law, except as modified by the statute.[110]

61. Under the uniform scheme, the problem of a publication being published in more than one jurisdiction was addressed. Where a publication has been published in multiple Australian jurisdictions, the relevant law to be applied will be the substantive law of the jurisdiction 'with which the harm occasioned by the publication as a whole has its closest connection'. In making this determination, the factors to be taken into account will be: the plaintiff's ordinary place of residence or business (in the case of a corporation); the extent of publication in each relevant Australian jurisdiction; the extent of harm sustained by the plaintiff in each relevant Australian jurisdiction; and, any other matter considered relevant.[111] The Stage One reforms have resulted in a statutory threshold of serious harm which the plaintiff must demonstrate as an element in the cause of action.[112] This is designed to discourage trivial claims at the outset, rather than rely on the defence of triviality which has now been abolished (*see* IX G *infra*). One issue that may arise is the interaction of the statutory threshold with the defence of contextual truth (*see* IX B *infra*).[113]

II. Libel and Slander

62. The uniform defamation laws have abolished the distinction between libel and slander.[114] At common law, there were two forms of defamation: libel and slander. Libel referred to defamation which appeared in a permanent form, such as in writing, whilst slander related to defamation that occurred in a transient form such as the spoken word. In the case of slander, it was usually necessary to establish actual damage. Broadcasting was declared to be publication in permanent form for the purposes of defamation law.[115] The abolition of the distinction means that it is no longer necessary to establish actual damage.[116]

III. Meaning

63. In determining whether there is a defamatory matter, it will be necessary to ascertain the imputations or meanings of the matter published. The meaning conveyed is assessed by reference to the ordinary reasonable member of the community who 'does not live in any ivory tower' and 'can, and does, read between the

110. Defamation Act 2005 (NSW), s. 6.
111. Defamation Act 2005 (NSW), s. 11.
112. Defamation Act 2005 (NSW), s. 10A.
113. *See* D Rolph, 'A Serious Harm Threshold for Australian Defamation Law' *Australian Bar Review* 51 (2022): 185 and J. O'Hara, 'Defamation: Serious Harm and Contextual Truth' *Australian Law Journal* 95 (2021): 348.
114. Defamation Act 2005 (NSW), s. 7.
115. Broadcasting Services Act 1992 (Cth), s. 206.
116. Defamation Act 2005 (NSW), s. 7(2).

lines, in the light of his general knowledge and experience of worldly affairs'.[117] The context will also be important for the reader in ascertaining the meaning. Hence, the type of publication, its form and the whole of the story or article will be relevant.[118] Accordingly, a tweet may convey the imputations pleaded, although it is hyperlinked to an article which does not carry the imputations.[119] Meaning can be conveyed through three avenues:

- The natural and ordinary meaning: the natural and ordinary meaning refers to the literal meaning which would be given to the matter by the ordinary reasonable person, relying on general knowledge only. If the plaintiff is alleging that the meaning is the natural and ordinary meaning, then no further evidence is produced to establish meaning.[120]
- False Innuendo: The ordinary reasonable person may also understand that material contains a meaning which can be implied or inferred, again without the aid of any special knowledge or extrinsic evidence. A distinction is drawn by the courts between 'implication' and 'inference'.[121]
- An implication is included in and is part of that which is expressed by the publisher. It is something which the reader (or listener or viewer) understands the publisher as having intended to say. An inference is something which the reader (or listener or viewer) adds to what is stated by the publisher; it may reasonably or even irresistibly follow from what has been expressly or impliedly said, but it is nevertheless a conclusion drawn by the reader (or listener or viewer) from what has been expressly or impliedly said by the publisher.[122]
- True innuendo: This is the third means for extracting meaning. Here, the meaning is conveyed because the reader has knowledge of special facts. In the absence of this extrinsic information, the material itself might not convey a defamatory meaning. The test for determining the meaning becomes whether the ordinary reasonable reader, armed with the relevant extrinsic facts, would understand the matter as conveying the meaning alleged by the plaintiff.[123]

IV. Tests for Determining Whether the Matter Is Defamatory

64. Having identified the meanings or imputations conveyed in the material, it is necessary to determine whether the meaning is defamatory. The uniform defamation scheme does not seek to define what is defamatory, and so the common law will be relevant. The common law has produced a number of tests for determining or ways to understand, what will be defamatory. The principal tests are explained in the following terms:

117. *Farquhar v. Bottom* [1980] 2 NSWLR 380, 386 (NSWSC).
118. *Charleston & Smith v. News Group Newspapers Limited* [1995] 2 All ER 313 (HL(UK)).
119. *Hockey v. Fairfax Media Publications Pty Limited* [2015] FCA 652.
120. *See Smith v. Lucht* [2015] QDC 289.
121. *See Smith v. Lucht* [2015] QDC 289.
122. *Amalgamated Television Services Pty Ltd v. Marsden* (1998) 43 NSWLR 158, 167 (NSWCA).
123. *Reader's Digest Services Pty Ltd v. Lamb* (1982) 150 CLR 500 (HCA).

- The reputation of the plaintiff is likely to be affected adversely by exposing the plaintiff to hatred, contempt or ridicule.[124] This test has been seen as too narrow, given the strong language used.[125]
- The matter is likely to lower the plaintiff in the estimation of others.[126]
- The matter is likely to cause the plaintiff to be shunned or avoided. In this test, there is not necessarily any disparagement or damage to the reputation of the plaintiff.[127]

65. In the decision, *Radio 2UE Sydney Pty Ltd v. Chesterton,* the High Court confirmed the general test for defamation as whether the ordinary reasonable person is likely to think less of the plaintiff or to shun and avoid the plaintiff. The test for defamation applies whether it is a personal, professional, or business reputation that is concerned.[128] Whilst determining the defamatory effect of matter is normally an issue to be judged according to the general community standards, in some instances, it may be appropriate to apply sectional standards where there may be an appreciable section of the community who would consider the matter defamatory.[129] Sectional standards are likely to be relevant where there are widely diverging views on social and moral, or religious, matters within the community.

V. Identification

66. To establish a cause of action, it will be necessary to establish that the defamatory matter referred to the plaintiff. It is not necessary for the plaintiff to be named, but the matter must be reasonably capable of referring to the plaintiff, and it is irrelevant that the reference was not intended. The test will be whether the ordinary reasonable person would understand the plaintiff to be the person referred to.[130] Identification can be established if it can be proved that at least one person who read the matter complained of would have identified the plaintiff as the person referred to.[131] Liability may still arise where the matter published was intended to refer to a particular person but is capable of referring to another person who has the same name.[132] This is because the intention of the publisher is not the relevant concern but the effect the matter produces on the reader.[133]

67. Prima facie groups cannot sue for defamation; however, it may be possible for one, or even the entire group, to sue for defamation if the member or members of the group can be sufficiently identified. If the defamatory matter refers to a group

124. *Parmiter v. Coupland* (1840) 6 M & W 105; 151 ER 340 (Ct Exchequer).
125. *Sim v. Stretch* [1936] 2 All ER 1237, 1240, per Ld Atkin (HL(UK)).
126. *Sim v. Stretch* [1936] 2 All ER 1237, 1240, per Ld Atkin (HL(UK)).
127. *Youssoupoff v. Metro-Goldwyn-Mayer Pictures Ltd* (1934) TLR 581 (CA(UK)).
128. *Radio 2UE Sydney Pty Ltd v. Chesterton* (2009) 238 CLR 460 (HCA).
129. *Hepburn v. TCN Channel Nine Pty Ltd* [1983] 2 NSWLR 682, 694 (NSWCA), per Glass JA.
130. *Morgan v. Odhams Press Ltd* [1971] 1 WLR 1239 (HL(UK)).
131. *Zoef v. Nationwide News Pty Ltd* [2016] NSWCA 283.
132. *Lee v. Wilson* (1934) 51 CLR 276 (HCA).
133. *Lee v. Wilson* (1934) 51 CLR 276, 295 (HCA), per Dixon J.

of persons, it will be necessary for the individual member of the group to establish that the matter is reasonably capable of referring to the individual plaintiff.[134] Factors such as the size of the group, the generality and extravagance of the accusation will be relevant to the process of identification.[135] The larger the class, the less likely an individual will be able to maintain an action.[136]

VI. Publication

68. For the requirement of publication to be satisfied, the defamatory matter must have been communicated or published to a third party. Without publication, no harm arises.[137] In this sense, the publication does not require, although, in the case of the media, it probably will involve, publication in the traditional sense or communication to a large number of people. However, the size of the audience may have an impact on the remedy.

69. A statement in a printed publication or one that is otherwise produced in a manner adapted for the production of numerous copies, that a particular person printed, produced, published or distributed, the publication is evidence of the fact that the document was printed, produced and so forth.[138]

70. It is possible that a defendant may be held liable for the republication of the defamatory matter initially published by him/her, where the 'natural and probable result of his act will be that his statement will be republished in the media … '.[139]

VII. Who Can Sue and Who Can Be Liable

71. Only living persons may sue for defamation. Actions for defamation must be brought within one year of the publication date, although there are provisions permitting the plaintiff to apply to the court for an extension of the limitation period, to a period of up to three years, if it can be established that it was not reasonable to have brought the action within the limitation period.[140] The Stage One review introduced the single publication rule meaning that the limitation period is one year from the date on which the matter was first published. This is relevant, particularly to

134. *Knupffer v. London Express Newspaper Ltd* [1944] AC 116, 124 (HL(UK)), per Ld Atkin & *McCormick v. John Fairfax & Sons Ltd* (1989) 16 NSWLR 485 (NSWSC).
135. *Knupffer v. London Express Newspaper Ltd* [1944] AC 116 (HL(UK)).
136. *David Syme & Co Ltd v. Canavan* (1918) 25 CLR 234 (HCA).
137. *Dow Jones & Co Inc v. Gutnick* (2002) 210 CLR 575 (HCA).
138. Defamation Act 2005 (NSW), s. 41(1). Section 41(2) applies to periodicals.
139. *Sims v. Wran* [1984] 1 NSWLR 317, 320 (NSWSC). In this case, the defendant was a prominent politician.
140. Limitation Act 1969 (NSW), ss 14B, 56A; Limitation of Actions Act 1974 (QLD), ss 10AA, 32A; Limitation of Actions Act 1936 (SA), ss 37, 37B; Defamation Act 2005 (TAS), ss 20A, 20AC; Limitation of Actions Act 1958 (VIC), ss 5(1AAA), 23B; Limitation Act 2005 (WA), ss 15, 40; Limitation Act 1985 (ACT); ss 21B, 21BB; Limitation Act (NT), ss 12(2)(b), 44A.

internet material whereby publication could arise on each occasion of download.[141] The estate or family of a deceased person cannot bring or continue an action for defamation on behalf of the deceased. This applies regardless of whether the defamatory matter has been published prior to or after death.[142]

72. A significant change brought by the uniform defamation laws is the limitation on corporations bringing actions for defamation. In general, it is no longer possible for a corporation to sue in defamation.[143] Only corporations that are classified as 'excluded corporations' are able to bring proceedings. An excluded corporation is:

– A corporation that is a not-for-profit corporation, and is not a public body.
– A corporation that employs fewer than ten persons and is not related to another corporation and is not a public body.[144]

73. The rights of government bodies that are not corporations, to bring defamation proceedings are determined by the common law. In *Ballina Shire Council v. Ringland,* the NSW Court of Appeal held that an elected council could not sue for defamation.[145]

74. Only living persons may be sued for defamation.[146] Each person who participates in the publication of the defamatory matter may be liable, regardless of the extent of the involvement.[147] Newspaper proprietors and broadcasting licensees will be liable for the defamatory material published and will generally be sued. The journalist responsible for the material will usually be sued also. Others who may be liable will include editors, distributors, and producers.[148] A party, such as a search engine provider, may be liable for the defamatory content of hyperlinks and paragraphs appearing in search results. In such a case, there could be said to be participation in publication because the search engine is doing what it was intended to do.[149] A media organization creating a public Facebook page and posting content will be the publisher of third-party comments on the Facebook pages, having facilitated the posting of such comments.[150] As noted, online platforms and liability have now been addressed as part of the Stage Two reforms (*see* para 59 *supra).*

141. Limitation Act 1969 (NSW), s. 14C; Limitation of Actions Act 1974 (QLD), s. 10AB, 32A; Limitation of Actions Act 1936 (SA), s. 37A; Defamation Act 2005 (TAS), s. 20AB; Limitation of Actions Act 1958 (VIC), s. 5A; Limitation Act 1985 (ACT); s. 21BA.
142. Defamation Act 2005 (NSW), s. 10.
143. Defamation Act 2005 (NSW), s. 9(1).
144. Defamation Act 2005 (NSW), s. 9(2). A public body is 'a local government body or other governmental or public authority constituted by or under a law of any country': s. 9(6).
145. (1994) 33 NSWLR 680 (NSWCA).
146. Defamation Act 2005 (NSW), s. 10(b). This rule does not apply in Tasmania.
147. *Webb v. Bloch* (1928) 41 CLR 331 (HCA).
148. *See Thompson v. Australian Capital Television Pty Ltd* (1996) 186 CLR 574 (HCA) & *Commisso v. United Telecasters Sydney Pty Ltd* [1999] NSWSC 51 (NSWSC).
149. *Google Inc v. Duffy* [2017] SASCFC 130.
150. *Fairfax Media Publications Pty Ltd v. Voller; Nationwide News Pty Limited v. Voller; Australian News Channel Pty Ltd v. Voller* (2021) 392 ALR 540.

VIII. Role of Judge and Jury

75. There is a divergence of approach between the jurisdictions with regard to the role of juries in defamation proceedings. Under the uniform defamation scheme, either party can elect to have a jury.[151] Following the Stage One reforms, an election can only be revoked with the consent of all parties or the leave of the court.[152] However, the court may order that the action proceeds without a jury where the proceedings are likely to involve a prolonged examination of records or technical, scientific or other issues that cannot be conveniently considered and resolved by a jury.[153] The jurisdictions, in addition to NSW, that have retained a role for juries are:

- Queensland
- Tasmania
- Victoria
- Western Australia.

South Australia, the ACT, and the Northern Territory have abolished jury trials in defamation proceedings.

76. Where a jury is involved, the matters for determination by the jury will be the factual ones of whether the defamatory matter has been published about the plaintiff and whether a defence has been established.[154] The determination of damages will be a matter for the judge.[155]

IX. Defences

77. Defences that can be raised in a defamation action are derived from the statutory uniform defamation scheme and the common law.

A. Justification

78. Under the uniform law, it is a complete defence to a claim of defamation if a defendant can establish the substantial truth of the defamatory imputations.[156] Each of the jurisdictions has adopted this aspect of the uniform scheme, which also reflects the common law position. However, this was one of the substantial changes introduced by the uniform defamation scheme. Prior to the uniform scheme, four jurisdictions required an additional element to be established before the defence of justification could be made out. For example, NSW required truth and publication

151. Defamation Act 2005 (NSW), s. 21(1).
152. Defamation Act 2055 (NSW), s. 21(3).
153. Defamation Act 2005 (NSW), s. 21(1A).
154. Defamation Act 2005 (NSW), s. 22(2).
155. Defamation Act 2005 (NSW), s. 22(3).
156. Defamation Act 2005 (NSW), s. 25.

in the public interest or publication on an occasion of qualified privilege to be established.[157] Three other jurisdictions (Queensland, Tasmania, and the ACT) required the defendant to establish, in addition to the truth, that the publication was for the public benefit.[158] The additional element required by these jurisdictions made the defence of truth difficult to establish.

79. As noted, the uniform defamation scheme justification defence requires the defendant to establish that the defamatory imputations were substantially true. The legislation defines 'substantially true' as meaning 'true in substance or not materially different from the truth'.[159] In establishing the defence, the motives or intention of the defendant, or what the plaintiff believed about the truth or falsity of the published matter is not relevant.[160] The defendant must establish the substantial truth of each defamatory imputation, including any innuendo that might be conveyed by the matter.[161] Further, the defendant must establish the substantial truth of all the defamatory imputations: a failure to justify all the imputations will lead to a failure of the defence.

80. The *Polly Peck* defence allows a defendant to establish the truth of the 'common sting' of the defamatory meanings pleaded by the plaintiff rather than the specific meanings pleaded by the plaintiff.[162] Whilst this defence has been available in Australia, there has also been criticism. In *Chakravarti v. Advertiser Newspapers Ltd*, two of the judges of the High Court were critical of the defence as contrary to the rules of common law pleadings.[163] Other jurisdictions have also been critical of the defence.[164] More recently there were conflicting judicial statements on whether the *Polly Peck* defence forms part of the law in Australia. In *John Fairfax Publications Pty Ltd v. Zunter*,[165] it was suggested that the defence was not part of the common law in Australia, whilst *Li v. Herald & Weekly Times Pty Ltd* took the opposite view.[166] The position remains unclear but has generally been regarded as unlikely to succeed as a defence at common law, whilst the statutory defence of contextual truth might provide a better path.

B. Contextual Truth

81. The Stage One reforms have amended the defence of contextual truth, largely to address drafting deficiencies which were seen to prevent the defence from

157. Defamation Act 1974 (NSW,) s. 15 (repealed).
158. Defamation Act 1889 (QLD), s. 15 (repealed), Defamation Act 1957 (TAS), s. 15 (repealed), Defamation Act 1901 (ACT), s. 6 (repealed).
159. Defamation Act 2005 (NSW), s. 4.
160. *E. Hulton & Co v. Jones* [1910] AC 20.
161. *Andrews v. John Fairfax & Sons Pty Ltd* [1980] 2 NSWLR 225 (NSWCA).
162. *Polly Peck (Holdings) Plc v. Trelford* [1986] QB 1000.
163. (1998) 193 CLR 519, 527 (HCA), per Brennan CJ. & McHugh J.
164. *See*, for example, *David Syme & Co Ltd v. Hore-Lacy* (2000) 1 VR 667 (VSCA) and *Setka v. Abbott & Anor* [2014] VCSA 287.
165. [2006] NSWCA 227 (NSWCA), per Handley JA.
166. [2007] VSC 109 (VSC).

achieving its legislative purpose.[167] The defence prevents a plaintiff from relying on relatively minor imputations where the publication contains content that can be justified.[168] Under the amended defence, the defendant must prove:

(a) the matter carried one or more imputations ('contextual implications') that are substantially true; and
(b) any defamatory imputations of which the plaintiff complains that are not contextual imputations and are also carried by the matter do not further harm the reputation of the plaintiff because of the substantial truth of the contextual imputations.[169]

82. Those jurisdictions which have not enacted the Stage One reforms will have to rely on the defence as originally drafted even though the defence is not seen as viable.[170]

C. *Absolute Privilege*

83. It would be a defence to a defamation claim if the defamatory matter was published on an occasion of absolute privilege.[171] Absolute privilege offers protection which is unqualified by, for example, the speaker's motives. The legislation sets out the occasions in which absolute privilege will arise, but this is not intended to be an exhaustive list. Under the common law and the uniform defamation scheme, parliamentary proceedings, judicial and quasi-judicial (such as tribunals) proceedings are such occasions.[172] The protection arises by reason of the occasion, so that the speaker of the defamatory matter, who will be protected if the defamatory matter is published on an occasion of absolute privilege, will have no protection if s/he publishes the defamatory matter outside the privileged occasion, subject, of course, to any other defence being available.

D. *Qualified Privilege*

84. Several defences come under the category of qualified privilege and are derived from the common law and the uniform defamation scheme. The defences which will be considered in this section are:

---

167. Council of Attorneys-General, *Review of Model Defamation Provisions: Discussion Paper* (February 2019), para. 5.7.
168. Council of Attorneys-General, *Review of Model Defamation Provisions: Discussion Paper* (February 2019), para. 5.3.
169. Defamation Act 2005 (NSW), s. 26.
170. *Fairfax Media Publications Pty Ltd v. Kermode* (2011) 81 NSWLR 157 (NSWCA).
171. Defamation Act 2005 (NSW), s. 27.
172. *Mann v. O'Neill* (1997) 191 CLR 204 (HCA) & Defamation Act 2005 (NSW), s. 27(2)(d) & Sch. 1. The legislation for each jurisdiction includes a lengthy list (in Sch. 1) of various bodies and offices that will attract the protection. The Ombudsman and Privacy Commissioner are two such examples.

- Extended common law qualified privilege with respect to political communications.
- Common law qualified privilege.
- Statutory defence of publication of public documents.
- Fair report of proceedings of public concern.
- Statutory defence of qualified privilege and the Stage One public interest defence.

85. An occasion of qualified privilege will arise where the public interest in the publication of the defamatory matter is considered to outweigh the interest of the plaintiff in vindicating his/her reputation. At common law, it is recognized that there are occasions when it is important that a person can speak freely, and those communications should be protected. The common law defence of qualified privilege protects a defamatory statement if it is made on an occasion where a person has a duty or interest to make the statement, and the recipient has a corresponding duty or interest to receive it.[173] It has been said that the requirement of reciprocity of duty or interest is the 'hallmark of the common law defence of qualified privilege'.[174] The defence contemplates situations where the audience for the communication is limited, such as where one might be providing a reference.[175] The defence is one which would be difficult for the media to rely upon because it would be unlikely that it could establish the requisite duty or interest and reciprocity. Unlike absolute privilege, qualified privilege is, as its name suggests, qualified because the defence cannot be relied upon if the defendant has used the privileged occasion for some improper purpose. However, the improper purpose must be the dominant motive for a claim of malice to succeed.[176]

86. The implied freedom of political communication (*see* Part I, section 2 *supra*) has had an impact on the common law defence of qualified privilege. In *Lange v. Australian Broadcasting Corporation,* the HCA held that the defamation law was not 'reasonably appropriate and adapted to serve a legitimate end'.[177] This was because the common law did not provide an 'appropriate defence for a person who mistakenly but honestly published government or political matter to a large audience'.[178] Accordingly, the High Court held that:

> each member of the Australian community has an interest in disseminating and receiving information, opinions and arguments concerning government and political matters that affect the people of Australia. The duty to disseminate such information is simply the correlative of the interest in receiving it. […]

173. *Adam v. Ward* [1917] AC 309, 334 (HL(UK)). *See also* recent Australian High Court statements of the common law qualified privilege defence: *Roberts v. Bass* (2002) 212 CLR 1 and *Bashford v. Information Australia (Newsletters) Pty Ltd* (2004) 218 CLR 366.
174. *Cush v. Dillon* (2011) 243 CLR 298, 305 (HCA), per French CJ., Crennan and Kiefel JJ.
175. However, a public reply to a public attack can be an occasion of qualified privilege: *Harbour Radio Pty Ltd v. Trad* (2012) 247 CLR 31, (HCA). *See* Ch. 4 *infra.*
176. *Roberts v. Bass* (2002) 212 CLR 1, 41 (HCA), per Gleeson CJ.
177. *Lange v. Australian Broadcasting Corporation* (1997) 189 CLR 520, 567–568 (HCA).
178. *Lange v. Australian Broadcasting Corporation* (1997) 189 CLR 520, 569–570 (HCA).

> The interest that each member of the Australian community has in such a discussion extends the categories of qualified privilege.[179]

87. This extended defence of common law privilege is likely to apply in circumstances where the communication is made to large numbers, by contrast to the traditional common law qualified privilege that contemplates a limited audience. Accordingly, the Court held that in such circumstances a requirement of reasonableness is necessary. In other words, the defendant must establish that its conduct in publishing the material was reasonable.[180] The defence will also fail if the publication was motivated by malice.[181]

88. Under the statutory defence of publication of public documents, the defence will be available if the defamatory matter is contained in:

(a) a public document or a fair copy of a public document; or
(b) a fair summary of, or a fair extract from, a public document.[182]

89. A 'public document' is defined to include documents such as those published by parliamentary or government bodies and court judgments.[183] Under the uniform defamation scheme, each jurisdiction can extend the types of public documents that will attract the defence by specifying them in Schedule 2.[184] The defence will be defeated if the plaintiff proves that the defamatory matter has not been 'published honestly for the information of the public or the advancement of education'.[185] What is fair in the context of section 28 is not defined. The statutory defence, which applied before the uniform defamation scheme, drew on common law tests that also applied to the defence of fair report of proceedings of public concern, discussed in the next paragraph.

90. The defence of fair report of proceedings of public concern is part of the uniform defamation scheme,[186] although a defence of fair and accurate report of parliamentary and judicial proceedings also exists at common law. The ability to report in respect of such proceedings is consistent with the principles of open justice and representative democracy.[187] The fair report defence is an important defence for the media because it can enable the media to publish matters which may have been originally published under absolute privilege. It is important, however, to remember

179. *Lange v. Australian Broadcasting Corporation* (1997) 189 CLR 520, 571 (HCA).
180. *Lange v. Australian Broadcasting Corporation* (1997) 189 CLR 520, 572–573, 574 (HCA).
181. *Lange v. Australian Broadcasting Corporation* (1997) 189 CLR 520, 574 (HCA).
182. Defamation Act 2005 (NSW), s. 28.
183. Defamation Act 2005 (NSW), s. 28(4).
184. Defamation Act 2005 (NSW), s. 28(4)(g).
185. Defamation Act 2005 (NSW), s. 28(3).
186. Defamation Act 2005 (NSW), s. 29.
187. *Waterhouse v. Broadcasting Station 2GB Pty Ltd* (1985) 1 NSWLR 58, 62 (NSWSC).

that the fair report defence is a defence of qualified privilege only. Hence, the common law fair and accurate report defence can be defeated by malice, and the statutory defence will be defeated, like the section 28 defence, if the matter is not published honestly for the information of the public or the advancement of education.[188]

91. The statutory defence encompasses a broad range within the meaning of 'proceedings of public concern' including, for example, international organizations, proceedings of a public meeting of corporate shareholders, and law reform bodies. What is a fair report is not defined but under the common law, a fair report will need to be '… a substantially accurate summary of the proceeding, neither more nor less. The question is not whether it is fair or unfair to any particular person; the question is whether it substantially records what was said and done …'.[189]

92. The uniform defamation scheme introduced a statutory defence of qualified privilege. The statutory defence was substantively different from the common law defence; the former was not dependent upon reciprocity of duty and interest but rather on reasonableness. It was intended that the statutory defence would offer a more viable defence for the media. However, in submissions to the Stage One review, media organizations raised concerns that courts had been overly restrictive in applying the reasonableness test.[190] The Stage One reforms introduced a new public interest defence.[191] The defence will be established if the defendant can prove:

(1)
  (a) the matter concerns an issue of public interest; and
  (b) the defendant reasonably believed that the publication of the matter was in the public interest.

(2) In determining whether the defence is established, a court must take into account all of the circumstances of the case.

(3) Without limiting subsection (2), the court may take into account the following factors to the extent the court considers them applicable in the circumstances:
  (a) the seriousness of any defamatory imputation carried by the matter published,
  (b) the extent to which the matter published distinguishes between suspicions, allegations and proven facts,
  (c) the extent to which the matter published relates to the performance of the public functions or activities of the person,
  (d) whether it was in the public interest in the circumstances for the matter published to be published expeditiously,

188. Defamation Act 2005 (NSW), s. 29(3).
189. *Waterhouse v. Broadcasting Station 2GB Pty Ltd* (1985) 1 NSWLR 58, 63 (NSWSC), per Hunt J.
190. Council of Attorneys-General, *Review of Model Defamation Provisions: Discussion Paper* (February 2019), para. 5.22.
191. Defamation Act 2005 (NSW), s. 29A.

(e) the sources of the information in the matter published and the integrity of those sources,
(f) if a source of the information in the matter published is a person whose identity is being kept confidential, whether there is good reason for the person's identity to be kept confidential (including, for example, to comply with an applicable professional code or standard),
(g) whether the matter published contained the substance of the person's side of the story and, if not, whether a reasonable attempt was made by the defendant to obtain and publish a response from the person,
(h) any other steps taken to verify the information in the matter published,
(i) the importance of freedom of expression in the discussion of issues of public interest.

Most of these factors to be considered have been taken from the statutory defence of qualified privilege, although consideration of the value of freedom of expression is new.

93. In view of the new public interest defence the statutory defence of qualified privilege has been amended to reduce the list of factors a court may take into account in considering reasonableness:

(a) the seriousness of any defamatory imputation carried by the matter published,
(b) the extent to which the matter published distinguishes between suspicions, allegations and proven facts,
(c) the nature of the business environment in which the defendant operates,
(d) whether it was appropriate in the circumstances for the matter published to be published expeditiously,
(e) any other steps taken to verify the information in the matter published.[192]

As with common law qualified privilege, the statutory defence will be unsuccessful if the publication was actuated by malice.[193] For those jurisdictions which have not adopted the Stage One reforms, the original statutory defence of qualified privilege will remain relevant.[194]

94. Whilst existing defences may have covered the ground, the Stage One reforms also introduced a defence for scientific or academic peer review to provide more robust protection for academics and scientists expressing their views as part of a peer review process. The defence will be established if the matter was published in a scientific or academic journal, relates to a scientific or academic issue, and, an independent review of the scientific or academic merit had been carried out.[195]

192. Defamation Act 2005 (NSW), s. 30.
193. Defamation Act 2005 (NSW), s. 30(4).
194. See Defamation Act 2006 (NT), s. 27 and Defamation Act 2005 (WA), s. 30.
195. Defamation Act 2005 (NSW), s. 30A.

E. Comment

95. At common law, the defence of fair comment provides protection to persons who have expressed an opinion or comment. It is a recognition of freedom of expression values and is a defence that can be particularly relevant to the media. A similar statutory defence exists under the uniform defamation scheme – the defence of honest opinion.[196] The defendant can put both defences forward. As the names of both defences indicate, not all opinions and comments will benefit from the defence.

96. A defence of fair comment at common law must establish:

- that comment, rather than statements of fact, has been made;
- the comment relates to matters of public interest;
- the comment is based on disclosed or sufficiently well-known facts; and
- the comment is one that can be honestly held.[197]

97. In order for the defence to be established, the facts upon which the comment is based must be able to be justified or be published on an occasion of privilege. It is essential to establish that the matter is comment and not fact, because, no matter how fair, the defence of fair comment does not protect statements of fact.[198] Whether the matter is a comment or fact will be determined by reference to how the matter would be understood by the ordinary reasonable recipient.[199]

98. Since the defence is one that protects the expression of comment and opinion, it might be thought that the test for public interest would be a broad one and that matters of public affairs would be matters of public interest.[200] However, the majority in *Bellino v. Australian Broadcasting Corporation* rejected the idea that a matter that affected 'people at large' would be a matter of public interest.[201] The majority ruled that a comment made on a matter of public interest would be:

> made in the course of or for the purposes of discussing the conduct of any person whose conduct, inherently, expressly or inferentially, invites public criticism or discussion. Thus, the discussion of the conduct of any person holding public office, participating in the administration of justice or public affairs,

196. Defamation Act 2005 (NSW), s. 31.
197. *Goldsbrough v. John Fairfax & Sons and another* (1934) 34 SR 524, 531 (NSWSC), per Jordan CJ.
198. *Goldsbrough v. John Fairfax & Sons and another* (1934) 34 SR 524, 531–532 (NSWSC), per Jordan CJ.
199. *Goldsbrough v. John Fairfax & Sons and another* (1934) 34 SR 524, 531–532 (NSWSC), per Jordan CJ.
200. *Bellino v. Australian Broadcasting Corporation* (1996) 185 CLR 183, [paras 13–15] (HCA), per Brennan CJ.
201. *London Artists Ltd v. Littler* (1969) 2 QB 375, 391 per Denning MR., quoted in *Bellino v. Australian Broadcasting Corporation* (1996) 185 CLR 183, 193 (HCA), per Brennan CJ.

offering goods or services to the public or otherwise engaging in public conduct that invites public criticism or discussion.[202]

99. To be protected, the comment must be fair. This is determined by reference to whether the opinion is one that 'a fair-minded man might ... reasonably form upon the facts on which it is put forward'.[203] Malice can defeat the defence of fair comment.

100. The statutory defence of honest opinion is in similar terms to the common law defence. The defence will be defeated if the plaintiff is able to prove that the opinion was not honestly held at the time the defamatory matter was published.[204] The statutory defence includes a defence where the comment is made by an employee or agent of the defendant or by a commentator.[205] There has been concern that the statutory defence created some uncertainty regarding what would constitute 'proper material' upon which the opinion must be based, and whether the defence was suitably adapted to the different communication styles found in digital publications.[206] The Stage One reforms have resulted in a broader definition of 'proper material' which includes digital means of accessing material.[207]

F. Innocent Dissemination

101. The uniform defamation scheme includes a defence of innocent dissemination. Although this defence also exists at common law, the statutory defence is broader because it includes a wider category of persons who may take advantage of the defence. The intention in the publication is not an element in determining liability for defamation, and so the potential for liability is quite broad, including anyone who voluntarily distributes, or publishes the defamatory matter. Thus, vendors, distributors, and libraries could find themselves liable in defamation. The defence of innocent dissemination lessens the scope for liability for these secondary publishers. Section 32(1) provides that it will be a defence if the defendant can prove that:

(a) the defendant published the matter merely in the capacity, or as an employee or agent, of a subordinate distributor; and
(b) the defendant neither knew nor ought reasonably to have known, that the matter was defamatory; and

---

202. *Bellino v. Australian Broadcasting Corporation* (1996) 185 CLR 183, 221 (HCA), per Dawson, McHugh & Gummow JJ.
203. *Goldsbrough v. John Fairfax & Sons and another* (1934) 34 SR 524, 532 (NSWSC), per Jordan CJ. *See also O'Shaughnessy v. Mirror Newspapers Ltd* (1970) 125 CLR 166, 176 (HCA) & *Channel Seven Adelaide Pty Ltd v. Manock* (2007) 232 CLR 245 (HCA).
204. Defamation Act 2005 (NSW), s. 31(4).
205. Defamation Act 2005 (NSW), s. 31(2)–(3).
206. Council of Attorneys-General, *Review of Model Defamation Provisions: Discussion Paper* (February 2019), paras 5.34–5.39.
207. *See* Defamation Act 2005 (NSW), s. 31(5)(a).

(c) the defendant's lack of knowledge was not due to any negligence on the part of the defendant.

102. A subordinate distributor is a person who is not the first or primary distributor of the matter, is not the author or originator of the defamatory matter, and who did not have the capacity to exercise editorial control over the matter before it was published.[208] The uniform defamation scheme provides a non-exhaustive list of the persons who may not be regarded as the first or primary distributor of the defamatory matter such as:

- Bookseller, newsagent, news-vendor.
- Librarian.
- Broadcaster of a live programme (television, radio, or otherwise) in circumstances where the broadcaster had no effective control over the person who makes the statement.
- Internet service providers.[209]

G. *Triviality*

103. The introduction of the serious harm threshold (*see* I, para. 61 supra) has rendered the defence of triviality unnecessary and as part of the Stage One amendments has been repealed. However, it will still apply to the jurisdictions which have not yet adopted the Stage One reforms. Thus, if the defamatory matter is unlikely to harm the plaintiff, the defendant may rely upon a defence of triviality. In a claim of defamation, the harm is presumed, and it will usually be a matter for the determination of damages to consider the extent of that harm. The defence of triviality was intended as a means to deter trivial claims being brought.

X. Remedies

A. *Damages*

104. The award of damages is the main remedy for a plaintiff who establishes successfully that the defendant is liable in defamation. In defamation proceedings, 'compensation for an injury to reputation operates as a vindication of the plaintiff to the public, as well as a consolation'.[210] For those jurisdictions that have retained juries (*see* VIII *supra*) under the uniform defamation scheme, the assessment of the

208. Defamation Act 2005 (NSW), s. 32(2).
209. Defamation Act 2005 (NSW), s. 32(3).
210. *Radio 2UE Sydney Pty Ltd v. Chesterton* (2009) 238 CLR 460, 466 (HCA), per French CJ., Gummow, Kiefel & Bell JJ. citing Windeyer J. in *Uren v. John Fairfax & Sons Pty Ltd* (1966) 117 CLR 118, 150 (HCA).

damages amount to be awarded is a matter for the judge.[211] Under the uniform defamation scheme, the damages awarded must constitute '… an appropriate and rational relationship between the harm sustained by the plaintiff and the amount of damages awarded'.[212]

105. The uniform defamation scheme provides a maximum award of AUD 250,000 for non-economic loss.[213] The Stage One reforms clarified that this amount is to be awarded only in the most serious case.[214] However, a court may award an amount that exceeds this if the court is satisfied that the circumstances of the publication are such as to warrant an award of aggravated damages.[215] Aggravated damages are compensatory in intent and are awarded because the defendant's conduct or the circumstances of the publication have increased the injury done to the plaintiff.[216] The uniform defamation scheme prohibits the award of exemplary damages.[217] Exemplary damages are not compensatory in nature but are intended to punish the defendant.[218]

106. A defendant may offer evidence in mitigation of the damages to be awarded. Section 38 sets out a list of matters that may be relevant to mitigation.[219] Matters relevant to mitigation will include:

- Whether an apology has been made or a correction published.
- The plaintiff has already recovered damages for defamation in relation to another publication of defamatory matter similar to the one in question.

The list of mitigating factors is not intended to be exhaustive.[220]

B. *Injunction*

107. An injunction preventing publication may be sought if the plaintiff is aware of the defamatory matter before it is published. An interlocutory injunction will not permanently restrain the publication but will apply pending the resolution of the claim. Injunctions are not a common remedy in defamation proceedings and will not be readily granted given the impact an injunction in this context will have on freedom of expression. The uniform defamation scheme does not cover injunctions, but

211. Defamation Act 2005 (NSW), s. 22(3).
212. Defamation Act 2005 (NSW), s. 34.
213. Defamation Act 2005 (NSW), s. 35(1). There is provision for this amount being adjusted annually calculated by reference to Australian weekly earnings: s. 35(3-4). The current maximum amount in NSW is AUD 443,000 as per 1 Jul. 2022.
214. Defamation Act 2005 (NSW), s. 35(2).
215. Defamation Act 2005 (NSW), s. 35(2A). *See also Wilson v. Bauer Media Pty Ltd* [2017] VSC 521 and *Bauer Media Pty Ltd v. Wilson (No 2)* [2018 VSCA 154.
216. *Uren v. John Fairfax & Sons Pty Ltd* (1966) 117 CLR 118, 131 (HCA), per Taylor J.
217. Defamation Act 2005 (NSW), s. 37.
218. *Uren v. John Fairfax & Sons Pty Ltd* (1966) 117 CLR 118, 130 (HCA), per Taylor J.
219. Defamation Act 2005 (NSW), s. 38.
220. Defamation Act 2005 (NSW), s. 38(2).

injunctions in defamation proceedings continue to be available under the uniform defamation scheme's preservation of the general law.[221]

108. As a general matter, the plaintiff seeking an injunction must establish that there is a serious question to be tried, that damages are unlikely to be an adequate remedy, and that the balance of convenience favours the granting of an injunction. In the context of defamation proceedings, these principles need to be considered in light of the public interest in free speech.[222] Accordingly, it is unlikely that an injunction will be granted unless the plaintiff is able to establish:

- That a finding by the jury that the matter is not defamatory would be set aside as unreasonable.
- There is no real basis for anticipating that a defence of privilege, justification or comment would succeed.
- More than nominal damages will be recovered.[223]

Where an injunction is sought, the court will exercise 'exceptional caution' given that the injunction will act as a prior restraint on the exercise of free speech.[224] A permanent injunction does not 'ordinarily follow success' in a defamation action, and will be only granted where it is 'reasonably necessary to address the risk or threat of repetition of the defamation'.[225]

C. *Offer of Amends*

109. A further remedy is offered under the uniform defamation scheme: the offer of amends procedure.[226] Rather than being a remedy for the end-stage of proceedings, the procedure is a way of resolving disputes at an earlier point. Hence, the publisher of the matter (the potential defendant) may make an offer of amends to the aggrieved either in relation to the whole of the complaint or with respect to particular alleged defamatory imputations.[227] The publisher may make the offer within twenty-eight days of the aggrieved person issuing a concerns notice or, where defamation proceedings have commenced before the defence is filed.[228] Under the Stage One reforms, a concerns notice is now mandatory prior to proceedings being commenced, and at least fourteen days must elapse before commencing proceedings.[229] The concerns notice requirement is designed to facilitate opportunities for settling

221. Defamation Act 2005 (NSW), s. 6.
222. *Australian Broadcasting Corporation v. O'Neill* (2006) 227 CLR 57, 68 (HCA), per Gleeson CJ. & Crennan J.
223. *Australian Broadcasting Corporation v. O'Neill* (2006) 227 CLR 57, 66–68 (HCA), per Gleeson CJ. & Crennan J.
224. *Australian Broadcasting Corporation v. O'Neill* (2006) 227 CLR 57, 73 (HCA), per Gleeson CJ. & Crennan J.
225. *Carolan v. Fairfax Media Publications Pty Ltd (No 7)* [2017] NSW SC 351, para. 56.
226. Defamation Act 2005 (NSW), ss 12–19.
227. Defamation Act 2005 (NSW), s. 13.
228. Defamation Act 2005 (NSW), s. 14(1).
229. Defamation Act 2005 (NSW), ss 12A–12B.

the dispute. A concerns notice is a written communication to the publisher setting out the defamatory imputations that the aggrieved person believes are conveyed by the matter.[230] If the concerns notice fails to particularize the imputations sufficiently, the publisher can request by written notice further particulars. The response must be given within fourteen days, and if further particulars are not provided, the concerns notice is deemed not to have been issued.[231]

110. If the publisher issues an offer of amends, it must include an offer to publish a correction and an offer to pay reasonable expenses incurred by the aggrieved person. The offer may also include an offer to apologize or an offer to pay compensation.[232] If the aggrieved person accepts the offer of amends, s/he cannot bring proceedings in respect of the defamatory imputations covered by the offer of amends procedure.[233] If the aggrieved person does not accept the offer of amends, the publisher may assert the offer of amends as a defence in any consequent proceedings.[234] To be successful, the court must be satisfied that:

- The offer was made as soon as reasonably practicable after the defendant was given a concerns notice, and.
- The defendant was ready and willing before the trial to carry out the terms of the offer if accepted, and
- The offer was, in all the circumstances, reasonable. In determining reasonableness, the court must have regard to whether a correction or apology was published before the trial, and the relative prominence of the offer or apology, and the lapse of time between the publication of the defamatory matter and the publication of the correction or apology.[235]

XI. Criminal Defamation

111. Although civil action for defamation is now the main way in which defamatory matter is dealt with, prosecutions for criminal defamation can still be brought. With the exception of Victoria, the common law offence of criminal libel has been abolished.[236] A common statutory offence of criminal defamation is found in all states and territories, with the exception of Victoria and the Northern Territory: both these jurisdictions have statutory provisions for criminal defamation, but they have not adopted the common approach.[237] There are some variations between the jurisdictions in the elements of the offence and penalties, but the main elements of the statutory provisions can be summarized as follows:

230. Defamation Act 2005 (NSW), s. 12A.
231. Defamation Act 2005 (NSW), s. 12A.
232. Defamation Act 2005 (NSW), s. 15.
233. Defamation Act 2005 (NSW), s. 17(1).
234. Defamation Act 2005 (NSW), s. 18.
235. Defamation Act 2005 (NSW), s. 18(1)-(2).
236. *See, e.g.*, Crimes Act 1900 (NSW), s. 529.
237. *See* Wrongs Act 1958 (VIC), s. 10 and Criminal Code (NT), s. 204.

(a) The elements of the offence are:
   - the publication of defamatory matter of another living person, without lawful excuse;
   - with the knowledge that the matter is false (or in some jurisdictions being reckless as to truth or falsity); and
   - the publication has been made with the intention of causing serious harm to the victim or some other person or being reckless as to whether any harm is caused.

(b) The defences that would have been available in a civil action will constitute a lawful excuse.
(c) The permission of the Director of Public Prosecutions must be obtained before proceedings can be brought. Criminal proceedings do not bar civil proceedings.
(d) The criminal proceedings will be heard before a jury.
(e) In most jurisdictions, a maximum penalty of three years imprisonment applies.[238]

Criminal prosecutions for defamation are not common.

§3. Privacy

I. The General Law and Privacy

112. The common law in Australia does not currently recognize a general right of privacy (*see also* Part III, Chapter 3, section 6 *infra*), although there is some uncertainty about the current position. For a long period, it was understood that as a result of a decision of the High Court, *Victoria Park Racing and Recreation Grounds Pty Ltd v. Taylor* [239] no legally enforceable right to privacy could be recognized. However, in a later decision of the High Court, *Australian Broadcasting Corporation v. Lenah Game Meats Pty Ltd,* it was stated that *Victoria Park* did not '... stand in the path of the development of ... ' a tort of invasion of privacy at common law.[240] However, in the circumstances of the case, the High Court held that there was no invasion of privacy. Moreover, another difficulty was the fact that the plaintiff, seeking to enforce a right to privacy, was a corporation. The majority of the High Court considered that if an invasion of privacy enforceable right were to develop, it should be for the benefit of individuals, not corporations.[241]

238. Crimes Act 1900 (NSW), s. 529; Criminal Code Act 1899 (QLD), s. 365; Criminal Law Consolidation Act 1935 (SA), s. 257; Criminal Code Act 1924 (TAS), s. 196; Criminal Code 1913 (WA), s. 345; Crimes Act 1900 (ACT), s. 439.
239. (1937) 58 CLR 479.
240. *Australian Broadcasting Corporation v. Lenah Game Meats Pty Ltd* (2001) 208 CLR 199, 248 (HCA), per Gummow and Hayne JJ.
241. *See*, e.g., *Australian Broadcasting Corporation v. Lenah Game Meats Pty Ltd* (2001) 208 CLR 199, 258 (HCA), per Gummow and Hayne JJ. & 279, per Kirby J.

113. Notwithstanding the *Lenah Game Meats* decision, the position regarding privacy at common law in Australia remains unclear. Several lower court decisions have recognized a tort of invasion of privacy, although the position has yet to be confirmed at the appellate level.

114. The first decision to recognize an enforceable right to privacy was a decision of a district court in Queensland, *Grosse v. Purvis.* [242] In *Grosse v. Purvis,* the plaintiff brought proceedings alleging that the defendant, with whom she had been in a former sexual relationship, had over a lengthy period stalked and harassed her, engaging in a variety of actions such as unauthorized entry to her home and intrusive telephone calls. The plaintiff pleaded a number of causes of action, including invasion of privacy. The court found that following *Lenah Game Meats*, it was open to it to find an invasion of privacy had occurred.[243] Skoien SDCJ held that the elements of the tort of an invasion of privacy were:

- a willed act by the defendant;
- which intrudes into the plaintiff's privacy or seclusion;
- in a manner which would be considered highly offensive to a reasonable person of ordinary sensibilities; and
- which causes detriment to the plaintiff in the form of physical, emotional, or mental distress, hindering the plaintiff from doing some lawfully entitled act.[244]

Skoien SDCJ awarded compensatory damages (AUD 108,000), aggravated damages (AUD 50,000), and exemplary (AUD 20,000).[245] The matter was settled before an appeal was heard.

115. In *Doe v. Australian Broadcasting Commission*, the plaintiff brought proceedings in the Victoria County Court against the ABC claiming a breach of statutory duty, negligence, breach of confidence, and invasion of privacy.[246] The plaintiff had been a victim of sexual assault committed by her estranged husband, who had been found guilty and imprisoned for the attacks. Journalists, employed by the ABC, had, in breach of the Judicial Proceedings Act 1958 (VIC), disclosed details of the victim's identity. The journalists pleaded guilty to offences under the Act. The plaintiff brought civil proceedings against the ABC. The court held that the High Court in *Lenah Game Meats* had held out an invitation to find that a breach of privacy arose in accordance with the normal principles of tort.[247] Hampel J. amended the first element set down in *Grosse v. Purvis* from a willed act of the defendant to the broader 'unjustifiable' act of the defendant.[248]

242. [2003] QDC 151 (16 Jun. 2003).
243. [2003] QDC 151 (16 Jun. 2003), para. 423.
244. [2003] QDC 151 (16 Jun. 2003), para. 444.
245. [2003] QDC 151 (16 Jun. 2003), paras 475, 480 & 482.
246. [2007] VCC 281, per Hampel J.
247. [2007] VCC 281, para. 157.
248. [2007] VCC 281, para. 163.

116. However, other decisions have doubted whether an action for invasion of privacy is part of the common law in Australia. In *Giller v. Procopets*,[249] the Victorian Supreme Court held that the law has not developed so as to recognize an action for breach of privacy in Australia.[250] Having found that the plaintiff had a claim in breach of confidence, the Court of Appeal found that it was unnecessary to consider the position concerning an action for privacy.[251] However, Ashley JA observed that no superior court in Australia had recognized a tort of invasion of privacy.[252] More recently, in *Sands v. State of South Australia,* Kelly J. stated:

> [t]he *ratio decidendi* of the decision in *Lenah* is that it would require further development in the law to acknowledge the existence of a tort of privacy in Australia. In my view, the statements of the majority in *Lenah* do not support the suggestion that the High Court in *Lenah* held out an invitation to intermediate courts in Australia to develop the tort of privacy as an actionable wrong.[253]

117. Within this context, there have been several inquiries into the development of privacy law in Australia. In 2008, the Australian Law Reform Commission (ALRC) recommended the introduction of a statutory cause of action for serious invasion of privacy.[254] In the following year, the New South Wales Law Reform Commission also recommended the introduction of a statutory general cause of action for invasion of privacy.[255] In 2013, the Australian Government commissioned the ALRC to undertake a further inquiry into the prevention of and remedies for serious invasions of privacy in the digital era. The ALRC was specifically charged with making recommendations for a statutory cause of action for invasion of privacy.[256] The ALRC reported in June 2014. The reported detailed the operation of a statutory course of action, and suggested statutory alternatives.[257] Calls by review bodies for a statutory tort for invasion of privacy have been repeated more recently.[258] A review of the Privacy Act 1988 (Cth) also proposed the introduction

249. [2004] VSC 113 (VSC), per Gillard J.
250. [2004] VSC 113, para. 188 (VSC).
251. [2008] VR 1, para. 168 (VSCA), per Ashley JA. & para. 452, per Neave JA.
252. [2008] VR 1, para. 167 (VSCA), per Ashley JA.
253. [2013] SASC 44, para. 614, per Kelly J. (SASC).
254. ALRC, *For your Information: Australian Privacy Law and Practice* (Report 108, May 2008), recommendation 74-1, http://www.alrc.gov.au/publications/report-108 (accessed 1 Mar. 2014).
255. New South Wales Law Reform Commission, *Invasion of Privacy* (Report 120, April 2009), 3, http://www.lawreform.lawlink.nsw.gov.au/agdbasev7wr/lrc/documents/pdf/report_120.pdf (accessed 1 Mar. 2014).
256. Australian Law Reform Commission, *Serious Invasions of Privacy in the Digital Era: Issues Paper* (IP 43, October 2013), http://www.alrc.gov.au/inquiries/invasions-privacy (accessed 1 Mar. 2014). Following the referral of this inquiry to the ALRC, a new government was elected. It was unclear if the new government was disposed towards a statutory cause of action in privacy. The ALRC is due to report in mid-2014.
257. Australian Law Reform Commission, *Serious Invasions of Privacy in the Digital Era.* (Final Report 123, September 2014) https://www.alrc.gov.au/publications/serious-invasions-privacy-digital-era-alrc-report-123 (accessed 4 Mar. 2019).
258. Australian Competition and Consumer Commission, *Digital Platforms Inquiry: Final Report* (June 2019) https://www.accc.gov.au/about-us/publications/digital-platforms-inquiry-final-report (accessed

of a statutory right of action for privacy invasions which fall outside the Privacy Act scope.[259] In its response, the Australian Government agreed in principle to the proposal, although it also recommended further consultation.[260]

118. Despite the position concerning a specifically enforceable right to privacy, there are other causes of actions which can be used to protect privacy indirectly. In the cases just reviewed, the plaintiff had generally also pleaded some of these other causes of action. The tort of trespass to land may provide some protection against invasion of privacy if a person has entered onto land or remains on land, without permission, which is in possession of the plaintiff. This action may be particularly relevant where media organizations have entered into the plaintiff's land or premises.[261] The courts have acknowledged that the protection of privacy interests is a social value provided by the tort of trespass.[262] Trespass can include interference with airspace, although this is limited. Trespass to land may not give adequate protection where new technologies such as drones may be being used.[263]

119. Indirect protection of privacy interests may also be achieved through the tort of private nuisance. Like trespass, the plaintiff in a nuisance action must establish that s/he has a possessory interest in land. The action in nuisance provides a remedy where there is an unlawful interference in the use or enjoyment of one's land. The action differs from trespass because it does not involve a physical entry onto the premises. The nuisance could be noise or fumes. It may also be persistent telephone calls.[264]

120. An action for breach of confidence may also provide protection for privacy interests and be a basis for a claim against media organizations. In *Giller v. Procopets*, the court accepted that a breach of confidence action could be available to protect against invasion of privacy, with Ashley JA noting that the case was '... an instance of the way in which the law has otherwise developed to address a particular situation'.[265] To establish a breach of confidence claim, it is necessary to establish a pre-existing relation of confidence. Such a requirement may limit the scope for media organizations to be held liable. In the UK, it is no longer necessary for a

---

22 Jun. 2024) and Australian Human Rights Commission, *Human Rights and Technology: Final Report* (March 2021) https://humanrights.gov.au/our-work/technology-and-human-rights/projects/final-report-human-rights-and-technology (accessed 22 Jun. 2024).

259. Australian Government, *Privacy Act Review: Report* (2022) https://www.ag.gov.au/rights-and-protections/publications/privacy-act-review-report (accessed 22 Jun. 2024), 280–287.

260. Australian Government, *Government Response: Privacy Act Review Report* (September 2023) https://www.ag.gov.au/rights-and-protections/publications/government-response-privacy-act-review-report (accessed 22 Jun. 2024), 19 and 36.

261. *TCN Channel Nine Pty Ltd v. Anning* (2002) 54 NSWLR 333 (NSWCA).

262. *TCN Channel Nine Pty Ltd v. Anning* (2002) 54 NSWLR 333, 344 (NSWCA), per Spigelman CJ.

263. Australian Law Reform Commission, *Serious Invasions of Privacy in the Digital Era: Issues Paper* (IP 43, October 2013), http://www.alrc.gov.au/inquiries/invasions-privacy (accessed 1 Mar. 2014), 47.

264. *Alma v. Nakir* [1966] 2 NSWR 396 (NSWSC).

265. [2008] VR 1, para. 168 (VSCA), per Ashley JA.

confidential relationship to be established. It is sufficient if the person receives information that s/he knew or should have known would be confidential.[266] The HCA also appears to have accepted this position.[267]

II. Personal Information Protection

121. The main general source for protection of personal information privacy is the Privacy Act 1988 (Cth).[268] The legislation adopts a principles-based framework. The Australian Privacy Principles (APPs) comprise a set of principles, thirteen, governing the collection, use, storage, and disclosure of personal information, and access to personal information.[269] The APPs apply to Australian Government agencies, organizations within the private sector that have an annual turnover of more than AUD 3,000,000, and to smaller organizations if the services they provide are, for example, health services or services that for a benefit disclose personal information.[270] An entity that is subject to the Privacy Act must have in place a privacy policy that complies with the APPs. Under the Privacy Act, the Australian Privacy Commissioner has the power to investigate complaints about APP entities and, *inter alia*, may apply to the Federal Court for civil penalty orders in relation to serious or persistent breaches. A Notifiable Data Breaches (NDB) Scheme was introduced in February 2018.[271] The NDB scheme applies to those entities already subject to obligations under the Privacy Act. Under the Scheme, such entities are required to notify affected individuals and the Office of the Australian Information Commissioner (OAIC) if a data breach is likely to result in serious harm to those individuals whose personal information is involved in the breach. The legislation has recently been reviewed (Privacy Act Review) to ensure it is fit for purpose in light of the growth of online activity and digital technologies.[272] The Review has proposed extensive changes to privacy laws to ensure adequate protection.

122. Acts done by a media organization in the course of journalism are exempt from the Privacy Act, provided that the media organization is publicly committed to observing published privacy standards.[273] The APC (*see* Chapter 6, section 1 *infra*)

266. *See Attorney-General v. Guardian Newspapers Ltd (No 2)* [1990] 1 AC 109 (HL(UK)) & *Campbell v. MGN Ltd* [2004] 2 AC 457 (HL(UK)).
267. *See*, e.g., *Australian Broadcasting Corporation v. Lenah Game Meats Pty Ltd* (2001) 208 CLR 199, 224 (HCA), per Gleeson CJ. & 271–272, per Kirby J.
268. There are also similar legislative schemes at state and territory level.
269. *See Privacy Commissioner v. Telstra Corporation Limited* [2017] FACAFC 4 where it was held that 'personal information' does not include all information that can be linked to an individual unless the information is also about that individual.
270. Privacy Act 1988 (Cth), s. 6D.
271. Privacy Amendment (Notifiable Data Breaches) Act 2017.
272. Australian Government, *Privacy Act Review: Report* (2022) https://www.ag.gov.au/rights-and-protections/publications/privacy-act-review-report (accessed 22 Jun. 2024). See also Australian Government, *Government Response: Privacy Act Review Report* (September 2023) https://www.ag.gov.au/rights-and-protections/publications/government-response-privacy-act-review-report (accessed 22 Jun. 2024).
273. Privacy Act 1988 (Cth), s. 7B(4).

is responsible for the Statement of Privacy Principles.[274] Most print media organizations and those with digital websites cite adherence to the Statement of Privacy Principles as constituting their commitment to published privacy standards. Under the APC self-regulatory regime, the Council can adjudicate on complaints about a breach of the Privacy Principles. The Principles cover the collection, use, disclosure, and security of personal information, as well as the handling of sensitive personal information and assurance of balance and fairness in the context of private information. Broadcast media will adhere to the privacy provisions through the relevant industry codes of practice (*see* Part III, Chapter 3, section 6 *infra*). The Privacy Act Review recommended that the journalism exemption should be retained but with increased accountability.[275]

III. Interception and Surveillance

123. In 2018 the Australian Government instituted a review of the national intelligence community. The review concluded that the security laws were complex, inconsistent, and outdated.[276] The review recommended that the Telecommunications (Interception and Access) Act 1979 (Cth), and the Surveillance Devices Act 2004 (Cth), along with other legislation, should be repealed and replaced with a new act.[277] The Government accepted this recommendation and has led further consultation.[278] However, the Government has stated that these reforms will be a long-term undertaking so that the current legal framework remains in place. The Telecommunications (Interception and Access) Act 1979 (Cth) regulates the privacy of communications over telecommunication systems. It is an offence to intercept, authorize or permit another person to intercept or to do any act that will enable interception.[279] Interception comprises listening to or recording a communication during its passage over a telecommunications system, without the knowledge of the person making the communication.[280] There are exceptions to the interception prohibition such as where a telecommunications service warrant has been obtained by an enforcement or security agency. The exceptions are of little benefit to media organizations. In the past few years, the Australian Government, mindful of national

274. Press Council, Statement of Privacy Principles (August 2014) www.presscouncil.org.au (accessed 1 Mar. 2019).
275. Australian Government, *Privacy Act Review: Report* (2022) https://www.ag.gov.au/rights-and-protections/publications/privacy-act-review-report (accessed 22 Jun. 2024), 84–92.
276. Australian Government, *Comprehensive Review of the Legal Framework of the National Intelligence Community by Mr Dennis Richardson AC* (December. 2019) https://www.ag.gov.au/national-security/publications/report-comprehensive-review-legal-framework-national-intelligence-community (accessed 29 Jun. 2024), *see* Ch. 6.
277. *Ibid.*, recommendation 75.
278. Australian Government, *Reform of Australia's electronic surveillance framework discussion paper* (2021) https://www.ag.gov.au/sites/default/files/2022-08/electronic-surveillance-framework-discussion-paper.pdf (accessed 29 Jun. 2024).
279. Telecommunications (Interception and Access) Act 1979 (Cth), s. 7(1).
280. Telecommunications (Interception and Access) Act 1979 (Cth), s. 6(1).

security concerns, has introduced legislation that increases the scope for surveillance and access to information, at the potential cost of privacy. The Telecommunications (Interception and Access) Amendment (Data Retention) Act 2015 (Cth) introduced a requirement for telecommunications companies and internet service providers to store customer metadata (relating to voice, SMS, email, and social media communications) for two years. Such data can be accessed by intelligence and law enforcement agencies without a warrant.[281] Because of concerns that the legislation could provide access to journalists' sources, a journalist information warrant scheme was introduced that applies to all agencies seeking access to a journalist's metadata.[282] In late 2018, the Australian Government enacted national security legislation requiring communication providers to provide access to security and law enforcement agencies of information on encrypted platforms.[283] The legislation does not prevent encryption methods being used but requires systems to be in a place that will enable access to information. The new scheme will apply to companies such as Facebook and Google. Proper authorizations and warrants are still required, and the information accessed will be in the context of serious criminal investigations. No protection is in place regarding journalists' information.

124. Media organizations also need to be mindful of the restrictions on dealing with intercepted information. Under section 63, it is an offence to communicate with another person, make use of, or record information, whether lawfully intercepted or intercepted in breach of section 7(1). In *John Fairfax Publications Pty Ltd v. Doe*, the media defendant had come into possession of transcripts of intercepted telephone conversations recorded by the Australian Federal Police.[284] The media defendant used extracts from the transcripts in a series of newspaper articles about race-fixing. An injunction restraining publication was ordered. The defendant had argued that the restraint on publication was an infringement of the implied freedom of political communication. The NSW Court of Appeal rejected this argument. The legislative scheme was designed to respect the privacy of communications and interception was only permitted in tightly controlled circumstances. The fundamental human right of privacy was as important as that of freedom of expression.[285]

125. Section 108(1) of the Telecommunications (Interception and Access) Act 1979 (Cth) makes it an offence to access, authorize or permit another person to access or to do any act that will enable another to access a stored communication without the knowledge of the sender or the recipient of the stored communication. In essence, a stored communication is one that is not passing over a telecommunications system but is held on a carrier's equipment.[286] This provision will apply to communications such as voice mail, email, and text messages. As with the interception regime, access can be authorized in limited circumstances.

281. Telecommunications (Interception and Access) Act 1979 (Cth), Part 5-1A.
282. Telecommunications (Interception and Access) Act 1979 (Cth), Part 4-1, Div. 4C.
283. Telecommunications and other Legislation Amendment (Assistance and Access) Act 2018 (Cth).
284. (1995) 37 NSWLR 81 (NSWCA).
285. (1995) 37 NSWLR 81, 97 (NSWCA), per Kirby P.
286. Telecommunications (Interception and Access) Act 1979 (Cth), s. 5.

126. The Australian Government has the constitutional power to regulate communications using telecommunications systems and the Telecommunications (Interception and Access) Act 1979 (Cth) covers this. However, if a telecommunications system is not used, state or territory surveillance legislation may apply. The Australian Government has enacted legislation governing surveillance devices. However, the Surveillance Devices Act 2004 (Cth) covers the use of surveillance devices by Australian Government agencies only. The regulation of surveillance devices otherwise is a matter for the states and territories. Each state and territory has enacted relevant legislation:

- NSW – Surveillance Devices Act 2007.
- Queensland – Invasion of Privacy Act 1971.
- SA –Surveillance Devices Act 2016.
- Tasmania – Listening Devices Act 1991.
- Victoria – Surveillance Devices Act 1999.
- WA – Surveillance Devices Act 1998.
- ACT – Listening Devices Act 1992.
- NT – Surveillance Devices Act 2007.

127. In general, these statutes prohibit the covert use of listening and optical surveillance devices to listen to or record conversations, to record visually or observe an activity, and tracking and data surveillance devices. The regulation of surveillance devices at the state and territory level means that there may be differences in regulation across Australia.[287] Current legislation also tends to be device-specific, which may mean that regulation is not able to encompass adequately new technology.[288]

128. Under the Surveillance Devices Act 2007 (NSW), the prohibition on the use of a listening device does not apply if a party to the conversation consents to the use of the listening device and the recording is necessary for the protection of that person's lawful interests.[289] In WA, the Surveillance Devices Act 1998 (WA) authorizes the publication of information that might otherwise have been prohibited if it is necessary to protect or further the public interest, provided that a judge has authorized the publication.[290]

---

287. Australian Law Reform Commission, *Serious Invasions of Privacy in the Digital Era: Issues Paper* (IP 43, Oct. 2013), http://www.alrc.gov.au/inquiries/invasions-privacy (accessed 1 Mar. 2014), 47.
288. Australian Law Reform Commission, *Serious Invasions of Privacy in the Digital Era: Issues Paper* (IP 43, October 2013), http://www.alrc.gov.au/inquiries/invasions-privacy (accessed 1 Mar. 2014), 47.
289. Surveillance Devices Act 2007 (NSW), s. 7(3). *See also* Invasion of Privacy Act 1971 (QLD); Surveillance Devices Act 2016 (SA); Listening Devices Act 1991 (TAS); Surveillance Devices Act 1999 (VIC); Listening Devices Act 1992 (ACT), and Surveillance Devices Act (NT).
290. Surveillance Devices Act 1998 (WA), s. 31(1).

Chapter 4. Right to Reply

129. No specific right of reply obligation is imposed on media in Australia (*see also* Part III, Chapter 3, section 5 *infra*). During the discussions which led to the uniform defamation scheme (*see* Chapter 3, section 2, I *supra*), the introduction of a right of reply was considered. It was not intended that a right of reply be compulsory, rather, if the media allowed a right of reply to a person claiming they had been defamed, damages would be reduced or not awarded if the matter went to trial.[291] This proposal was not included in the agreed uniform defamation scheme.

130. In the MEAA Journalists' Code of Ethics, journalists are encouraged to 'do your utmost to give a fair opportunity for reply'.[292] The APC General Statement of Principles also encourages an opportunity for a response:

> Ensure that where material refers adversely to a person, a fair opportunity is given for subsequent publication of a reply if that is reasonably necessary to address a possible breach of General Principle 3 [fairness and balance].[293]

131. The MEAA and the APC schemes are both self-regulatory schemes (*see* Chapter 6 *infra*). The ABC also encourages a right of reply in its editorial policies (*see* Part III, Chapter 3, section 5 *infra*).

132. Within the context of defamation proceedings, there is an understanding that the common law defence of qualified privilege (*see* Chapter 3, section 2, IX, D *supra*) offers a de facto right of reply. It may be that the defendant in publishing the alleged defamatory matter has responded to an attack on his/her reputation. In such circumstances, the reply would be an occasion of privilege.[294] To gain the defence of qualified privilege, the reply must be commensurate with the attack. Thus, if the plaintiff had made the attack in the public press, the defendant may choose to reply using the same medium.[295]

291. Australian Government, Attorney-General's Department, *Revised Outline of a possible National Defamation Law* (July 2004) http://www.auscheck.info/www/agd/rwpattach.nsf/VAP/(CFD7369FCAE9B8F32F341DBE097801FF)~0+0+defamationV5+19+August.pdf/$file/0+0+defamationV5+19+August.pdf (accessed 10 Feb. 2014), 32–33.
292. MEAA Journalists' Code of Ethics, cl. 1.
293. APC General Statement of Principles, General Principle 4.
294. *Loveday v. Sun Newspapers Ltd* (1938) 59 CLR 503, 511 (HCA), per Latham CJ. See also *Harbour Radio Pty Ltd v. Trad* (2012) 247 CLR 31, (HCA).
295. *Loveday v. Sun Newspapers Ltd* (1938) 59 CLR 503, 512 (HCA), per Latham CJ.

Chapter 5. Access to Public Information

§1. Public Documents

133. A right of access to government information is accorded by the Australian government and each state and territory government. Freedom of Information (FOI) was first introduced in Australia in 1982 by the Australian Government and the Victorian state government. In general, the FOI legislative model provides a statutory right to access official documents, subject to certain exemptions. The laws in place are as follows:

– Cth – Freedom of Information Act 1982.
– NSW – Government Information (Public Access) Act 2009.
– Queensland – Right to Information Act 2009.
– SA – Freedom of Information Act 1991.
– Tasmania – Right to Information Act 2009.
– Victoria – Freedom of Information Act 1982.
– WA – Freedom of Information Act 1992.
– ACT – Freedom of Information Act 2016.
– NT – Information Act 2002

134. Section 11 of the Freedom of Information Act 1982 (Cth) (FOI(Cth)) sets out the general approach to access:[296]

(1) Subject to this Act, every person has a legally enforceable right to obtain access in accordance with this Act to:
   (a) a document of an agency, other than an exempt document; or
   (b) an official document of a Minister, other than an exempt document.
(2) Subject to this Act, a person's right of access is not affected by:
   (a) any reasons the person gives for seeking access; or
   (b) the agency's or Minister's belief as to what are his or her reasons for seeking access.

135. Agencies under the FOI(Cth),[297] and the state and territory equivalents, may be government departments, statutory bodies, and in the case of state legislation, local authorities.[298]

296. The equivalent provisions in the states and territory legislation are: Government Information (Public Access) Act 2009 (NSW), s. 9; Right to Information Act 2009 (QLD), s. 23; Freedom of Information Act 1991 (SA), s. 12; Right to Information Act 2009 (TAS), s. 7; Freedom of Information Act 1982 (VIC), s. 13; Freedom of Information Act 1992 (WA), s. 10; Freedom of Information Act 2016 (ACT), s. 7; Information Act 2002 (NT), s. 15.
297. Freedom of Information Act 1982 (Cth), s. 4.
298. *See*, for example, Government Information (Public Access) Act 2009 (NSW), s. 4.

136. In NSW, the emphasis is slightly different. The Government Information (Public Access) Act 2009 refers to a presumption in favour of disclosure of government information unless there is an 'overriding public interest against disclosure',[299] although section 9 refers to a person, who makes an access application for government information having a legally enforceable right to be provided with access, subject to the public interest constraint.

137. The FOI statutory schemes tend to operate along similar lines. Accordingly, the Federal scheme under the FOI (Cth) will be described, and any notable state or territory differences will be mentioned. Access applications are made in writing in the prescribed manner, and there is no standing or qualification required for the person applying.[300] A fee for the application may be required.[301] Once an application is made, the requested Minister or agency, must within thirty days, take all reasonable steps to enable the applicant to be notified of a decision.[302] There is some scope for extensions. The time frame for responses tends to be between twenty-five and forty-five days across the states and territories.[303] Under the FOI (Cth), if a decision has been made to provide access, access must be provided as soon as reasonably practicable after the applicant has been notified of the decision, any charges for access have been paid, and the time period in which a third party may seek review of the decision has expired.[304]

138. An internal review of a decision on access can be sought by an applicant in the case of a refusal, or a third party in the case of a decision to grant access unless the decision was made by the Minister or by the principal officer, personally, of an agency.[305] If the person seeking review is not satisfied with the outcome of the internal review, a review by the Office of the Australian Information Commissioner (OAIC) may be sought.[306] It is not obligatory to seek an internal review before seeking a review by the OAIC, but the Commissioner regards it as good practice to proceed first with an internal review.[307] Where an internal review is not available, the person may seek a review by the OAIC. A person dissatisfied with the outcome of the OAIC's review may apply to the Administrative Appeals Tribunal.[308]

---

299. Government Information (Public Access) Act 2009 (NSW), s. 5.
300. Freedom of Information Act 1982 (Cth), s. 15.
301. Following reforms in 2010 to the Freedom of Information Act 1982 (Cth), there are no longer fees imposed for making an application.
302. Freedom of Information Act 1982 (Cth), s. 15(5).
303. *See*, for example, Right to Information Act 2009 (QLD), s. 18(1) (twenty-five days) and Freedom of Information Act 1992 (WA), s. 13 (forty-five days).
304. Freedom of Information Act 1982 (Cth), ss 20, 2629.
305. Freedom of Information Act 1982 (Cth), Pt VI.
306. Freedom of Information Act 1982 (Cth), Pt VII.
307. Office of the Australian Information Commissioner, *FOI Guidelines*, https://www.oaic.gov.au/freedom-of-information/foi-guidelines/part-10-review-by-the-information-commissioner (accessed 30 Jun. 2024), s. 10.2.
308. Freedom of Information Act 1982 (Cth), Pt VIIA.

139. Charges may be imposed in relation to the provision of access.[309] The amount of these charges may, in practical terms, limit accessibility. For example, a journalist was presented with a charge of approximately AUD 13,000 to access documents from an Australian Government department. On review by the Administrative Appeals Tribunal, the decision was affirmed.[310] However, following legislative amendments in 2010 (*see infra*), an agency has the discretion of whether to impose a charge and should consider the 'lowest reasonable cost' of the statutory objectives.[311] A journalist sought a review of a decision to charge AUD 265.73 to process documents. The documents related to asylum seeker decisions. The OAIC considered the charge reasonable but decided that the charge should be waived in full because of the public interest in these documents. The Commissioner noted that there was no presumption that the public interest test was satisfied because the applicant was a journalist, nor that a charge should not be waived because the applicant was a journalist.[312]

140. Not surprisingly, there is a wide range of exemptions and qualifications affecting the freedom to access public information. Some government agencies are expressly exempted from the operation of the FOI (Cth). For example, the Auditor-General, the Parliamentary Budget Office, and security organizations such as the Australian Security Intelligence Organisation (ASIO) are exempted agencies,[313] whilst some agencies may be exempt in relation to certain matters. For example, the ABC and the Special Broadcasting Service are exempt in relation to programme material and datacasting content, whilst the Australian Postal Corporation is exempt in relation to commercial activities.[314] Certain types of documents will have the effect of exempting agencies in relation to those documents, although there may be some discretion over whether to allow disclosure. Thus, for example, documents that relate to national security, defence, and international relations are exempt documents if disclosure would cause damage.[315] In other circumstances, documents may be conditionally exempt. Access to such documents will depend upon meeting a public interest test. For example, a document will be conditionally exempt if disclosure would, or could reasonably be expected to, damage Commonwealth and state or territory relations,[316] or because it relates to the deliberative processes exercised by Government, ministers, or agencies, and is the form of advice, opinion, or recommendations.[317] Documents are conditionally exempt if disclosure would involve the unreasonable disclosure of personal information of a person, including

309. Freedom of Information Act 1982 (Cth), s. 29.
310. *Peatling and Department of Employment and Workplace Relations* (2007) 44 AAR 494.
311. Office of the Australian Information Commissioner, *FOI Guidelines*, https://www.oaic.gov.au/freedom-of-information/foi-guidelines/part-4-charges-for-providing-access Pt 4.3.
312. *Australian Associated Press Pty Ltd and Department of Immigration and Border Protection* [2015] AICmr 65 (2 October 2015) http://www8.austlii.edu.au/cgi-bin/viewdoc/au/cases/cth/AICmr/2015/65.html (accessed 30 Jun. 2024).
313. Freedom of Information Act 1982 (Cth), s. 7(1) & Sch. 2, Pt I, div. 1.
314. Freedom of Information Act 1982 (Cth), s. 7(2) & Sch. 2, Pt II.
315. Freedom of Information Act 1982 (Cth), s. 33.
316. Freedom of Information Act 1982 (Cth), s. 47B.
317. Freedom of Information Act 1982 (Cth), s. 47C.

one who has died.[318] Access to documents that are classified as conditionally exempt under FOI (Cth) must be provided unless access '… at that time would, on balance, be contrary to the public interest'.[319]

141. It was noted above that the NSW FOI legislation, the Government Information (Public Access) Act 2009, operates on a principle of a presumption in favour of disclosure of government information. In 2010, the Federal Government made significant changes to the approach to FOI. The FOI Amendment (Reform) Act 2010 (Cth) created a new culture of openness and disclosure.[320] The statutory objectives were amended and now include the following statements:

(1) The objects of this Act are to give the Australian community access to information held by the Government of the Commonwealth, by:
   (a) requiring agencies to publish the information; and
   (b) providing for a right of access to documents.
(2) The Parliament intends, by these objects, to promote Australia's representative democracy by contributing towards the following:
   (a) increasing public participation in Government processes, with a view to promoting better-informed decision-making;
   (b) increasing scrutiny, discussion, comment and review of the Government's activities.
(3) The Parliament also intends, by these objects, to increase recognition that information held by the Government is to be managed for public purposes, and is a national resource.
(4) The Parliament also intends that functions and powers given by this Act are to be performed and exercised, as far as possible, to facilitate and promote public access to information, promptly and at the lowest reasonable cost.[321]

142. Thus, the expectation is that information should be provided unless there is an overriding reason not to do so,[322] and there should generally be a culture of agencies publishing as much information as possible on websites.[323] Each agency must publish an information publication plan that explains '… what the agency does and the way it does it, as well as information dealt with or used in the course of its operations, some of which is called operational information'.[324] The process for making FOI requests was also made simpler, and application fees were removed.

318. Freedom of Information Act 1982 (Cth), s. 47F.
319. Freedom of Information Act 1982 (Cth), s. 11A(5).
320. Amendments made by the Freedom of Information Amendment (Reform) Act 2010 (Cth) have been incorporated into the Freedom of Information Act 1982 (Cth) and references will be to the latter.
321. Freedom of Information Act 1982 (Cth), s. 3(1)–(4).
322. Freedom of Information Act 1982 (Cth), s. 11A.
323. Freedom of Information Act 1982 (Cth), Pt II.
324. Freedom of Information Act 1982 (Cth), s. 7A.

§2. COURT HEARINGS AND DOCUMENTS

I. Access to Courts

143. The long-established principle of open justice guides the determination of access to courts and to court-related documents, and the reports and commentary on court proceedings. Under the open justice principle, it is expected that courts will sit in public. An open court is assumed to encourage scrutiny and to maintain confidence in the courts and the judicial process.[325] The open justice principle has particular relevance to the media because it will often be the vehicle through which the public is made aware of legal proceedings and the court process. However, as part of a commitment to open justice, some courts now livestream selected proceedings, particularly where there might be a strong public interest.[326] The open justice principle is not unqualified and will be overridden, where it may be necessary to ensure the proper administration of justice.[327] In late 2018, a senior Catholic official, and Australia's most senior, the late Cardinal George Pell, was found guilty of charges of child sexual abuse (later acquitted on appeal). A suppression order, pursuant to sections 17 and 18 of the Open Courts Act 2013 (Vic.), was made which prevented any reporting on the proceedings. Cardinal Pell faced further criminal charges. The order, on the application of the prosecution, was made to ensure a fair trial of the second proceedings. That trial did not proceed, and so in February 2019, the suppression orders were lifted. Given the profile of Cardinal Pell, the suppression order was understandable, but it also illustrates the challenge of such orders in a modern media environment, especially when a case may attract international interest. Whilst Australian media could not report on the proceedings, it was possible to find coverage online.[328]

144. At common law, a superior court has an inherent jurisdiction to close a court whilst an inferior court has an implied jurisdiction to exercise power to close the court.[329] Given that the media are accorded no special status, the media will also be excluded from access if a court is closed. The common law power to override the open justice principle is used cautiously. It should only be used in 'wholly exceptional' circumstances, not merely where it might be useful or desirable or whether it may save distress or embarrassment.[330] Whilst the circumstances in

325. *Hogan v. Hinch* (2011) 243 CLR 506, 530 (HCA), per French CJ.
326. *See*, for example, the Federal Court of Australia: https://www.fedcourt.gov.au/digital-law-library/videos.
327. *Hogan v. Hinch* (2011) 243 CLR 506, 531 (HCA), per French CJ.
328. M. Douglas & J. Bosland, 'We knew George Pell was guilty of child sex abuse. Why couldn't we say it until now?', *The Conversation,* 26 Feb. 2019, https://theconversation.com/we-knew-george-pell-was-guilty-of-child-sex-abuse-why-couldnt-we-say-it-until-now-112521 (accessed 17 Mar. 2019).
329. *Hogan v. Hinch* (2011) 243 CLR 506, 531 (HCA), per French CJ. A superior court is a court having a general jurisdiction whilst an inferior court will have a jurisdiction that is limited in scope.
330. *See John Fairfax Publications Pty Ltd v. Ryde Local Court* (2005) 62 NSWLR 512, 516 (NSWCA), per Spigelman CJ.; *Attorney-General (NSW) v. Mayas Pty Ltd* (1988) 14 NSWLR 342, 347 (NSWCA), per Mahoney JA.; *John Fairfax Group Pty Ltd v. Local Court of NSW* (1991) 26 NSWLR 131, 142–143 (NSWCA), per Kirby P.

which a court will be closed are not circumscribed, there are some well-recognized situations, such as protection of an informer, protection of blackmail victims and matters of national security.[331] The circumstances in which the open justice principle will be departed from will be extended in exceptional circumstances only.[332]

145. The open justice principle also contemplates that, in the absence of any restriction, a fair and accurate report of proceedings may be published. This may include identification of the parties and witnesses and details of the evidence and testimonies.[333] Orders prohibiting the publication of reports of proceedings or the publication of aspects of those proceedings should also only be made where it is necessary for the due administration of justice.[334]

146. In addition to the common law qualifications to the open justice principle, there are a large number of statutory exceptions. Like the common law, the statutory exceptions may affect whether or not the court is closed or the extent to which material about the proceedings may be published. There are statutory exceptions at the federal level as well as state and territory levels. It is not practicable to describe every statutory exception, but some examples will be given to illustrate the type of matters where it has been thought appropriate to provide exceptions to the open justice principle. Courts will often have a general statutory power to close a court. For example, the Federal Court of Australia Act 1976 (Cth) affirms the principle of open justice but provides that there is a power to override that principle where necessary:

> (1) Except where, as authorized by this Act or another law of the Commonwealth, the jurisdiction of the Court is exercised by a Judge sitting in Chambers, the jurisdiction of the Court shall be exercised in open court.
>
> (1A) For the purposes of subsection (1), the circumstances in which the jurisdiction of the Court is exercised in open court include where the exercise of jurisdiction is made accessible to the public by way of video link, audio link or other appropriate means.
>
> … .
>
> (4) The Court may order the exclusion of the public or of persons specified by the Court from a sitting of the Court where the Court is satisfied that the presence of the public or of those persons, as the case may be, would be contrary to the interests of justice.
>
> (5) The reference in subsection (4) to a sitting of the Court includes a reference to a sitting of the court that is conducted by way of video link, audio link or other appropriate means. [335]

331. *See John Fairfax Group Pty Ltd v. Local Court of NSW* (1991) 26 NSWLR 131, 159 (NSWCA), per Mahoney JA.; *John Fairfax Publications Pty Ltd v. District Court of NSW* (2004) 61 NSWLR 344, 353 & 358 (NSWCA), per Spigelman CJ.; *Raybos Australia Pty Ltd v. Jones* (1985) 2 NSWLR 47, 54 (NSWCA), per Kirby P.
332. *Hogan v. Hinch* (2011) 243 CLR 506, 531 (HCA), per French CJ.
333. *Hogan v. Hinch* (2011) 243 CLR 506, 532 (HCA), per French CJ.
334. *John Fairfax & Sons Ltd v. Police Tribunal of New South Wales* (1986) 5 NSWLR 465, 476 (NSWCA), per McHugh JA.
335. Federal Court of Australia Act 1976 (Cth), s. 17.

147. The Federal Court of Australia Act 1976 (Cth) also makes provisions for non-publication orders and suppression orders. Non-publication orders are orders that restrict or prohibit the publication of information (including documents), whilst suppression orders are orders that prohibit or restrict the disclosure of information (including documents).[336] In deciding whether to make a suppression or non-publication order, the Court must 'take into account that a primary objective of the administration of justice is to safeguard the public interest in open justice'.[337] The grounds upon which the court may make a publication or suppression order are because the order is necessary to:

- prevent prejudice to the proper administration of justice;
- prevent prejudice to the interests of the Commonwealth or a state or territory in relation to national or international security;
- protect the safety of any person;
- avoid causing undue distress or embarrassment to a party or witness in a criminal proceeding involving an offence of a sexual nature.[338]

148. The types of matters covered by the order include:

- information relating to the identity of a party, witness, or any person related to a party or witness in proceedings before the court;
- information that is evidence or about evidence;
- information produced under a subpoena;
- information lodged or filed in the Court.[339]

149. The making of a non-publication order or a suppression order will obviously have relevance to the media, and the legislation permits a news publisher to be heard by the Court on an application for a non-publication order or suppression order.[340] A news publisher is defined as 'a person engaged in the business of publishing news or a public or community broadcasting service engaged in the publishing of news through a public news medium'.[341]

150. The legislative provisions dealing with suppression and non-publication orders enacted in the Federal Court of Australia Act 1976 (Cth) are based on model provisions that were agreed to in 2010 by the Standing Committee of Attorneys-General, a council comprising the Attorneys-General of the Federal Government and each state and territory government (as well as the New Zealand Minister for Justice).[342] The Court Suppression and Non-publication Orders Model Bill was developed to streamline the process for making suppression and non-publication orders but within the context of the open justice principle. To date, only NSW and

336. Federal Court of Australia Act 1976 (Cth), s. 37AA.
337. Federal Court of Australia Act 1976 (Cth), s. 37AE.
338. Federal Court of Australia Act 1976 (Cth), s. 37AG.
339. Federal Court of Australia Act 1976 (Cth), s. 37AF.
340. Federal Court of Australia Act 1976 (Cth), s. 37AH.
341. Federal Court of Australia Act 1976 (Cth), s. 37AA.
342. It is now known as the Council of Attorneys-General.

the Federal Government have enacted the model legislation, although Victoria's Open Courts Act 2013 is based to some extent on the principles of the model bill.[343] The Court Suppression and Non-Publication Orders Act 2010 (NSW) has been considered by the NSW Court of Appeal.[344] The appeal concerned the granting of a suppression order in relation to proceedings over a family trust dispute.[345] A suppression order had been granted by the trial judge and was appealed against by some of the plaintiff's family members and a number of media organizations also intervened. The trustee, Gina Rinehart, had sought a suppression order on the basis that the proceedings were an abuse of process because they were commenced without compliance with the trust deed's alternative dispute resolution procedures, which would have been confidential. The Court of Appeal noted that:

> The principle of legality favours a construction of legislation such as the [… Court Suppression and Non-Publication Orders Act 2010] which, consistently with the statutory scheme, has the least adverse impact upon the open justice principle and common law freedom of speech and, where constructional choices are open, so as to minimize its intrusion upon that principle.[346]

The Court of Appeal upheld the appeal. In the view of the majority, the judge at first instance in considering whether to grant a suppression order had failed to consider whether there was a basis that had the least impact on the open justice principle and had been dismissive of the public interest element in the dispute involving alleged misconduct of the trustee.[347] Further, the trial judge had erred by treating the terms of the trust deed as effectively determinative of the question of whether a suppression order should be made.[348]

151. Beyond general provisions affirming the open justice principle or providing for circumstances in which the open justice principle may be overridden, most jurisdictions will have statutory exceptions covering particular circumstances or proceedings.[349] For example, the Criminal Procedure Act 1986 (NSW) requires the proceedings, or parts of the proceedings, in relation to certain sexual offences to be closed. In some situations, the Court will be closed where the complainant is giving

343. The Victorian legislation has been under review: The Hon. Frank Vincent AO QC, *Open Courts Act Review*, Sept. 2017, https://engage.vic.gov.au/open-courts-act-review (accessed 17 Mar. 2019). The Victorian Government has announced that it will adopt many of the recommendations: S. Ilanbey, 'Andrews vows to implement suppression order overhaul this term', *The Age*, 13 Dec. 2018, https://www.theage.com.au/national/victoria/andrews-vows-to-implement-suppression-order-overhaul-this-term-20181213-p50lz7.html (accessed 17 Mar. 2019).
344. *Rinehart v. Welker* [2011] NSWCA 403 (NSWCA).
345. The proceedings relate to a dispute within the family of Gina Rinehart. Ms Rinehart is one of Australia's wealthiest women, because of extensive mining interests. Any matters concerning Ms Rinehart and her family tend to generate considerable media interest.
346. *Rinehart v. Welker* [2011] NSWCA 403, [26] (NSWCA), per Bathurst CJ. & McColl JA.
347. *Rinehart v. Welker* [2011] NSWCA 403, [49] & [52] (NSWCA), per Bathurst CJ. & McColl JA.
348. *Rinehart v. Welker* [2011] NSWCA 403, [51] (NSWCA), per Bathurst CJ. & McColl JA.
349. The examples provided here are from the Federal or NSW legislation.

evidence whilst the whole of the proceedings relating to incest offences must be closed.[350] The Court does have the discretion to permit media organizations to view or hear the evidence.[351]

152. Specific arrangements are also made for criminal proceedings involving children. In NSW, the court has the power to exclude from proceedings anyone not directly interested where the proceedings involve children.[352] A family victim may remain,[353] and so may media representatives unless the court otherwise directs.[354] There are also restrictions on the publication or broadcast of the names of children who may be connected with criminal proceedings as an offender, witness, victim, or brother or sister of a victim.[355] However, there are exceptions to these restrictions, including the following circumstances:

- An official report of the proceedings is being published or broadcast.[356]
- A person has been convicted of a serious children's indictable offence, and the court has authorized the publication or broadcast of the name.[357]
- A person who is 16 years or older at the time of publication or broadcasting has consented, or the court has consented.[358]

153. Another area where the open justice principle may be overridden relates to matters concerning national security. Under the Criminal Code, the court may order that the court is closed or prohibit a report of the whole or part of the proceedings.[359] In defamation proceedings brought by a former member of the Special Air Service Regiment, the Commonwealth Attorney-General gave notice that the National Security Information (Criminal and Civil Proceedings) Act 2004 (Cth) applied to the proceedings. The result was that evidence was given in open court and closed court.[360]

154. The Family Law Act 1975 (Cth) restricts the publication of any account of family law proceedings if it identifies a party to the proceedings; a witness; or a person who is related to or associated with a party to the proceedings.[361] Adoption proceedings are to be heard in a closed court, although the court has the discretion to permit persons who are not parties to the proceedings to be present.[362]

350. Criminal Procedure Act 1986 (NSW), ss 291, 291A, 291B.
351. Criminal Procedure Act 1986 (NSW), s. 291C.
352. Children (Criminal Proceedings) Act 1987 (NSW), s. 10.
353. Children (Criminal Proceedings) Act 1987 (NSW), s. 10(1)(c).
354. Children (Criminal Proceedings) Act 1987 (NSW), s. 10(1)(b).
355. Children (Criminal Proceedings) Act 1987 (NSW), s. 15A.
356. Children (Criminal Proceedings) Act 1987 (NSW), s. 15B.
357. Children (Criminal Proceedings) Act 1987 (NSW), s. 15C.
358. Children (Criminal Proceedings) Act 1987 (NSW), s. 15D.
359. Criminal Code Act 1995 (Cth), s. 93.2.
360. *Roberts-Smith v. Fairfax Media Publications Pty Ltd (No 41)* [2023] FCA 555.
361. Family Law Act 1975 (Cth), s. 114Q.
362. Adoption Act 2000 (NSW), s. 119.

II. Access to Court Documents

155. Another element of the open justice principle will be the capacity for accessing the court file, created when proceedings commence.[363] The documents contained within the court file may be important for the media reporting on the trial in order to provide context and to understand the issues in the proceedings. Access to the court file has become more crucial as modern court practice has moved away from former practices where documents, evidence and submissions were always read aloud in court. However, at common law, the principle of open justice does not create a freestanding right of access to court documents.[364] Nevertheless, in considering whether to provide the media with access to documents within the court file, the courts will be guided by the principle of open justice.[365]

156. Although there is no right of access to the court file, court practices accommodate requests for access. There is no uniform approach across Australia, and as there are multiple courts, taking into account the Federal, state and territory jurisdictions, pursuing access can be complex for media organizations. A recent review of the operation of open justice and access to information in NSW noted that current access regimes were overly complex and created barriers to access.[366] As it is not practicable to describe the approaches used across all jurisdictions, a few examples to illustrate the approaches taken will be provided.

157. The Federal Court of Australia provides non-parties (which includes media representatives) to proceedings with a right of access to certain documents such as the originating claim, pleadings, interlocutory applications, judgments, Court orders, a notice of change of lawyer, reasons for judgment, and a notice of appeals.[367] However, documents that are confidential, or restricted or prohibited from publication may not be accessed if the prohibition covers the person or class of persons the applicant is part of.[368] A person may apply to the Court for access to documents not encompassed within the access provision.[369] By contrast, the Supreme Court of New South Wales prohibits access except with the leave of the

363. *John Fairfax Publications Pty Ltd v. Ryde Local Court* (2005) 62 NSWLR 512, 520 (NSWCA), per Spigelman CJ.
364. *John Fairfax Publications Pty Ltd v. Ryde Local Court* (2005) 62 NSWLR 512, 520 (NSWCA), per Spigelman CJ.
365. *John Fairfax Publications Pty Ltd v. Ryde Local Court* (2005) 62 NSWLR 512, 520 (NSWCA), per Spigelman CJ.
366. NSW Law Reform Commission, *Open Justice: Court and tribunal information: access, disclosure and publication* (Report 149, May 2022) https://lawreform.nsw.gov.au/documents/Publications/Reports/Report%20149.pdf (accessed 29 Jun. 2024), para. 4.11 and Ch. 4 generally.
367. Federal Court Rules 2011 (Cth), r. 2.32(2). A similar approach is taken in some state jurisdictions also; for example: Supreme Court of Victoria (General Civil Procedure) Rules 2015 (VIC), ord. 28.05 and Uniform Civil Procedure Rules 1999 (QLD), r. 975H.
368. Federal Court Rules 2011 (Cth), r. 2.32(3).
369. Federal Court Rules 2011 (Cth), r. 2.32(4).

Court.[370] Thus, no person may search a registry or inspect any document or thing in any proceeding.[371] The effect of this rule is that access must be determined on a case-by-case basis; however, the rules indicate when access will normally be provided to non-parties, in respect of:

- pleadings and judgments in proceedings that have been concluded, except where a confidentiality order has been made;
- documents that record what was said or done in open court;
- material, normally including evidence in electronic mediums such as video and audio tapes, DVDs and CD-ROMs, that was admitted into evidence; and
- information that would have been heard or seen by a person present in open court.[372]

158. Access to other documents will only be permitted if the court is satisfied that exceptional circumstances exist.[373] The Practice Note also explains the reasoning for the Supreme Court's approach:

> 14. It should not be assumed that material held by the Court comes within paragraph 7. Affidavits and witness statements that are filed in proceedings are often never read in open court. This can occur because they contain matter that is objected to and rejected on any one of a number of grounds or because the proceedings have settled before coming on for hearing. Affidavits, statements, exhibits and pleadings may contain matter that is scandalous, frivolous, vexatious, irrelevant or otherwise oppressive … .
> 15. If access to material were to be given prior to the conclusion of the proceedings to which it relates, material that is ultimately not read in open court or admitted into evidence would be seen. Thus access will not normally be allowed prior to the conclusion of the proceedings.
> 16. Even where material has been read in open court or is included in pleadings, there may be good reasons for refusing access. Material that has been rejected or not used or struck out as being scandalous, frivolous, vexatious, irrelevant or otherwise oppressive, may still be legible. Where access to material would be otherwise unobjectionable, it may concern matters that are required to be kept confidential by statute … or by public interest immunity considerations.[374]

159. A different approach in NSW is taken to criminal proceedings. A right is given expressly to the media to inspect any document at any time after the proceedings commence until two working days after the completion of the proceedings, for the purpose of compiling a fair report of the proceedings for publication. This right

370. Supreme Court (NSW), Practice Note SC Gen 2 (4 Oct. 2019), para. 6. These rules apply to the Court of Appeal, the Court of Criminal Appeal, and each of the divisions of the Supreme Court (NSW).
371. Supreme Court (NSW), Practice Note SC Gen 2 (4 Oct. 2019), para. 6.
372. Supreme Court (NSW), Practice Note SC Gen 2 (4 Oct. 2019), para. 7.
373. Supreme Court (NSW), Practice Note SC Gen 2 (4 Oct. 2019), para. 7.
374. Supreme Court (NSW), Practice Note SC Gen 2 (4 Oct. 2019), paras 14–16.

does not override any restrictions there may be on proceedings or material pursuant to a non-publication or suppression order, or that is otherwise prohibited from publication.[375] As may be expected, proceedings that may be required to be conducted in closed court, will also normally mean that access to court documents is restricted. Thus, for example, access to the court records in adoption proceedings is prohibited.[376]

160. As noted above, there is a variety of practices across the Australian court system. Even where access to court documents is possible, the practice adopted at the court registry level may result in limiting access because of costs, unclear processes, and delays.[377] There have been attempts to try to harmonize the rules and practices concerning access to court documents. Legislation passed by NSW, the Court Information Act 2010,[378] was intended to form the basis of a model law to be considered by the, then, Standing Committee of Attorneys-General. However, this has not progressed, and at a meeting of the Standing Committee, it was resolved that this matter would be removed from the agenda of the Standing Committee, and governments would be left to review their own systems.[379]

III. Contempt of Court

161. Contempt of court is concerned with conduct that interferes or is likely to interfere with the administration of justice. It encompasses a wide range of situations including disobedience to an order or judgment of the court, but there are some forms of contempt that are of particular relevance to the media, and it is these forms that will be considered here. Contempt of court has also been categorized into two areas: criminal contempt and civil contempt. The latter form of contempt is usually more concerned with, for example, disobedience to a court order, undertaking, or judgment. Civil contempt has been seen as remedial or coercive, a matter more for the parties to the proceedings to be concerned with, whilst criminal contempt has been viewed as being '… in the public interest to vindicate judicial authority or maintain the integrity of the judicial process …'.[380] However, although still

375. Criminal Procedure Act 1986 (NSW) s. 314.
376. Adoption Act 2000 (NSW), s. 143.
377. In 2008, a report was commissioned by a group of media organizations reviewing practices in relation to suppression orders and access to court documents. The report showed the variety of practices and difficulties that could arise accessing documents: Innes, P., *Report of the Review of Suppression Orders and The Media's Access to Court Documents and Information* (13 Nov. 2008) http://www.australiasrighttoknow.com.au/files/docs/Reports2008/13-Nov-2008ARTK-Report.pdf (accessed 6 Apr. 2014), 44 & Ch. 3 generally.
378. This law has never come into operation.
379. Standing Committee of Attorneys-General, Communiqué (December 2010) http://www.sclj.gov.au/agdbasev7wr/sclj/documents/pdf/scag_public_oos_decisions_december_2010_final.pdf (accessed 6 Apr. 2014).
380. *Witham v. Holloway* (1995) 183 CLR 525, 531 (HCA).

referred to, the distinction between criminal and civil contempt is becoming less relevant, and the basis for the distinction has been criticized by the HCA as illusory.[381] In the Court's view, there is a public interest in all forms of contempt as a vindication of the Court's authority.[382]

162. However, the types of contempt that are likely to be of most relevance to the media fall within the category of criminal contempt, and the consequences can be serious with the possibility of penalties such as fines and imprisonment. In late 2013, a radio journalist, Derryn Hinch, was fined AUD 100,000 in the Supreme Court of Victoria for contempt. He refused to pay the fine and subsequently spent fifty days in gaol. The journalist was found guilty of contempt for breach of a non-publication order having published details of the past life of an accused murderer.[383] The main aspects of contempt likely to be relevant to the media concern:

- Disclosure of sources.
- Breach of a non-publication order or disclosure of material related to closed proceedings.
- Sub judice contempt.
- Scandalizing the court.
- Revealing jury deliberations.

163. Journalists are particularly vulnerable to contempt of court charges if they refuse to disclose their sources when required to do so by the court. Disclosure of sources and shield laws was considered earlier in Part II (*see* Chapter 2, section 3, I *supra*). The absence of any general privilege for journalists means that journalists must evaluate their position and obligations on a case-by-case basis. As shown earlier, contempt convictions for refusal to disclose sources are of contemporary relevance.

164. Qualifications to the open justice principle in the form of closed courts and restrictions on what can be disclosed or published will restrict the capacity of the media to report on court proceedings (*see* section 2, I *supra*). Disobedience will constitute a contempt of court, as was the case in the Derryn Hinch matter (*supra*).

165. Sub judice contempt prohibits the publication of material that might prejudice legal proceedings. The concern is that the publication might interfere with the proper administration of justice. Sub judice contempt does not arise until the proceedings are pending. Thus, the fact that proceedings are imminent will not give rise to a liability for contempt of court, although there could be some other liability such as defamation.[384] In the case of criminal proceedings, a matter is generally sub

381. *Witham v. Holloway* (1995) 183 CLR 525, 534 (HCA). *See also Australasian Meat Industry Employees' Union v. Mudginberri Station Pty Ltd* (1986) 161 CLR 98, 107 (HCA), where the distinction was described as unsatisfactory.
382. *Witham v. Holloway* (1995) 183 CLR 525, 532 (HCA).
383. *R v. Hinch (No. 2)* [2013] VSC 554 (18 Oct. 2013). The journalist, something of a 'shock-jock', had a number of previous convictions for contempt.
384. *James v. Robinson* (1963) 109 CLR 593, 607 (HCA).

judice from the time that a person is arrested or charged and will remain pending until the proceedings are resolved. This may occur when the person has been acquitted or sentenced, or when charges have been withdrawn, or when the time for lodging an appeal has expired. If an appeal has been lodged, then the proceedings will remain pending until all appeals have been heard. Civil proceedings will be considered pending once some initiating action has taken place, such as a statement of claim, and will remain pending until the matter has been decided.

166. Sub judice contempt will arise if the publication has a tendency to interfere with the administration of justice in the requisite proceedings.[385] Actual interference does not have to be established.[386] Further, the risk of interference should be a substantial risk.[387] It is not necessary to establish an intention to interfere with the administration of justice, although an intention to publish the material must be established.[388] However, in the case of the media, this is not problematic.

167. To publish a comment about the guilt or innocence of a person facing trial will almost certainly constitute contempt.[389] This is particularly the case where the trial is before a jury, and the stronger the language used, the more likely will be the seriousness of the contempt.[390] Both the then Premier of NSW, Neville Wran, and the media organization which published the statements made by the Premier, were liable for contempt when the Premier spoke of his 'very deep conviction' that Mr Justice Murphy (a then judge of the HCA) was innocent of a charge of perverting the course of justice. At the time of the statement, a retrial had just been ordered. The court rejected an argument that there was a distinction between a statement that someone was innocent and a statement of belief about a person's innocence.[391] If the media publishes details of an accused person's previous convictions, it is likely to constitute contempt.[392]

168. Sub judice contempt may also arise if a publication might influence witnesses in the relevant proceedings. In the course of a coroner's inquest, into the deaths of seven people during a fire at a 'fun park', a witness suggested that a park attendant might have been responsible for the deaths of at least two boys. Following this evidence, a newspaper conducted a doorstop interview with the attendant, who had yet to give evidence at the inquest. The interview was reported on its front page. Whilst the Court considered that the possibility of the report affecting the coroner was so remote as to be disregarded, it took the view that the report could

385. *John Fairfax & Sons Pty Ltd and Reynolds v. McRae* (1955) 93 CLR 351 (HCA).
386. *Ex parte Bread Manufacturers Ltd; Re Truth and Sportsman Ltd* (1937) 37 SR(NSW) 242, 248 (NSWSC), per Jordan CJ.
387. *Hinch v. Attorney-General (Vic)* (1987) 164 CLR 15, 27–28 (HCA), per Mason CJ.
388. *Hinch v. Attorney-General (Vic)* (1987) 164 CLR 15, 69 (HCA), per Toohey J.
389. *Attorney-General (NSW) v. Radio 2UE Sydney Pty Ltd* [1998] NSWSC 28 (NSWCA).
390. *Attorney-General (NSW) v. Radio 2UE Sydney Pty Ltd* [1998] NSWSC 28 (NSWCA).
391. *Director of Public Prosecutions v. Wran* (1987) 7 NSWLR 616, 626–627 (NSWCA).
392. *Attorney-General (NSW) v. Willesee* [1980] 2 NSWLR 143 & *Hinch v. Attorney-General (Vic)* (1987) 164 CLR 15. *See also R v. Hinch (No. 2)* [2013] VSC 554 (18 Oct. 2013) where the same journalist, Derryn Hinch was found liable for sub judice contempt by broadcasting details of previous convictions.

have an effect on the attendant and other witnesses and the manner in which they might give their evidence.[393] An exacerbating factor was the use of emotional and other devices in the reporting of the matter.[394]

169. By contrast, the reporting of matters, which were the subject of another coronial inquest, was held not to be contemptuous. In this case, the radio report took place after the Coroner had given notice of the inquest, but several months before the actual hearing. The inquest was established to investigate a plane crash in which a number of passengers died. The report included interviews with several witnesses who had been at the airport and with two air safety experts. In relation to the eye-witness accounts, the Court of Appeal considered that these interviews did not constitute contempt as they were merely stating their personal account of what they saw on the night and it was unlikely that anything they had said would interfere with the evidence of other witnesses. Moreover, they would not be giving evidence as to the cause of the crash or the deaths.[395] The reports of the interviews with the air safety experts were also held not to be contemptuous as they relied upon notes that they had made shortly after the accident and which had been admitted into evidence. Hence, it was unlikely that the interviews would interfere with the evidence they were to give. As expert witnesses, they were likely to be less vulnerable to influence from the reporting.[396] The Court of Appeal also noted that the facts of this case were different from the circumstances of the reporting in *Attorney-General (NSW) v. Mirror Newspapers Ltd.* In the former, the radio report was broadcast months before the actual inquest. It did not rely on sensationalist reporting or doorstop interviews as was the case in *Attorney-General (NSW) v. Mirror Newspapers Ltd,* nor was there any evidence of serious inconsistencies in the evidence as there was in *Mirror Newspapers.* [397] Although the conclusions drawn by the reporter attributing blame to the airline company were contentious, the majority did not consider that they were contemptuous or that the public would not be able to distinguish the journalist's angle.[398] Kirby P made it clear that it was not the role of the law of contempt to act as some form of media quality control.[399]

170. Whilst the Court in *Civil Aviation Authority v. Australian Broadcasting Corporation* referred to the undesirability of trial by media, it acknowledged the importance of matters of public interest, such as matters before the Court, being

393. *Attorney-General (NSW) v. Mirror Newspapers Ltd* [1980] 1 NSWLR 374, 387–388 (NSWCA).
394. *Attorney-General (NSW) v. Mirror Newspapers Ltd* [1980] 1 NSWLR 374, 388 (NSWCA).
395. *Civil Aviation Authority v. Australian Broadcasting Corporation* (1995) 39 NSWLR 540, 551 (NSWCA), per Kirby P.
396. *Civil Aviation Authority v. Australian Broadcasting Corporation* (1995) 39 NSWLR 540, 551 (NSWCA), per Kirby P.
397. *Civil Aviation Authority v. Australian Broadcasting Corporation* (1995) 39 NSWLR 540, 552 (NSWCA), per Kirby P.
398. *Civil Aviation Authority v. Australian Broadcasting Corporation* (1995) 39 NSWLR 540, 560–561 (NSWCA), per Kirby P.
399. *Civil Aviation Authority v. Australian Broadcasting Corporation* (1995) 39 NSWLR 540, 557 (NSWCA), per Kirby P.

aired.[400] Thus, whilst the administration of justice is an important principle to be maintained, it must be balanced with interest in the public discussion of matters of concern.[401] Accordingly, a fair and accurate report of proceedings may be published.[402]

171. Another form of contempt of court referred to as 'scandalizing the court', may be committed if someone engages in criticism of the court that might have a real tendency to undermine public confidence in the administration of justice. Unlike sub judice contempt, scandalizing the court does not have to be related to particular proceedings. Scandalizing the court contempt is not intended to protect the judges personally from imputations, nor is it intended to restrict honest and fair criticism. The contempt is there to protect against criticism that undermines the authority of the courts and legal system.[403] Deciding where the boundary falls between honest criticism, that might be 'wrong-headed' or discourteous, and criticism that will constitute contempt will involve 'questions of degree'. It has been suggested that criticism that is 'merely scurrilous abuse' will constitute contempt. Unjustified allegations of personal bias or some judicial mala fides will also probably constitute contempt.[404] In a recent appeal which concerned the contempt of a party to the proceedings, the Court of Appeal upheld the contempt convictions on the ground that the statements constituted scurrilous abuse, a sub-category of 'scandalizing the court' contempt.[405] Assertions that a judge tampered with court proceedings transcripts that the District Court was corrupt and that another judge engaged in corruption were not legitimate criticisms of court decisions, but scurrilous abuse.[406] Whilst the assertions were unlikely to have had the effect of influencing the outcome of proceedings still pending, those assertions were calculated to induce a lack of confidence in the administration of justice.[407]

172. Clearly scandalizing the court contempt runs the risk of shutting down legitimate public debate and infringing freedom of expression. Prosecutions for scandalizing the court are not frequent, and in contemporary times judges seem more willing to engage in the public debate through the media when criticism is made of the judicial system. The media frequently publish strong criticism of judges' sentencing decisions, often ignoring the application of sentencing rules and guidelines within which the judiciary may have to operate. However, this form of contempt of court – scandalizing the court – is not dead. In 2006, the NSW Industrial Relations Commission (NSWIRC) gave consideration to whether proceedings

---

400. *Civil Aviation Authority v. Australian Broadcasting Corporation* (1995) 39 NSWLR 540, 560 (NSWCA), per Kirby P.
401. *Ex parte Bread Manufacturers Ltd; Re Truth and Sportsman Ltd* (1937) 37 SR(NSW) 242, 249 (NSWSC), per Jordan CJ.
402. *See Hinch v. Attorney-General (Vic)* (1987) 164 CLR 15 (HCA).
403. *R v. Dunbabin* (1935) 53 CLR 434, 442–443 (HCA), per Rich J. *See also Gallagher v. Durack* (1983) 152 CLR 238 (HCA).
404. *Attorney-General for New South Wales v. Mundey* [1972] 2 NSWLR 887, 908, 910–911 (NSWCA), per Hope JA.
405. *Mahaffy v. Mahaffy* [2018] NSWCA 42, para. 214 (NSWCA), per Simpson JA.
406. *Mahaffy v. Mahaffy* [2018] NSWCA 42, para. 223 (NSWCA), per Simpson JA.
407. *Mahaffy v. Mahaffy* [2018] NSWCA 42, para. 223 (NSWCA), per Simpson JA.

for contempt should be initiated against the then Federal Minister for Employment and Workplace Relations in relation to a media release that he had issued under the heading 'NSW Industrial Relations Commission shows no Interest in National Consistency and Fairness'.[408] The NSWIRC's consideration of the matter provides a useful recent analysis of the approach to criticism:

> Were it not for the last paragraph of the press statement, however, we would have more readily dismissed the Media Release, notwithstanding its distorted interpretation of the Statement of 17 May [statement of the Full Bench] and our earlier interlocutory decisions. Industrial tribunals are not immune from robust – even unfair – criticism, provided it does not descend into the realm of contempt for being malicious, designed to undermine the proper administration of justice or involving some other factor making it contemptuous. A balance has to be struck between the maintenance of the Commission's reputation for fairness, objectivity and integrity on the one hand and the freedom to criticize on the other. .... .
>
> However, the final paragraph of the Media Release transcended the field of legitimate 'public scrutiny and criticism' even in the 'highly charged, contentious world of industrial relations' and had, as we have noted, the real potential to bring the commission, into disrepute. Despite the attempt to cloak the reference with some third party concerned about the Commission's process, the inference seemed to us to be clearly available that the Minister was conveying his own view that the commission might be 'playing politics'.
>
> In our view, the inference was reasonably available that the Minister was conveying that either this Full Bench did not conform to the Commonwealth's expressed desire to have one body determined minimum wage adjustments, ..., for political motives or, the Full Bench was seeking to have the Commonwealth state its position on wages for political reasons and not for reasons associated with its duty as an independent quasi-judicial tribunal. On either view, serious issues arise, particularly when statements of this kind are made in connection with proceedings to which the maker of the statement is a party or intervener.[409]

173. The NSWIRC sought an explanation from the Minister and assurances that there was no intention to bring the Commission into disrepute. On that basis it decided not to initiate contempt proceedings; however, it explained that it had taken these steps in order to avoid any perception that it was 'amenable to intimidation or pressure from the Minister'.[410]

408. *Re State Wage Case 2006 (No. 5)* [2006] NSWIRComm 190 (26 Jun. 2006) (www.austlii.edu.au).

409. *Re State Wage Case 2006 (No. 5)* [2006] NSWIRComm 190, paras 15–17 (26 Jun. 2006) (www.austlii.edu.au).

410. *Re State Wage Case 2006 (No. 5)* [2006] NSWIRComm 190, para. 18 (26 Jun. 2006) (www.austlii.edu.au). *See also Environment Protection Authority v. Pannowitz* [2006] NSWLEC 219 (9 May 2006) (www.austlii.edu.au). In this matter, the accused was found guilty of contempt for suggesting that the NSW Land and Environment Court was being investigated for corruption.

174. At common law, it may also be contempt to disclose the deliberations of a jury.[411] However, the law in Australia is not settled. Whilst the disclosure of jury deliberations is considered inappropriate, it is not entirely clear whether disclosure by a juror would constitute contempt.[412] However, a media organization that published the disclosures by a juror might face contempt charges.[413]

175. Notwithstanding the uncertainty at common law, all Australian states and territories now have legislation in place dealing with the information about jurors and disclosure of deliberations:

- NSW – Jury Act 1977.
- Queensland – Jury Act 1995.
- SA – Criminal Law Consolidation Act 1935.
- Tasmania – Juries Act 2003.
- Victoria – Juries Act 2000.
- WA – Juries Act 1957.
- ACT – Juries Act 1967.
- NT – Juries Act 1962.

176. The legislative provisions generally deal with three main matters: disclosure of the identity of jurors; soliciting information from jurors; and, disclosure of information by jurors. Under section 68 of the Jury Act 1977 (NSW), it is an offence to publish wilfully, broadcast, or otherwise disclose information that is likely to lead to the identification of a juror or former juror, unless that person has consented.[414] Each of the other jurisdictions has a similar provision.[415]

177. In NSW there is a prohibition on soliciting information from a juror or former juror or harassing that juror, in order to obtain information about the deliberations of a jury or how conclusions were arrived at.[416] Queensland, Tasmania, and Victoria have similar provisions.[417] However, in the other four jurisdictions, the prohibition only applies to soliciting or obtaining information for the purposes of publication or

411. *Attorney-General v. New Statesman and Nation Publishing Co Ltd* [1981] QB 1.
412. In *Re Donovan's Application* [1957] VR 333 (14 Feb. 1957) (www.austlii.edu.au) the judge suggested that no constraint could be imposed on a juror who wanted to discuss his experiences of the trial, including what took place in the jury room.
413. *Attorney-General v. New Statesman and Nation Publishing Co Ltd* [1981] QB 1.
414. Jury Act 1977 (NSW), s. 68(1)–(2). There are exceptions for disclosure to authorities and for approved research purposes: s. 68(4)–(5).
415. Jury Act 1995 (QLD), s. 70(11); Criminal Law Consolidation Act 1935 (SA), s. 246; Juries Act 2003 (TAS), s. 57; Juries Act 2000 (VIC), s. 77; Juries Act 1957 (WA), s. 56B; Juries Act 1967 (ACT), s. 42C; and Juries Act 1962 (NT), s. 49B.
416. Jury Act 1977 (NSW), s. 68A. Again, there are exceptions for disclosure to authorities and for approved research purposes.
417. Jury Act 1995 (QLD), s. 70(3); Juries Act 2003 (TAS), s. 58(1)(b); and Juries Act 2000 (VIC), s. 78(1)(b).

facilitating the publication of the information.[418] With the exception of NSW, it is also an offence to publish information about jurors' deliberations.[419]

178. In NSW, there is a prohibition on a juror, save with the consent of the judge or coroner, wilfully disclosing, during the trial or coronial inquest, information about the deliberations of a jury or how conclusions were reached.[420] It should be noted that this prohibition applies only during the course of the trial. There is a more general prohibition that covers completed trials also, but this only operates when some form of reward is involved. Thus, a juror or former juror is not permitted, for a fee or reward, to disclose or offer to disclose information about the jury's deliberations or how conclusions were reached.[421] Deliberations are defined to include statements made, opinions expressed, arguments advanced or votes cast by jury members.[422] The effect of the NSW provisions is that a juror may publicly discuss information about jury deliberations provided the trial is completed, no solicitation is involved, and, no reward is given. A different position is adopted by other jurisdictions. In those jurisdictions, jurors or former jurors are not permitted to disclose information about jury deliberations if they are aware that the information is likely to be published to the public.[423]

---

418. Criminal Law Consolidation Act 1935 (SA), s. 246(3); Juries Act 1957 (WA), s. 56C(1); Juries Act 1967 (ACT), s. 42C(3); and Juries Act 1962 (NT), s. 49A(3).
419. Jury Act 1995 (QLD), s. 70(2); Criminal Law Consolidation Act 1935 (SA), s. 246(4); Juries Act 2003 (TAS), s. 58(1); Juries Act 2000 (VIC), s. 78(1); Juries Act 1957 (WA), s. 56D; Juries Act 1967 (ACT), s. 42C(4); and Juries Act 1962 (NT), s. 49A(4).
420. Jury Act 1977 (NSW), s. 68B(1).
421. Jury Act 1977 (NSW), s. 68B(2).
422. Jury Act 1977 (NSW), ss 68A(2) & 68B(3).
423. Jury Act 1995 (QLD), s. 70(4); Criminal Law Consolidation Act 1935 (SA), s. 246(2); Juries Act 2003 (TAS), s. 58(2)-(3); Juries Act 2000 (VIC), s. 78(2); Juries Act 1957 (WA), s. 56B(1); Juries Act 1967 (ACT), s. 42C(2); and Juries Act 1962 (NT), s. 49A(2).

Chapter 6. Supervision: Press

§1. The Press Council

179. Although the print media is mainly regulated through the general law, a self-regulatory scheme is in place to deal with complaints about newspapers, magazines and the associated websites of these print media outlets. With the advent of digital media, the APC also now manages complaints in relation to online-only publishers.[424] The APC was established in 1976 and is funded by contributions from its constituent members, although funding comes mainly from the print media industry.[425] In addition to adjudicating on complaints, the Council also takes responsibility for promoting good standards of practice within the media industry, and it may also make statements of policy on matters that might be relevant to access to information and freedom of expression. The Council is comprised of between 22 to 30 members comprising nine to twelve public members (all independent of media organizations); nine to twelve nominees of member media organizations (and the MEAA, the main union body for journalists); and, four to six journalists, as well as an independent chair.[426] The APC is constituted by its constituent bodies. These include the major print media publishers and now some online-only publishers. The constituent bodies provide funding for the APC and are entitled to select industry nominees on the Council. There is no mandatory obligation for a publisher to belong to the APC. This means that the position of the APC and its role in the adjudication of complaints can be sensitive.[427]

180. The Council has a set of Standards of Practice that comprise the Statements of Principles, Specific Standards, and non-binding advisory guidelines.[428] There is a General Statement of Principles and a Statement of Privacy Principles (in relation to the latter, *see* Chapter 3, section 3, II *supra*). The General Statement covers matters such as accurate, fair and balanced reporting; correction of inaccuracies; representation of facts and transparency; and, fair investigation. The APC has developed standards to assist with the application of the Statement of Principles in specific contexts. Currently, there are two specific standards addressing coverage of suicide and contacting patients. There are around thirteen advisory guidelines covering matters such as advertorials; digital alteration of images; opinion polls; reporting of 'race'; reporting elections; reporting on family and domestic violence; reporting on diverse sexual orientation; and, health and medical matters reporting.

424. https://presscouncil.org.au/complaints/information-for-complainants/.
425. *See*, for example, Australian Press Council, *Annual Report 2020-2021* (No. 44, 30 Jun. 2021) https://presscouncil.org.au/wp-content/uploads/2022/03/8416_AnnualReport_2020-2021_R17_WEB.pdf (accessed 14 Jun. 2023), 18.
426. Constitution of the Australian Press Council Inc, ss 11 and Annexure.
427. Most Australian newspapers and publishers are part of the APC scheme. One major newspaper, the *West Australian* (the only newspaper in WA) is not part of the scheme. It left the APC in 2012 and established its own council, the Independent Media Council to deal with complaints: http://independentmediacouncil.com.au/index.html. The publisher of the *West Australian* is the only publisher covered by the Independent Media Council.
428. http://www.presscouncil.org.au/standards/.

181. The complaints process undertaken by the APC is intended to be '… as informal, prompt and economical as possible'.[429] The APC will consider complaints about any published material whether it be a news report, editorial, general article, an image, or a cartoon.[430] It only considers complaints about advertising where the issue is whether the printed material is capable of being identified as advertising. The APC can consider complaints about publications that are not published by a constituent body, but its determinations will have no persuasive force. Any person may complain to the APC. A complaint can be made directly to the APC without first complaining to the publication although the APC may decide to request the complainant to raise the matter first with the publication. In general, a complaint must be made within thirty days of the first publication of the material being complained about. An APC complaint does not prevent a complainant from separately commencing legal action in relation to the publication, although the complainant must inform the APC if legal proceedings have been initiated or are likely to be. Where legal proceedings have commenced or may do so, the publisher being complained about can request the APC to delay adjudication of the complaint or require a confidentiality agreement from the complainant, or a commitment by the complainant not to commence proceedings. Because the APC adjudication of complaints is intended to be a speedy and informal process, the APC generally requires complainants to pursue complaints themselves and not to use lawyers or other professional representatives. Similarly, the publishers are expected to deal with the APC directly and not through lawyers.

182. An initial assessment is made when a complaint is received, and if it is to proceed, the complaint receives an informal consideration (referred to as Level 1). The executive director of the APC or another member of the complaints-handling staff usually deals with Level 1 complaints. One outcome of the Level 1 consideration is a referral to a Level 2 adjudication. The Council's Adjudication Panel undertakes this. An Adjudication Panel comprises the Chair (or one of the two vice-chairs) and an equal number of public and industry members. The Adjudication Panel will usually decide the matters on the paper. If the Panel recommends a full adjudication, then oral representations can be made by the complainant and media organization. The parties have an opportunity to review the provisional adjudication, following which the final adjudication is published on the APC's website.

183. The APC has limited sanctions available to it. It has no power to impose financial sanctions or to order compensation, nor can it require the publisher to take action such as making an apology or correction. In fact, the only action available to the APC is to declare a reprimand or censure, although it may call upon the publisher to make an apology or retraction, or to take some other form of remedial action. A publisher concerned in a complaint must publish the Council's adjudication promptly; for a daily publication, within seven days of notification of the adjudication. As part of the Level 1 consideration, the parties may agree to an outcome that involves an apology, correction, or some other action. Most matters are resolved

429. http://www.presscouncil.org.au/complaints/.
430. The complaints process is detailed at http://www.presscouncil.org.au/complaints/.

at the Level 1 stage. In the year ending 30 June 2021, 797 complaints were received. Of those complaints, fourteen were considered by an adjudication panel and 78% of those were upheld or partially upheld.[431]

184. In an inquiry into media regulation in Australia, the Inquiry's Final Report acknowledged that self-regulation through the APC had played a significant role in upholding standards of journalism, but concluded that the effectiveness of the APC was limited because of structural and funding weaknesses, and the ability of publishers to withdraw.[432] Although the Inquiry recommended the establishment of a new statutory regulatory body, a News Media Council, the recommendations were not taken up and are unlikely to be.[433] In 2021, the MEAA gave notice that it would withdraw its membership of the APC in 2025. It attributed its decision to the failure of the self-regulatory framework to manage a converged media framework.[434]

§2. Journalists' Code of Ethics

185. The APC complaints process is directed at publishers, and the complaint is about the actual publication, not individual journalists. There is no direct regulation of journalists aside from the liability that might arise under the general law. However, the MEAA, the professional organization and union for, *inter alia*, journalists, has in place a self-regulatory scheme that manages complaints in relation to breaches of the MEAA Journalists' Code of Ethics.[435] The Code of Ethics covers twelve standards relating to matters such as fairness and honest reporting; avoidance of conflicts of interest and commercial interests; respect for privacy and grief; and, avoidance of plagiarism. Overall, journalists are expected to commit themselves to honesty, fairness, independence, and, respect for the rights of others. The Code and complaints process only applies to members of the MEAA. As a result of concerns about the rise of hate speech in Australia, the MEAA has also developed guidelines on Reporting Hate Speech and Extremism (introduced in 2020)[436] and Reporting on LGBTQIA+ Issues (introduced in 2021).[437] These guidelines are designed as a practical tool for journalists; sitting alongside, and not excluding, the Code of Ethics.

431. Australian Press Council, *Annual Report 2020-2021* (No. 44, 30 Jun. 2021) https://presscouncil.org.au/wp-content/uploads/2022/03/8416_AnnualReport_2020-2021_R17_WEB.pdf (accessed 14 Jun. 2023), 9.
432. Australian Government, *Report of the Independent Inquiry into the Media and Media Regulation* (Canberra, Commonwealth of Australia, Feb. 2012), paras 6 & 8.123.
433. *Ibid.*, paras 8 ff.
434. Media Entertainment & Arts Alliance, *Journalists' Union gives notice to quit Australian Press Council* (21 Apr. 2021) https://www.meaa.org/mediaroom/journalists-union-gives-notice-to-quit-australian-press-council/ (accessed 14 Jun. 2023).
435. https://www.meaa.org/meaa-media/code-of-ethics/ (accessed 19 Jun. 2023).
436. https://www.meaa.org/meaa-media/code-of-ethics/hate-speech-guidelines/ (accessed 19 Jun. 2023).
437. https://www.meaa.org/meaa-media/code-of-ethics/lgbtqia-guidelines/ (accessed 19 Jun. 2023).

186. If someone believes that the Code has been breached a written complaint may be lodged with the MEAA.[438] Complaints are referred to the MEAA's National Ethics Committee, which will establish a Complaints Panel if it considers that the complaint requires investigation. The membership of the Complaints Panel comprises three members of the Ethics Committee (including at least one general public member). Aside from dismissing the complaint, the Committee may uphold the complaint without hearing further evidence, attempt to mediate, request further information in writing, or, hold a hearing. If a hearing is held, both the complainant and journalist are present, but legal representation is not permitted. If a complaint is upheld, the MEAA has the power to issue a warning or reprimand to the journalist, impose a monetary penalty of up to AUD 1,000, suspend the journalist's membership for up to a year, or, expel the journalist from the MEAA. It does not have the power to, for example, require correction because, from a practical perspective, a journalist would rarely have the power to place such a correction. As such, complaints to the APC may be a more effective avenue for complaints about the print or related digital media.

187. Except where a complaint has been dismissed, the complainant or journalist may appeal against the outcome of a complaint. The National Ethics Committee will establish an Appeals Panel comprising five members of the Ethics Committee, of which two must be general public members; and none of whom can have sat on the Complaints Panel. The Appeals Panel is limited to correcting errors in the decision of the Complaints Panel. The Appeals Panel can direct that a new Complaints Panel be convened to reconsider the complaint.

438. *See* https://www.meaa.org/download/how-meaas-journalist-code-of-ethics-complaints-process-works/ (accessed 19 Jun. 2023).

Part III. Regulation of Audiovisual Media (Broadcasting)

188. There are three main broadcasting sectors in Australia. National broadcasting service is the statutory term for the two public broadcasters, the ABC and the Special Broadcasting Service Corporation (SBS).[439] Commercial broadcasting is the dominant sector in Australia. Commercial radio and television services in Australia began broadcasting at much the same time as the ABC. Commercial broadcasting is provided free-to-air and by subscription, although the former dominates the commercial market. A third sector, community broadcasting, can be seen as a form of public broadcasting, and, indeed, this was its original title, when it began in the seventies. It serves local or special interest communities. Community broadcasting services must be non-profit making. They tend to be relatively small in operation and reach as they must rely on member subscriptions and sponsorship for funding. There is only very limited government funding for community services.

189. The main statute governing the provision and regulation of radio and television services is the Broadcasting Services Act 1992 (Cth) (BSA). The BSA has some relevance to the operation of the public broadcasters, the ABC and the SBS, although there is specific legislation covering the activities of each public broadcaster: the Australian Broadcasting Corporation Act 1983 (Cth) (ABC Act) and the Special Broadcasting Service Act 1991 (Cth) (SBS Act), respectively.

190. When the BSA came into force in 1992, it was the product of a major redesign of broadcasting regulation, and was intended to shift the emphasis away from statutory supervision to a greater reliance upon industry regulation: '[It] … represented a conscious attempt to implement good regulatory practice and was a major step towards a more market based, less interventionist approach to broadcasting regulation.'[440]

191. The resulting regulatory scheme is one of direct regulatory supervision in some areas, such as ownership and control regulation, and a co-regulatory approach in other areas, such as most aspects of content regulation. Under the co-regulatory approach, the relevant industry body has responsibility for code-setting and monitoring of compliance, whilst the statutory body is responsible for enforcement.

439. Broadcasting Services Act 1992 (Cth), s. 13.
440. Productivity Commission, *Broadcasting*, Report No. 11 (Canberra: AusInfo, 2000), 450.

192. The statutory regulator is the ACMA. The ACMA was established in 2005 and is the product of a merger between the former regulatory authorities: the Australian Broadcasting Authority (ABA) and the Australian Communications Authority (responsible for telecommunications and spectrum planning). Accordingly, the ACMA, in addition to its responsibilities for broadcasting, is responsible for telecommunications and spectrum. The ACMA has some regulatory authority in relation to public broadcasters, but its main broadcasting remit is in relation to the other broadcasting services, especially the commercial sector. (*See* further Part V *infra.*)

Chapter 1. Public Service Broadcasting

§1. The Concept and Mission of Public Service Broadcasting

193. Australia does not have the same public service broadcasting tradition as can be seen in the UK and other European jurisdictions. The burden of public service broadcasting traditions mainly rests with the public broadcasters, the ABC and the SBS. Although the commercial broadcasting sector has some specific obligations, such as the promotion of Australian content, it is not regarded as a public service broadcaster.

194. However, the BSA does include in its statutory objectives statements which can be seen as akin to traditional public service broadcasting concepts. Thus:

(a) to promote the availability to audiences throughout Australia of a diverse range of radio and television services offering entertainment, education and information; and
(b) to promote the role of broadcasting services in developing and reflecting a sense of Australian identity, character and cultural diversity; and
(c) to promote the provision of high-quality and innovative programming by providers of broadcasting services.[441]

195. Despite these objectives, there is little in the way of a specific regulation that addresses the objective, for example, of providing quality and innovative content, nor any measure to assess whether this has been achieved. There are some general programming formats specified. For example, commercial broadcasting services are expected to provide programmes of general appeal.[442] However, in Australia, the approach is to focus less on the individual broadcasting services and their programme provision, and more on creating diversity structurally across the sector. The object of providing the public with radio and television programming which will entertain, educate, and inform is intended to be achieved through the provision of differently constituted and funded sectors such as public, commercial, and community. Thus, sectoral diversity provides an environment which implicitly acknowledges public service broadcasting traditions, whilst imposing express public service broadcasting obligations on the public broadcasters.

§2. The Organization of Public Service Broadcasting

I. ABC

196. ABC radio broadcasting began in 1932 and television broadcasting in 1956, initially in Sydney only, but by 1960, nationally. The ABC represents the more

441. Broadcasting Services Act 1992 (Cth), s. 3(1).
442. Broadcasting Services Act 1992 (Cth), s. 14(1)(a).

traditional public broadcaster with its general public service broadcasting mandate. Its main functions and obligations are set out in the ABC Act, and it is governed by the ABC Board which is responsible for ensuring the independence and integrity of the ABC and for the performance of the ABC's statutory obligations.[443] It must also ensure that the functions of the ABC are 'performed efficiently and with the maximum benefit to the people of Australia'.[444] The ABC Board consists of a chairperson, a managing director, a staff-elected director, and between four and six other directors. The board members are appointed by the Governor-General on the recommendation of the Australian Government following a merit-based selection process for the non-executive directors.[445] The merit-based process was introduced in 2010 and is a step in helping to strengthen the independence of the ABC. Prior to this process, there was a strong perception that appointments were politically motivated, and there have certainly been examples of appointments to the ABC Board of persons openly critical of the ABC. Under the selection process, the Prime Minister must consult with the Leader of the Opposition before recommending to the Governor-General the person to be appointed as chairperson of the Board.[446] The Board appoints the managing director of the ABC. In keeping with the independence of the ABC, the broadcaster deals with its own complaints although the ACMA has the power to investigate if the ABC has failed to deal with a complaint within sixty days of the complaint being made, or the response is inadequate (*see* Part V, Chapter 3, section 2 *infra*).[447]

197. Section 6 of the ABC Act sets out the ABC Charter. The Charter specifies the functions of the ABC, and the traditional public service broadcasting principles can be seen in that charter:

(1) The functions of the Corporation are:
  (a) to provide within Australia innovative and comprehensive broadcasting services of a high standard as part of the Australian broadcasting system consisting of national, commercial and community sectors and, without limiting the generality of the foregoing, to provide:
    – broadcasting programs that contribute to a sense of national identity and inform and entertain, and reflect the cultural diversity of, the Australian community; and
    – broadcasting programs of an educational nature.
  (b) to transmit to countries outside Australia broadcasting programs of news, current affairs, entertainment and cultural enrichment that will:
    – encourage awareness of Australia and an international understanding of Australian attitudes on world affairs; and
    – enable Australian citizens living or travelling outside Australia to obtain information about Australian affairs and Australian attitudes on world affairs; and
  (ba) to provide digital media services; and

443. Australian Broadcasting Corporation Act 1983 (Cth), s. 8(1).
444. Australian Broadcasting Corporation Act 1983 (Cth), s. 8(1)(a).
445. Australian Broadcasting Corporation Act 1983 (Cth), Pt IIIA.
446. Australian Broadcasting Corporation Act 1983 (Cth), s. 24X(1).
447. Broadcasting Services Act 1992 (Cth), s. 150(1).

(c) to encourage and promote the musical, dramatic and other performing arts in Australia.

(2) In the provision by the Corporation of its broadcasting services within Australia:

(a) the Corporation shall take account of:

- the broadcasting services provided by the commercial and community sectors of the Australian broadcasting system;
- the standards from time to time determined by the ACMA in respect of broadcasting services;
- the responsibility of the Corporation as the provider of an independent national broadcasting service to provide a balance between broadcasting programs of wide appeal and specialized broadcasting programs;
- the multicultural character of the Australian community; and
- in connection with the provision of broadcasting programs of an educational nature – the responsibilities of the States in relation to education; …

198. The statutory charter expressly requires the ABC to provide digital media services. This amendment to the Charter was made in 2013 and was done to remove any doubt about the role of the ABC in offering online content and services. Until digital transmission, the ABC broadcast one national television channel (ABC TV), but digital has allowed it to expand its offerings and it now provides, in addition to ABC TV, four digital channels which specialize in children's programming, comedy, and news.

The ABC provides four national radio services:

- Radio National – a mainly talk-based service.
- News Radio – a twenty-four-hour news service.
- Classic FM – a dedicated classical music station.
- Triple j FM – a service aimed at a young audience.

199. ABC TV remains the main channel offering the broadest range of programming and original news and current affairs programming. In addition, the ABC offers local radio services from more than fifty locations across Australia and a range of additional digital radio channels, mainly offering music. The ABC provides a catch-up television service, views, and streams all its digital radio services, as well as making available via the Internet considerable additional content. ABC provides two international broadcasting services. Radio Australia is a radio and online service broadcasting to Asia and the Pacific in a number of languages. ABC Australia is a service provided to around forty countries in Asia and the Pacific offering a television via service providers or satellite and online service.

200. As the more mainstream of the two public service broadcasters, the ABC has also been more vulnerable to criticism from the government of the day, regardless of the government's political affiliation. There is a long-standing practice of accusing the ABC of bias.

II. SBS

201. Although also considered a public service broadcaster, the SBS has a more distinctive multicultural and multilingual remit. SBS was established in 1978 to provide radio broadcasting and began television services in 1980. It is also a national broadcaster. It is incorporated under the SBS Act and governed by the SBS Board. The Board comprises a chairperson and between three and seven directors as well as the managing director.[448] One director must be an Indigenous person, and collectively the directors should represent a diversity of cultural perspectives.[449] Like the ABC, the non-executive board members are appointed by the Government following a merit-based selection process.[450] The Board appoints the managing director.[451] The SBS Board is responsible for deciding the objectives, strategies and policies of the SBS and for ensuring that 'the SBS performs its functions in a proper, efficient and economical manner and with the maximum benefit to the people of Australia'.[452] It is interesting to compare the slightly different wording in this responsibility compared with the obligation imposed upon the ABC Board. The SBS also handles its own complaints, but the ACMA has the power to consider a complaint in the same manner as complaints made to the ABC.[453]

202. The SBS' public service remit is set out in its statutory charter, found in section 6 of the SBS Act:

(1) The principal function of SBS is to provide multilingual and multicultural broadcasting and digital media services that inform, educate and entertain all Australians and, in doing so, reflect Australia's multicultural society.
(2) SBS, in performing its principal function, must:
   (a) contribute to meeting the communications needs of Australia's multicultural society, including ethnic, Aboriginal and Torres Strait Islander communities; and
   (b) increase awareness of the contribution of a diversity of cultures to the continuing development of Australian society; and
   (c) promote understanding and acceptance of the cultural, linguistic and ethnic diversity of the Australian people; and
   (d) contribute to the retention and continuing development of language and other cultural skills; and
   (e) as far as practicable, inform, educate and entertain Australians in their preferred languages; and
   (f) make use of Australia's diverse creative resources; and

448. Special Broadcasting Service Act 1991 (Cth), s. 8.
449. Special Broadcasting Service Act 1991 (Cth), s. 17(2)(b) & (d).
450. Special Broadcasting Service Act 1991 (Cth), Pt 3A.
451. Special Broadcasting Service Act 1991 (Cth), s. 28.
452. Special Broadcasting Service Act 1991 (Cth), s. 9.
453. Broadcasting Services Act 1992 (Cth), s. 150(1).

(g) contribute to the overall diversity of Australian television and radio services, particularly taking into account the contribution of the ABC and the community broadcasting sector; and
(h) contribute to extending the range of Australian television and radio services, and reflect the changing nature of Australian society, by presenting many points of view and using innovative forms of expression.

203. The SBS Act was also amended in 2013 to expressly include the provision of digital media services. The main television service offered by SBS is SBS. SBS offers a range of news, current affairs, documentary, and entertainment programming in English and other languages. Since the introduction of digital transmission, SBS has offered additional television services covering world film, food and international news as well as SBS VICELAND which offers programming aimed at a younger adult audience. SBS Radio provides a range of analogue and digital radio services covering more than sixty languages. Via its online service, SBS also streams its radio language programmes and offers a catch-up viewing service. Since 2012, SBS has also provided the first national free-to-air Indigenous channel, the National Indigenous Television Service (NITV). NITV, funded by the Australian Government, was established in 2007 and originally broadcast to remote and regional communities. NITV programming is mainly produced by Aboriginal and Torres Strait Islander people.

§3. The Financing of Public Service Broadcasting

I. ABC

204. The ABC is funded by Australian Government grants[454] and is prohibited from broadcasting advertisements.[455] Funding via government grant constitutes around 80% of the ABC's income; the balance is earned through sales of programming and related products. Funding is allocated on a triennial basis which assists the ABC in its planning, but this is still a relatively short-term form of funding and is likely to add to the vulnerability of the broadcaster and its independence. In recent years, the ABC (and the SBS) have been subject to other funding constraints such as a freeze on indexation and efficiency reviews. In the 2020 Australian Government Budget, the ABC was allocated AUD 1,065.3 million.[456] The ABC has estimated that its operational revenue from the Government has declined by AUD 83.7 million over the three-year period 2019-20 to 2021-22 due to an indexation pause.[457] The Australian Government also conducted an inquiry into both the ABC and the SBS in 2018 in relation to competitive neutrality. The Government was of

454. The ABC was initially funded by a licence fee, but this was abolished in 1948.
455. Australian Broadcasting Corporation Act 1983 (Cth), s. 31(1) (relating to its broadcasting services) and s. 31(4) (relating to its digital media services). This prohibition does not prevent the ABC from advertising its own activities. The ABC is permitted to broadcast advertising on its international services: s. 31(2).
456. Australian Broadcasting Corporation, *Annual Report 2021*, 133.
457. Australian Broadcasting Corporation, *Annual Report 2021*, 134.

the view that the national broadcasters should not gain a competitive advantage, by reason of their public ownership when competing with the private sector. The Inquiry found that national broadcasters were abiding by a 'best endeavours approach to competitive neutrality'[458], although it found some areas for improvement regarding transparency and internal procedures.[459]

II. SBS

205. Like the ABC, the SBS also receives triennial funding from the Australian Government. Unlike the ABC, it is permitted to raise revenue through a limited amount of advertising and sponsorship announcements.[460] No more than five minutes in an hour of broadcasting is permitted, and the advertising must only run before programmes commence, after programmes end, or during natural programme breaks.[461] Announcements publicizing its own programmes and other activities are not included in this limitation.[462] The SBS is also permitted to transmit advertising and sponsorship announcements on its digital media services.[463]

206. Government funding accounts for around 70% of SBS revenue. In the 2019-20 to 2021-22 triennial funding period, SBS received funding from the Australian Government of AUD 897 million.[464]

458. Australian Government, *Inquiry into the Competitive Neutrality of the National Broadcasters: Report by Expert Panel* (September 2018), 11.
459. *Ibid.*
460. Special Broadcasting Service Act 1991(Cth), s. 45(1).
461. Special Broadcasting Service Act 1991(Cth), s. 45(2).
462. Special Broadcasting Service Act 1991(Cth), s. 45(3).
463. Special Broadcasting Service Act 1991(Cth), s. 45A(1).
464. Special Broadcasting Service, *Corporate Plan 2021-22,* 12.

Chapter 2. Private Broadcasting

§1. Different Categories of Private Broadcasters

207. The categories of private broadcasting services are defined in the BSA. The category definitions provide a description of a service that would fall within that category and apply to both radio and television services unless specified. It is possible to obtain an opinion from the ACMA as to the category in which a service or proposed service falls. An opinion can provide useful protection because it prevents action from being taken against the person providing the service that the service should be provided according to a different category.[465] The licensing arrangements and regulatory obligations of service will vary according to the degree of influence a service is able to exert in shaping community views in Australia (section 4(1) BSA). The following are the private broadcasting categories:

(1) *Commercial broadcasting services* are operated for profit, available for free to the general public and usually funded by advertising revenue. The service should be available via commonly available equipment and provide programmes intended to appeal to the general public.
(2) *Community broadcasting services* are not-for-profit services that are available free to the public via commonly available equipment, for community purposes.
(3) *Subscription broadcasting services* like commercial broadcasting services provide programmes which are intended to appeal to the general public, although the services are only available on payment of subscription fees.
(4) *Subscription narrowcasting services* are only available on payment of subscription fees, and the service is intended to have limited reception. The reception may be limited: by being targeted to a special interest group; by being intended for a limited location; by being provided for a limited period; because they provide programmes of limited appeal; or, for some other reason.[466]
(5) *Open narrowcasting services* are available free-to-air but with reception limited in the same manner as subscription narrowcasting services.
(6) *International broadcasting services* are broadcasting services targeted to a significant extent to audiences outside of Australia and delivered via the use of a radiocommunications transmitter in Australia.[467]

208. There is a further category of service, known as 'datacasting'. Datacasting services use the broadcasting service bands and deliver content in the form of text, data, speech, music or other sounds, or visual images, or, in any combination. Datacasting services were established in 2000 and designed to take advantage of the

465. Broadcasting Services Act 1992 (Cth), s. 21.
466. The regulator, the Australian Communications and Media Authority (ACMA), has published guidelines giving guidance on determining whether a service is a narrowcasting service: https://www.acma.gov.au/industry-codes-practice (accessed 27 Jun. 2023).
467. Broadcasting Services Act 1992 (Cth), ss 14–18A.

digital capacity and offer something different from traditional broadcasting services. However, the content that a datacasting service could provide was extremely limited so the service would not be a television-like or radio-like service. A datacasting service can provide the following forms of content: information-only programmes; educational programmes; interactive computer games; text or still visual image content; Parliamentary broadcasts; electronic mail; and internet content.[468] Because of the content limitations, datacasting services have not been seen as an attractive form of offering, and only very few licences have been issued. These are mainly used to provide teleshopping services. Unless specifically relevant to broadcasting service regulation, datacasting services will not be considered further.

§2. Licensing Requirements

I. General Licensing Matters

209. The communications regulator, the ACMA, issues licences. All broadcasting services must be licensed. Unless covered by a class licence, broadcasting services will require an individual licence.[469]

II. Commercial Television Broadcasting Services

210. Licences for the provision of Commercial Television Broadcasting (CTB) services cannot be allocated unless the applicant is a company with a share capital incorporated under the Corporations Act 2001 (Cth).[470] The ACMA is also prohibited from allocating a licence if it decides that the company is not a suitable applicant or licensee.[471] Suitability is determined by whether allowing the company to provide or continue to provide the service would lead to a significant risk of an offence against the BSA (or associated regulations) being committed; a breach of a civil penalty provision occurring; or a breach of a licence condition occurring.[472] In making such a determination, the ACMA can take into account matters such as the company's business record, the business record of persons who would be in a position to control the licensee, the record of the company and other persons in situations of trust and candour.[473] However, the ACMA is not required to consider the suitability of an applicant before allocating a licence.[474]

211. CTB services are licensed differently according to whether they are broadcasting services bands licences or not. A broadcasting services bands licence means

468. Broadcasting Services Act 1992 (Cth), Sch. 6.
469. Broadcasting Services Act 1992 (Cth), s. 12.
470. Broadcasting Services Act 1992 (Cth), s. 37.
471. Broadcasting Services Act 1992 (Cth), s. 41.
472. Civil penalties are offences where liability is determined by the civil standard of proof, rather than the criminal standard. *See* further Part V, Ch. 3, s. 1 *infra*.
473. Broadcasting Services Act 1992 (Cth), s. 41(3).
474. Broadcasting Services Act 1992 (Cth), s. 37(2).

that a CTB service will be broadcast via the radiofrequency spectrum and on the part of the spectrum reserved for broadcasting.[475] A non-broadcasting services bands CTB service will use other delivery technologies. Broadcasting services bands CTB licences have been allocated by means of a price-based mechanism determined by the ACMA.[476] However, no new CTB licences using the broadcasting services bands can be issued, as there is a limit on the number (three) of licences that can be allocated per licence area.[477] This prohibition was initially introduced to assist the existing free-to-air licensees who had to absorb the costs of digital transmission. Licences are issued for a term of five years, and the ACMA must renew the licence for a further term of five years unless it decides that the licensee is unsuitable according to section 41.[478]

212. CTB licences for non-broadcasting services bands are not covered by the limitation on the number of licences that can be issued and can be applied for at any time.[479] Unlike the broadcasting services bands CTB licences which cover both content and delivery, a section 40 licence will license the content service only, and an applicant will have to arrange separately for any licences or authorizations which may be necessary to cover the means of delivering the service. Licences are allocated on the basis of one licence per service and must be provided in digital mode. Before allocating a licence, the ACMA must notify the Minister of the application, who may direct the ACMA not to issue the licence if s/he is of the opinion that the service would be contrary to the public interest.[480]

III. Commercial Radio Broadcasting Services

213. In general, the licensing of CRB services follows a pattern similar to CTB licensing.[481] The same preliminary requirements apply with regard to the corporate nature of the applicant and the suitability requirement. The differentiation between services using the broadcasting services bands and services using the non-broadcasting services bands also applies to CRB licences. Hence, licences for CRB services using the broadcasting services bands are allocated using a price-based mechanism determined by the ACMA, whilst licences for CRB services using the non-broadcasting services bands are allocated on an application basis. Unlike CTB licences, the ACMA is not required to notify the Minister when an application for a non-broadcasting services bands licence is received.

---

475. *See* Part 3 of the BSA in relation to the ACMA's planning powers of the broadcasting services bands.
476. Broadcasting Services Act 1992 (Cth), s. 36(1).
477. Broadcasting Services Act 1992 (Cth), s. 37A.
478. Broadcasting Services Act 1992 (Cth), ss 45 & 47.
479. Broadcasting Services Act 1992 (Cth), s. 40(1).
480. Broadcasting Services Act 1992 (Cth), s. 40(9).
481. Part 4 of the Broadcasting Services Act 1992 (Cth) covers the allocation of both CTB and CRB licences and the statutory provisions are the same.

214. If the ACMA plans to allocate a licence using the broadcasting services bands, it will advertise its intention and provide details of the licence area for that licence.[482] Licences are allocated to provide either an analogue or digital CRB service.[483]

215. The terms for duration and renewal of CRB licences are the same as those applying to CTB licences also apply to CRB licences.

IV. Community Broadcasting Services

216. Like CTB services, community broadcasting (CB) services are licensed according to whether or not they will be licensed to broadcast within the broadcasting services bands. The process for awarding licences for CB services within the broadcasting services bands differs from commercial broadcasting license processes. CB licences are issued on a merit basis and can only be applied for when the ACMA advertises its intention to allocate CB licences, providing details of the licence area.[484] In deciding whether to award a licence, the ACMA must have regard to the extent to which the proposed service would meet existing and perceived future needs of the community within the licence area and the capacity of the applicant to provide the proposed service.[485] As part of the allocation process, the ACMA must consider the nature and diversity of the community's interests and the nature and diversity of other broadcasting services provided within that licence area. 'Community interests' are not defined in the BSA, but it is understood that the term does not refer only to the community in the geographical sense. Licences have been allocated to serve particular religious and ethnic communities, and interests such as specialist music genres. The ACMA is also required to take into account the undesirability of one licensee being in a position to exercise control of more than one CB licence, using the broadcasting services bands, within the relevant licence area; and, of the Commonwealth, a state, or a territory, or a political party being in a position to exercise control of a CB licence.[486] CB licences for non-broadcasting services bands can be allocated at any time on an application basis.[487] As with other broadcasting service licences, the preliminary licensing requirements of corporate form and suitability apply to CB licences.[488]

482. Broadcasting Services Act 1992 (Cth), s. 38.
483. Broadcasting Services Act 1992 (Cth), s. 36A(3).
484. Broadcasting Services Act 1992 (Cth), s. 80.
485. Broadcasting Services Act 1992 (Cth), s. 84.
486. Broadcasting Services Act 1992 (Cth), ss 84(e)–84(f).
487. Broadcasting Services Act 1992 (Cth), s. 82(1).
488. Broadcasting Services Act 1992 (Cth), s. 83. CB licences can be held by companies or incorporated associations (a type of non-profit voluntary association having corporate status): s. 79. CB licences for television require the licence holder to be a company limited by guarantee: s. 81(1)(a).

V. Subscription Television Broadcasting Services

217. Preliminary licensing requirements, such as corporate form and suitability, apply to Subscription Television Broadcasting (STB) services.[489] Licences per service are allocated on an application basis and are allocated for an indefinite term.[490] This means that they continue in force until they are surrendered or cancelled.

VI. Class Licences

218. Some services do not require an individual licence. These are subscription radio broadcasting and narrowcasting services. These services operate under class licences, the regime for which is governed by Part 8 of the BSA. A class licence is in effect a standing authority to provide the service. Pursuant to section 117, the ACMA may determine a class licence for these different services. A broadcaster wishing to provide a service under a class licence may commence the service without application, and operate the service indefinitely, subject to compliance with the class licence conditions. It is not necessary for a service operating within the class licence regime to notify the ACMA of its operation.

VII. International Broadcasting Services

219. An individual licence is required to provide an international broadcasting service. Like the other individually licensed services, the preliminary licensing requirements apply.[491] An application can be made at any time, and a licence will continue in force until surrendered or cancelled. Once the ACMA is satisfied that the preliminary licensing requirements are met it must, before deciding to grant the licence, refer the application to the Minister for Foreign Affairs with a report as to whether the proposed service complies with the ACMA's international broadcasting guidelines.[492] The guidelines deal mainly with content matters. The Minister will consider whether the proposed service is likely to be contrary to Australia's national interest, and if the Minister is of that opinion will direct the ACMA not to allocate the licence.[493] For these purposes, the national interest to be considered by the Minister is the likely effect of the service on Australia's international relations.[494] It is possible to hold an international broadcasting service licence and a licence for another category for the same service. In other words, the content service provided under the international broadcasting service licence might also be provided to an Australian audience.[495]

489. Broadcasting Services Act 1992 (Cth), s. 95.
490. Broadcasting Services Act 1992 (Cth), s. 96.
491. Broadcasting Services Act 1992 (Cth), s. 121FB.
492. Broadcasting Services Act 1992 (Cth), s. 121FB(1).
493. Broadcasting Services Act 1992 (Cth), s. 121FD(1).
494. Broadcasting Services Act 1992 (Cth), s. 121FD(3).
495. Broadcasting Services Act 1992 (Cth), s. 11A.

VIII. Licence Conditions

220. With the exception of international broadcasting services, a set of minimum licence conditions applies to all private broadcasting services. These are listed in Schedule 2 to the BSA. Some of these conditions are covered in more detail in the following chapters. The minimum set of licence conditions are:

- If during an election period, a broadcaster broadcasts election matter, the broadcaster must give reasonable opportunities for the broadcasting of election matter to all political parties contesting the election. The obligation does not require the broadcast to be free of charge (*see* Chapter 4 *infra*).
- Election advertisements cannot be broadcast from the end of Wednesday before polling day until after the close of the poll on the polling day (*see* Chapter 4 *infra*).
- Where a broadcaster broadcasts political matter at the request of another person (which includes a political party), the details of the person making the request must be identified.
- Tobacco advertising is not permitted.

221. There is a range of other common licence conditions such as not using the service in the commission of an offence and compliance with relevant programme, industry and technical standards. Certain broadcasting services have additional licence conditions imposed, and these are covered in the following chapters.

Chapter 3. Programme Standards

222. Content rules are imposed through three regulatory forms. They may be licence conditions such as the schedule 2 minimum set of conditions (Chapter 2, section 2, VIII *supra*). Content rules are also imposed through standards. Some standards are incorporated into the BSA, such as the standard on Australian content (*see* section 2, II *infra*). The ACMA also has the power to impose a standard if it considers that a code of practice is not effective (*see* Chapter 5, section 4 *infra*).[496] Compliance with standards is a condition of a licence. Finally, content rules may be imposed through industry codes of practice. Compliance with a code of practice is not a licence condition. The codes contain the majority of the content rules and are administered through the co-regulatory scheme. They are developed by industry groups, representing each category of broadcasting service. Each category of broadcasting service has its own industry code of practice. The codes of practice are registered by the ACMA.[497] The ABC and SBS are also required to develop codes of practice and to notify them to the ACMA.[498] *See* Part V for further information about enforcement of the content rules.

§1. Impartiality

223. The approach to impartiality differs between the broadcasting sectors. Australia does not impose a general obligation of impartiality, in the sense of no-editorializing, upon broadcasting services. Rather the stricter obligations are left to the public broadcasting sector whilst the private broadcasting sector must observe obligations of fairness and accuracy.

224. The ABC, as the primary public broadcaster, has, not surprisingly, the most onerous obligations. The Board of the ABC is required to ensure that the gathering and presentation of news and information are 'accurate and impartial according to the recognized standards of objective journalism'.[499] The legislation does not provide any further guidance on this obligation or the meaning of the term, 'objective journalism'. However, the ABC's Code of Practice stipulates that the ABC takes no editorial stance.[500]

225. The SBS, although also a public broadcaster, has a slightly relaxed obligation reflecting the different nature of the service. As a multilingual broadcaster, the SBS relies heavily on foreign-language news broadcasts, over which it has little editorial control. As such, impartiality obligations would be difficult to ensure. Hence, the statutory obligation refers to the responsibility of the Board to ensure that 'the

496. Broadcasting Services Act 1992 (Cth), s. 125.
497. Broadcasting Services Act 1992 (Cth), ss 123–124.
498. Australian Broadcasting Corporation Act 1983 (Cth), s. 8(1)(e) & Special Broadcasting Service Act 1991 (Cth), s. 10(1)(j).
499. Australian Broadcasting Corporation Act 1983 (Cth), s. 8(1)(c).
500. Australian Broadcasting Corporation, Editorial Policy 4 (December 2023), https://www.abc.net.au/edpols/4-impartiality-and-diversity-of-perspectives/13635402 (accessed 12 Jul. 2024).

gathering and presentation of news and information is accurate and balanced over time and across the schedule of programmes broadcast'.[501] However, the SBS also produces its own news and current affairs content and adopts a similar approach to the ABC in relation to the pursuit of impartiality and balance.[502] In relation to the broadcasting of news services from other countries, the SBS identifies the source of the programme so that the audience will have the opportunity to exercise their own judgment about the issues being presented.[503]

226. In the private sector, impartiality obligations, in the sense of no-editorializing obligations, do not apply, except in relation to news. Fairness and accuracy are the main focus. These obligations are neither statutorily imposed nor are they licence conditions. They form part of the co-regulatory scheme and are covered by the industry codes of practice. Section 123(2)(d) of the BSA refers to the promotion of accuracy and fairness in news and current affairs programmes as one of the areas to which the codes of practice may relate. In general, the codes of practice do not elaborate much on this obligation. For example, the Commercial Television Industry Code of Practice provides the following:

> 3.3.1 In broadcasting a News or Current Affairs Program, a Licensee must present factual material accurately and ensure viewpoints included in the Program are not misrepresented.
> 3.4.1 In broadcasting a news Program, a Licensee must:
>
> 1. present news fairly and impartially;
> 2. clearly distinguish the reporting of factual material from commentary and analysis.[504]

227. The Commercial Radio Code of Practice addresses the issue of balance is a slightly different manner. Code 3.9 states that a licensee in preparing and presenting a current affairs programme must provide:

> – reasonable opportunities for significant alternative viewpoints to be presented when dealing with controversial issues of public importance, while the issue has immediate relevance to the community.

> Code 3.2.3 requires a licensee to use reasonable efforts to ensure that viewpoints expressed to the licensee for broadcast are not misrepresented or presented in a misleading manner by giving wrong or improper emphasis or by editing material out of context.[505]

228. Reflecting the particular mandate of community broadcasting services, the Community Radio Code of Practice provides that news and current affairs 'shall

501. Special Broadcasting Service Act 1991 (Cth), s. 10(1)(c).
502. SBS, Code of Practice (2021), code 3.3.1.
503. *Ibid.*, code 3.3.2.
504. FTV, Commercial Television Industry Code of Practice (2015).
505. CRA, Commercial Radio Code of Practice (2017)

provide access to views not adequately represented by other broadcasting sectors'.[506] Community Television includes general provisions to ensure the accuracy and fairness of news and current affairs.[507] In relation to the other services, STB and narrowcasting services, the main focus in the codes is presenting news accurately, fairly, and impartially[508] or presenting accurate and fair news and current affairs.[509] In general, for these services, there is only minimal detail in setting out the obligations.

§2. Cultural Diversity

I. Sectoral Diversity

229. The preferred regulatory approach for the promotion of cultural diversity in Australian broadcasting is in the main to focus on sectoral diversity. By providing broadcasting services and sectors with different mandates, recognition is given to the cultural diversity within Australia and access to programming is provided, which acknowledges the different ethnic groups settled in Australia. The statutory objectives of the BSA seek to 'promote the role of broadcasting services in developing and reflecting a sense of Australian identity, character and cultural diversity'.[510]

230. The public service broadcasters play an important role here. ABC's statutory charter includes an obligation to provide programming that will 'reflect the cultural diversity of the Australian community'.[511] SBS, with its specific multilingual and multicultural mandate, is a key plank in the promotion of cultural diversity and a means of providing access to in-language programming. The community broadcasting sector is another element in reflecting the cultural diversity of the country. As of 30 June 2018, approximately 2% of community radio licences represent ethnic community interests and 26% the Aboriginal and Torres Strait Islander community.[512] NITV provides another means whereby cultural diversity is promoted, especially with the provision of the national free-to-air television channel, accessible to all Australians. Despite the BSA statutory objective, it can be observed that the burden of cultural diversity (save as noted in the following sections) rests on the public and community broadcasting sectors, and not on the private commercial sectors.

506. CBAA, Community Radio Broadcasting Codes of Practice (2008), cl. 3.6.
507. ACTA, Community Television Broadcasting Codes of Practice (2011), cls 3.11–3.13.
508. ASTRA, Subscription Broadcast Television Codes of Practice (2013), code 2.2.
509. *See*, e.g., ASTRA, Subscription Narrowcast Radio Codes of Practice (2013), code 1.2.
510. Broadcasting Services Act 1992 (Cth), s. 3(1)(e).
511. Australian Broadcasting Corporation Act 1983 (Cth), s. 6(1)(a)(i).
512. Australian Communications and Media Authority, *Communications Report 2017-18*, https://www.acma.gov.au/theACMA/communications-report, (accessed 10 Mar. 2019), 25.

II. Australian Content Obligations

231. It will be noted that the statutory objective referred to above is also concerned with the development and reflection of a sense of Australian identity. The ABC, as the public broadcaster with the broad remit, is expected to play a key role in providing programming which will meet this objective, and a similar obligation is identified in its statutory charter. However, a specific obligation is also imposed upon commercial television broadcasting services in the form of an obligation to broadcast a certain quota of Australian content. Such specific forms of content regulation are unusual within the commercial broadcasting regulatory scheme, but it can be seen to reflect the concern that without such an obligation, commercial broadcasters will be tempted to import cheaper programming, especially from the United States. The importance of this obligation is also apparent when one observes the manner in which this obligation is imposed upon commercial broadcasters. It is not imposed through the industry code of practice but by means of a standard. Under the BSA regulatory scheme, compliance with a standard is a condition of a licence. Accordingly, a breach of a standard will constitute a breach of licence.[513]

232. Australian content obligations were introduced in the sixties. The current obligations, for commercial television services, are derived from the Broadcasting Services (Australian Content and Children's Television) Standards 2020:

> The [object] ... is to promote the role of commercial television broadcasting services in developing and reflecting a sense of Australian identity, character and cultural diversity by supporting the community's continued access to television programs produced under Australian creative control.[514]

Prior to 2013, Australian content obligations were imposed only on the main commercial broadcasting service offered by the licensee, not on any additional digital multichannel. However, since January 2013, commercial television licensees must also meet Australian content requirements across their multichannel services. Licensees are required to provide 1,460 hours of Australian content per annum across their multichannels (not including the primary service).[515] The obligations for the licensee's primary service are outlined below.

233. The core obligation of the Standard requires 55% of the content broadcast annually between 6:00 am and midnight on the licensees' primary channels to be Australian content.[516] Australian content is determined by reference to creative control – in other words, whether or not those involved in the making of the content are

513. Broadcasting Services Act 1992 (Cth), Sch. 2, cl. 7(1)(ba), in the case of commercial television broadcasting service licences. It is also a condition of a commercial television broadcasting licence that the quota for Australian content is met: *see* Sch. 2, cl. 7(1)(aa) and s. 121G.
514. Broadcasting Services (Australian Content and Children's) Standards 2020, s. 6(a).
515. Broadcasting Services Act 1992 (Cth), s. 121G(2).
516. Broadcasting Services Act 1992 (Cth), s. 121G(1).

Australian.[517] In fact, because of a trade agreement between Australian and New Zealand, the Standard also recognizes that content will be Australian content if it is produced under the creative control of New Zealanders.[518] All types of programming can be used in the computation of the quota, and both first-run and repeat programming can be included, thus making the quota readily achievable. However, there is an additional quota requirement which must be met:

- The licensee must broadcast a certain minimum quota of first-release Australian programs between 6:00 am and midnight.[519] The quota can be satisfied across a range of genres as specified in the Standard including drama, documentary, film, and children's programs. This is a change from the previous Standard which specified specific genres per quota.[520] The quota is determined by a score which is calculated by reference to the duration of the programme and the format, and in some instances, the production budget.
- There is a restriction on the number of points that can be claimed in relation to commissioned first-release Australian documentary programs.[521]
- Points may be accrued by a licensee on any combination of its primary service and authorized multichannels, which excludes content on video-on-demand services.

234. A further standard requires commercial television licensees to ensure that 80% of total advertising time broadcast annually between 6 am and midnight is comprised of Australian-produced advertisements.[522]

235. The commercial television broadcasting sector has in the past argued, not without success, that the burden of the Australian Content obligations was such that the broadcasters should be protected from competition.[523] The degree of this regulatory burden was debatable, although as the growth of digital platforms changes the way in which content can be delivered, it is questionable whether obligations such as Australian content can continue to be justified if they are to be imposed upon one form of broadcaster or delivery platform only. The revision of the 2020 Standard which removed a range of specific quotas and focused on prime time viewing hours is a response to this challenge.[524] In 2004, Australia entered into a free trade agreement with the US. Under this agreement, the existing cultural content quotas can be maintained, but new obligations cannot be imposed. This adds to the complexity of preserving cultural diversity and addressing the regulatory imbalance.

517. *See Project Blue Sky Inc v. Australian Broadcasting Authority* (1998) 194 CLR 355 (HCA) which considered the determination of 'Australian content'.
518. Broadcasting Services (Australian Content and Children's) Standards 2020, s. 12.
519. *Ibid.*, s. 13(1).
520. *Ibid.,* Schedule 1.
521. *Ibid.*, s. 13(2).
522. Broadcasting Services (Australian Content in Advertising) Standard 2018, s. 8.
523. Productivity Commission, *Broadcasting,* Report No. 11 (Canberra: AusInfo, 2000), 55.
524. Australian Communications and Media Authority and Screen Australia, *Supporting Australian Stories on our Screens,* Options Paper (March 2020), chrome-extension://efaidnbmnnnibpcajpcglclefindmkaj/ https://www.infrastructure.gov.au/sites/default/files/documents/supporting-australian-stories-on-our-screens-options-paper.pdf (accessed 17 Jul. 2023).

Under the CRB code of practice, licensees are required to broadcast a certain proportion of Australian music, defined as music performed by Australians. The amount of the quota varies depending upon the type of music format.[525]

III. Australian Drama Expenditure Obligations

236. Subscription television licensees who offer services predominantly focused on drama programming are required to spend at least 10% of their total programme expenditure on new drama programmes that originate from Australia or New Zealand.[526] The obligation is in the form of a licence condition under the BSA. If the obligation is not met within a given year, the shortfall is carried over.[527] In the same way, excess expenditure in one year can be carried forward.[528] The expenditure obligation does not require the drama programme to be broadcast on a subscription television service.

IV. Regional Content Obligations

237. There has been ongoing concern about the lack of access in regional and rural communities to local news and information, especially with the closure of many local television newsrooms by regional television networks. In part, this was the product of government policy in the 1980s and early 1990s which encouraged the aggregation of smaller regional and rural television areas into larger zones in order to provide these areas with access to three commercial television services, as was, in this pre-digital period, the case for metropolitan areas. However, with licensees now operating over much larger markets, the fallout of this policy was that small markets tended to be ignored. Relaxation of media ownership and control rules also raised concerns about local content in regional areas. In 2004, the then broadcasting regulator, the ABA, imposed a licence condition on some regional television broadcasters requiring the broadcasting of a minimum amount (measured through a points system) of the material of local significance.[529] Regional content obligations continued for commercial television and were introduced for commercial radio following media ownership reforms in 2006. The media ownership and control reforms in 2017 (*see* Part IV *Infra)* brought changes to the rules.

238. The BSA imposes obligations on licensees in regional aggregated markets to broadcast to each local area within the licence area a minimum amount of material of local significance during certain periods of the day.[530] The content requirements are based on a point system determined by the type of local content and the

525. CRA, Commercial Radio Code of Practice (2017), code 5. Digital-only services are exempt: code 5.10.
526. Broadcasting Services Act 1992 (Cth), Pt 7, div. 2A.
527. Broadcasting Services Act 1992 (Cth), s. 103P.
528. Broadcasting Services Act 1992 (Cth), s. 103NA.
529. Broadcasting Services (Additional Television Licence Condition) Notice (7 Apr. 2003).
530. Broadcasting Services Act 1992 (Cth), s. 61CW(3).

number of minutes of content.[531] Local significance material is understood as material that relates directly to the local area or the licensee's licence area, and advertising and sponsorship are excluded.[532] Additional requirements, in the form of the number of points required, are imposed upon regional aggregated market licensees, and obligations arise for non-aggregated licensees if a trigger event occurs.[533] A trigger event arises when a CTB licensee is in a position to control two or more CTB licences, the combined licence area population exceeds 75% of the Australian population, and at least one of the licences is for a regional broadcaster.[534]

239. Media ownership and control reforms have largely driven the imposition of and changes in, regional content obligations for the commercial radio sector.[535] Three sets of requirements may apply to regional CRB licences. Pursuant to section 43C(1) of the BSA, the ACMA must have in place at all times a licence condition that requires regional CRB licensees to broadcast a certain amount of material of local significance each business day during daytime hours.[536] In the case of licences serving areas with a population of fewer than 30,000 people, the minimum level is thirty minutes and, in other areas, three hours.[537] Pursuant to section 43B(1A), the ACMA must have in place a licence condition requiring certain regional CRB licensees to maintain a local presence.[538] The condition applies if there has been a trigger event. In that event, the licensee must ensure that at least existing local presence requirements are maintained for a period of twenty-four months after the trigger event. Local presence relates to local staffing levels and the use of local studios and other production levels.[539] With some limited exceptions, in essence, a trigger event will arise when there is a change in control or in a position to exercise control of a regional CRB licence or the formation or change of control of a registrable media group that includes a regional CRB licence.[540] The third requirement also applies if a trigger event occurs, and requires regional CRB licensees to meet minimum service standards for local news, weather, community service announcements, and emergency warnings.[541] The standards are mainly quantitative requirements. Licensees under this obligation must submit local content plans to the ACMA for approval.[542]

---

531. Broadcasting Services Act 1992(Cth), s. 61CY.
532. Broadcasting Services Local Programming Determination 2018, s. 6.
533. Broadcasting Services Act 1992 (Cth), s. 61CW(1) & s. 61CX(1).
534. Broadcasting Services Act 1992 (Cth), s. 61CV.
535. Australia also has remote area radio licences, but these obligations do not apply: Broadcasting Services Act 1992 (Cth), s. 43C(2A).
536. Broadcasting Services (Regional Commercial Radio – Material of Local Significance) Licence Condition 2014. Daytime Hours are defined as between 6:00 am and 6:00 pm: Broadcasting Services Act 1992 (Cth), s. 43C(8).
537. Broadcasting (Hours of Local Content) Declaration No. 1 of 2017, s. 6.
538. *See* Broadcasting Services (Regional Commercial Radio –Local Presence) Licence Condition 2014.
539. Broadcasting Services Act 1992 (Cth), s. 43B(3) and Broadcasting Services (Regional Commercial Radio –Local Presence) Licence Condition 2014, s. 6.
540. Broadcasting Services Act 1992 (Cth), s. 61CB. A registrable media group effectively means a group of two or more media operations.
541. Broadcasting Services Act 1992 (Cth), ss 61CD-E.
542. Broadcasting Services Act 1992 (Cth), Pt 5, Div. 5C, Subdiv. C.

§3. Protection of Minors

240. One of the matters which licensees should address in their codes of practice, and it is noted as a high priority, is the need to ensure means for protecting 'children from exposure to programme material which may be harmful to them'.[543] The main focus is television broadcasting.

241. The Commercial Television Industry Code of Practice for commercial television broadcasting services includes a scheme for the classification of programmes.[544] The broadcast day is divided into time zones, based on the type of audience likely to be watching during that time period and only material which is suitable for a particular classification time zone is broadcast.[545] Oral warnings and classification symbols are also provided. Television programmes, other than films, are classified by licensees according to the Television Classification Guidelines.[546] The Television Classification Guidelines and guidelines are informed by the national classification scheme (*see* section 7 *infra*). In relation to films, licensees use the classification given to a film under the national classification scheme and modify films as necessary for the time zone chosen for the broadcast.[547]

242. The main category for programmes suitable for children is the 'G' (or General) category, but two other categories apply under the (Broadcasting Services (Australian Content and Children's Television) Standards 2020 and programmes with these two classifications – C (Children's) and P (Pre-school) – can also be shown in the 'G' classification time zone. C and P categorized material is material intended for children, whereas G classified material may not have been intended for children but is, nevertheless, very mild in impact and does not contain any material which would be unsuitable for children to watch without supervision.[548]

243. The (Broadcasting Services (Australian Content and Children's Television) Standards 2020 regulate programming suitable for children (younger than fifteen years) (C Programme) and pre-school children (children who have not yet started school) (P Programme) should be broadcast each year and provide protections for children from harmful programming. The Standards also set out what will constitute material which is suitable for children. A children's programme will have the following elements:

(a) is made specifically for children or groups of children [for C programs of school age, for P programs of pre-school age]; and

543. Broadcasting Services Act 1992 (Cth), s. 123(2)(b).
544. FTV, Commercial Television Industry Code of Practice (2015), cl. 2.
545. *Ibid.,* cl. 2.1.1.
546. *Ibid.,* app. 1. News, current affairs, and sporting events do not have to be classified, although care must be taken in the selection of material for broadcast having regard to the likely audience: cl. 2.3.3.
547. *Ibid.*, cl. 2.3.1. Community television broadcasting uses a similar approach: ACTA, Community Television Broadcasting Codes of Practice (2011), code 4.
548. FTV, Commercial Television Industry Code of Practice), app. 1.

(b) is entertaining; and
(c) is well produced using sufficient resources to ensure a high standard of the script, cast, direction, editing, shooting, sound and other production elements; and
(d) enhances a child's understanding and experience; and
(e) is appropriate for Australian children.[549]

For a programme to be classified as a 'C' or 'P' programme, it must meet these criteria of suitability and, interestingly, must have been classified as a 'C' or 'P' programme by the ACMA before it can be broadcast.[550]

244. Both public broadcasters also have television classification schemes in place.[551]

245. CRB codes do not address children specifically in relation to the content broadcast, although there is a requirement that programme content should have regard to the 'demographic characteristics of the audience' for the relevant programme.[552] However, in relation to live-hosted entertainment radio programmes, there is a specific requirement that such programmes must not be broadcast if they treat 'children participating in live hosted entertainment radio programs in a demeaning or exploitative manner'. Children here are defined as under 16 years of age.[553] This rule arose following an investigation conducted by the ACMA into the adequacy of community safeguards in relation to such programmes.[554] The investigation had been launched by the ACMA following complaints from the public about a live programme on a high-rating breakfast show in which a 14-year-old girl was attached to a lie detector and asked about her sexual history.

246. For subscription television services, the same process of classification occurs. Programmes are classified according to the national classification scheme, and appropriate classification markings are broadcast and oral warnings provided. However, the different nature of subscription services compared with free-to-air means that time zones are not used.[555]

549. (Broadcasting Services (Australian Content and Children's Television) Standards 2020, section 8.
550. Children's Television Standards 2009, CTS 5. The ACMA can appoint another body to carry out the classification but currently carries out the task itself, although it draws on expertise of children development experts and television production experts.
551. SBS, Code of Practice (2021), code 4 and ABC, Code of Practice (2024) and Associated Standard: Television Programme Classification (2019).
552. CRA, Commercial Radio Code of Practice (2017), s. 2.2.
553. *Ibid.*, s. 8.
554. Australian Communications and Media Authority, *ACMA Investigation: Live Hosted Entertainment Radio Programs: Adequacy of community safeguards for the protection of participants* (January 2010), http://www.acma.gov.au/webwr/_assets/main/lib311265/live_hosted_entertainment_radio_programs_investigation.pdf.
555. ASTRA, Subscription Broadcast Television Codes of Practice (2013), code 3 and ASTRA, Subscription Narrowcast Television Codes of Practice (2013), code 3.

§4. Human Dignity

247. In developing industry, codes of practice that are in accordance with community attitudes, licensees are required to take into account 'the portrayal in programs of matter that is likely to incite or perpetuate hatred against, or vilifies, any person or group on the basis of ethnicity, nationality, race, gender, sexual orientation, age, religion or physical or mental disability'.[556] Each of the codes of practice addresses these matters in similar terms, although with some differences with regard to detail. For example, the Commercial Television Industry Code of Practice, which applies to free-to-air television broadcasting services, prohibits the broadcasting of any programme or other matter ' … .which is likely, in all the circumstances, to provoke or perpetuate intense dislike, serious contempt or severe ridicule against a person or group of persons on the grounds of age, colour, gender, national or ethnic origin, disability, race, religion or sexual preference'.[557]

248. A set of advisory notes is also maintained in conjunction with the Commercial Television Industry Code of Practice to help broadcasters in the portrayal of Aboriginal and Torres Strait Islander Peoples, people with disabilities, cultural diversity, and, gender.[558]

249. The public broadcasters include similar provisions in their editorial policies to ensure that content which might vilify members of the community is not broadcast. The SBS Codes of Practice reflect the more delicate balance the broadcaster must sometimes maintain between its multicultural mandate and the need to avoid any discrimination: '[w]hile remaining consistent with its mandate to portray diversity, SBS will avoid programming which clearly condones, tolerates or encourages discrimination on these grounds'.[559]

250. The general law also applies to broadcasters, and there is legislation at both federal and state and territory levels addressing hate speech; for example, the Racial Discrimination Act 1975 (Cth) (*see* Part I, section 4 *supra*).

§5. Right of Reply

251. No general right of reply exists in Australia. However, the ABC's editorial policies require the ABC to make reasonable efforts to provide a fair opportunity to

556. Broadcasting Services Act 1992 (Cth), s. 123(3)(e).
557. FTV, Commercial Television Industry Code of Practice (2015), cl. 2.6.2. *See also* CRA, Commercial Radio Code of Practice (2017), s. 2.1.4; CBAA, Community Radio Broadcasting Codes of Practice (2008), cls 3.1(a), 3.3 & 4; ACTA, Community Television Broadcasting Codes of Practice (2011), cls 3.2(c) & 3.4; ASTRA, Subscription Broadcast Television Codes of Practice (2013), cls 2.1(a)-(b).
558. Free TV Australia, https://www.freetv.com.au/resources/advisory-notes/ (accessed 8 Apr. 2024).
559. SBS, Code of Practice (2021), code 5.1.

respond to persons or organizations about whom allegations have been made by the ABC[560] (*see* also Part II, Chapter 4 *supra*).

§6. Privacy

252. The common law in Australia does not currently recognize a general right to privacy. The broadcasting sector will be bound by a range of generally applicable laws that provide privacy protection in specific contexts, such as personal information and communications (*see* Part II, Chapter 3, section 3 *supra*). However, almost all of the industry codes of practice contain some recognition of personal privacy, although it is debatable how effective the provisions are in practice.

253. The privacy provisions in the Commercial Television Industry Code of Practice apply to the broadcasting of news and current affairs, and they prohibit the licensee from using material:

- 3.5.1 … relating to a person's personal or private affairs, or which invades a person's privacy, unless:
  a) there is a public interest reason for the material to be broadcast; or
  b) the person has provided implicit or explicit consent for the material to be broadcast (or in the case of a person under 16, a parent or guardian has given implicit or explicit consent).
- 3.5.2 For the purpose of clause 3.5.1, a Licensee must exercise special care before broadcasting material relating to a Child's personal or private affairs in a report of a sensitive matter concerning the Child.[561]

254. There are also provisions requiring the licensee to be sensitive in broadcasting interviews with (or images of) bereaved relatives and survivors or witnesses of traumatic incidents.[562] Commercial television broadcasters are also guided by an Advisory Note on Privacy, although this does not add a great deal of detail and does provide guidance on what might be in the 'public interest'.[563] The ACMA also publishes a set of privacy guidelines for broadcasters, Privacy Guidelines for Broadcasters.[564] These Guidelines seek to give some more detailed guidance, including the 'public interest', and provide case studies.

---

560. Australian Broadcasting Corporation, Editorial Policy: Fair and Honest Dealing (Revised December 2023), standard 5.3.
561. FTV, Commercial Television Industry Code of Practice (2015). A 'Child' is defined as under 15 years of age: cl. 8.
562. *Ibid.*, cls 3.2.1(d) & (e).
563. Free TV Australia, *Advisory Note: Privacy*, https://www.freetv.com.au/wp-content/uploads/2019/07/Privacy.pdf, (accessed 1 Jul. 2024).
564. Australian Communications and Media Authority, Privacy Guidelines for Broadcasters, Sept. 2016, https://www.acma.gov.au/sites/default/files/2019-12/Privacy%20guidelines%20for%20broadcasters.pdf, (accessed 1 Jul. 2024). The Guidelines apply also to the national broadcasting services (the public broadcasters, ABC & SBS).

255. A matter that arose in 2010 illustrates some of the difficulties in this area and the extent to which the Code of Practice provisions are respected by licensees and journalists. In May 2010, a reporter for one of the commercial television channels, Channel 7, confronted an NSW state government minister. Channel 7 planned to run a report that the minister had used a ministerial car to convey him to a gay bathhouse. The station had secretly filmed him leaving the bathhouse. Presented with this information, the minister resigned.[565] Channel 7 then broadcast news of his resignation, taking the opportunity to broadcast the secretly filmed footage. Although the licensee argued a number of public interest grounds such as misuse of the ministerial car, not performing ministerial duties, hypocrisy, and vulnerability to blackmail, there was no evidence to support any of these grounds. The matter came before the ACMA, and it had to decide whether, by reporting the information and footage of the visit to the bathhouse, there had been a breach of the Commercial Television Industry Code of Practice.[566]

256. As is commonly understood, what may interest the public is not necessarily in the public interest. Determining whether something is in the public interest can however require finely balanced judgment. But, this was not one of those situations, and this was swiftly evident. There was widespread criticism from the public and from other sections of the media. The ACMA found that Channel 7 had used material that constituted an invasion of privacy, and it rejected categorically each of the public interest justifications put forward by the licensee. However, curiously, the ACMA found that Channel 7 had not breached the Code. Although the licensee had used material which constituted an invasion of privacy, the ACMA accepted that there was a justifiable public interest. The justification was that the public was entitled to know the circumstances of the resignation. This seemed a curious decision given that the resignation was triggered by the fact that Channel 7 was about to expose the minister's private information. If the invasion had not taken place in the first instance, there would have been no occasion for the resignation. In light of this decision, it would seem that the protection provided under the codes of practice is only likely to be effective if the licensee is willing to take seriously in the first instance the entitlement to privacy and whether or not there is a serious public interest case to be made.

257. The code of practice for commercial radio treats privacy protection succinctly, preserving a public interest exception.[567] The provisions in the other industry codes of practice are generally specified to cover news and current affairs programming only, although in some cases they apply to programming generally.[568] Both the ABC and the SBS apply their privacy provisions to programming generally.[569]

565. The minister was married and had kept his homosexuality private.

566. Australian Communications and Media Authority, Investigation Report 2431 (December 2010), www.acma.gov.au. This matter is also one of the case studies in the ACMA Privacy Guidelines.

567. CRA, Commercial Radio Code of Practice (2017), cl. 3.3.

568. CBAA, Community Radio Broadcasting Codes of Practice (2008), cl. 3.5 (applies generally); ACTA, Community Television Broadcasting Codes of Practice (2011), cl. 3.5 (applies generally); ASTRA, Subscription Broadcast Television Codes of Practice (2013), cl. 2.2(c) (applies to news

§7. OFFENSIVE AND HARMFUL MATERIAL

I. Classification of Content Likely to Cause Offence

258. In Australia, the main means of protecting the public from offensive content is achieved through a national statutory scheme which classifies publications, films, and computer games. The National Classification Scheme is the product of a cooperative arrangement between the Australian Government and the governments of the states and territories. The Classification (Publications, Films and Computer Games) Act 1995 (Cth) establishes the Classification Board, which makes classification decisions, and sets out classification procedures. State and territory authorities enforce classification decisions. Legislative amendments, which came into effect in early 2024, are designed to manage the increasing classification load. The legislation enables the industry to self-classify content in-house or use third-party classifiers (trained and accredited by the Government).[570] Further reforms are designed to clarify the scope of the classification scheme, ensure classification guidelines are aligned with community standards, and appropriate regulatory arrangements are in place for consultation.[571] The National Classification Code made pursuant to section 6 of the Classification (Publications, Films and Computer Games) Act 1995 (Cth), sets out the classification categories. Films are classified as follows:

- 'G' – films not otherwise classified.
- 'PG' – films that cannot be recommended for viewing by persons under 15 years of age, without parental guidance.
- 'M' – films that cannot be recommended for viewing by persons under 15 years of age.
- 'MA 15+ – films that depict, express or otherwise deal with sex, violence or coarse language in such a manner as to be unsuitable for viewing by persons under 15 years of age.
- R 18+ – films that are unsuitable for a minor to see.
- X 18+ – films that contain real depictions of actual sexual activity between consenting adults, but otherwise contain no violence, coercion, or purposefully demeaning depictions; and, are unsuitable for a minor to see.
- RC – films classified as RC are banned.[572]

---

and current affairs only); ASTRA, Subscription Narrowcast Television Codes of Practice (2013), cl. 1.3 (applies to news and current affairs only); ASTRA, Subscription Narrowcast Radio Codes of Practice (2013), cl. 1.3 (applies to news and current affairs only); and, ANRA, Open Narrowcast Radio Codes of Practice (2011), cl.1.8 (makes reference to observing the ACMA Privacy Guidelines).

569. ABC, Code of Practice (2024) and SBS, Code of Practice (2021), code 5.5.

570. Classification (Publications, Films and Computer Games) Amendment (Industry Self-Classification and Other Measures) Act 2023.

571. See https://www.infrastructure.gov.au/have-your-say/modernising-australias-national-classification-scheme-stage-2-reforms (accessed 3 Jul. 2024).

572. National Classification Code (May 2005), cl. 3. The Code can be accessed at: https://www.legislation.gov.au/F2005L01284/latest/text (accessed 3 Jul. 2024).

259. The National Classification Code informs the manner in which offensive content within the broadcasting context is dealt with. Classification zones are used to determine suitable free-to-air television content and viewing times.[573] When broadcasting films, broadcasters rely on the classification applied under the National Classification Scheme. In relation to other programmes, broadcasters determine their own classification, although they are guided by the National Classification Code categories. The commercial television sector has additional categories: Children (C) and Pre-school (P) (*see* section 3 *supra*).

260. The community television sector is guided by the National Classification Scheme categories and does not have any additional categories.[574] The ABC is similar in approach to the commercial free-to-air sector.[575] SBS has a similar approach.[576]

261. Although STB services also classify programmes, applying the classification categories under the National Classification Scheme, it does not operate a classification time zone scheme.[577] This is consistent with the different relationships a subscription service has with its audience, compared with free-to-air television: 'subscription TV is in the nature of an invited guest, brought into the home in the full and prior knowledge of the guest's character'.[578]

II. Prohibited Classified Content

262. Although the National Classification Code categories are relevant to the material that is shown on television, certain categories cannot be broadcast. Material that cannot be classified as MA 15+ or below cannot be broadcast on commercial television broadcasting services.[579] Subscription narrowcasting television services are subject only to the proscription on showing 'RC' and 'X 18+' content.[580]

263. Subscription television broadcasting services are also prohibited from showing 'RC' and 'X 18+' content.[581] The broadcasting of 'R 18+' content is also restricted:

573. FTV, Commercial Television Industry Code of Practice (2015), s. 2 and app. 1.
574. ACTA, Community Television Broadcasting Codes of Practice (2011), code 4.
575. ABC, Code of Practice (2024) and Associated Standard: Television Programme Classification, https://www.abc.net.au/edpols/associated-standard-on-tv-program-classification/13637634 (accessed 3 Jul. 2024).
576. SBS, Code of Practice (2021), code 4.1.3.
577. ASTRA, Subscription Broadcast Television Codes of Practice (2013), s. 3.
578. *Ibid.,* cl. 1.1.
579. FTV, Commercial Television Industry Code of Practice (2015), s. 2.6.1.
580. Broadcasting Services Act 1992 (Cth), Sch. 2, cl. 11(4).
581. Broadcasting Services Act 1992 (Cth), Sch. 2, cl. 10(1)(f).

> The licensee will ensure that access to programs classified as 'R 18+' by the Classification Board is restricted by disabling devices acceptable to the ACMA but will not broadcast such an 'R 18+' classified program until the ACMA has completed extensive, Australia-wide qualitative and quantitative research on community standards of taste and decency in relation to classifications for pay television and on what levels of violence and depiction of sex should be allowed, and the ACMA has recommended, and the Parliament has, by resolution of each House, approved, the broadcast of such programs.[582]

These steps have never occurred, and so the restriction remains in place.

III. Harmful Content

264. The industry codes of practice contain provisions concerning a matter which if broadcast might cause harm, although, as might be expected, the more comprehensive protections are found in the television codes. The Commercial Television Industry Code of Practice serves as an example. Thus, news and current affairs programming must provide warnings of material that is likely to distress or offend a substantial number of the audience seriously.[583] Suicide or attempted suicide must only be reported where there is a public interest, and the broadcast must exclude detailed descriptions of the method and graphic details or images.[584]

IV. Anti-terrorism Provisions

265. Open and subscription narrowcasting television licensees are subject to an ACMA standard which prohibits the broadcasting of terrorism-related content.[585] Terrorism-related content is understood as a programme that advocates the doing of a terrorist act, including, directly or indirectly, providing instruction on the doing of a terrorist act, and promoting or urging the doing of a terrorist act.[586]

266. A 'listed terrorist' is determined by reference to a list of terrorist organizations prescribed in the Criminal Code (Cth), and to the persons or entities who have been listed in the *Commonwealth Gazette* by the Minister for Foreign Affairs because of their association with the commission of terrorist acts.[587]

582. Broadcasting Services Act 1992 (Cth), Sch. 2, cl. 10(1)(g).
583. FTV, Commercial Television Industry Code of Practice (2015), cl. 3.2.1(a)(b).
584. FTV, Commercial Television Industry Code of Practice (2015), cl. 3.2.1(c).
585. Australian Communications and Media Authority, Broadcasting Services (Anti-Terrorism Requirements for Television Narrowcasting Services) Standard 2021. The ACMA has also produced guidelines: Guidelines to the Anti-Terrorism Standard 2021.
586. Australian Communications and Media Authority, Broadcasting Services (Anti-Terrorism Requirements for Television Narrowcasting Services) Standard 2021, s. 11.
587. Australian Communications and Media Authority, Broadcasting Services (Anti-Terrorism Requirements for Television Narrowcasting Services) Standard 2021, s. 5.

§8. Online Content

267. Regulation of online content commenced in 1999 with the passing of the Broadcasting Legislation Amendment (Online Services) Act 1999 (Cth) which sought to regulate all Internet content whether or not it was hosted in Australia or outside in relation to offensive material. The early regulation applied only to stored Internet content, and by the early 2000s, it was apparent that there were gaps in the regulatory scheme as audiovisual-rich content was increasingly being distributed over mobile telephones and other digital devices.[588] An incident in 2006 propelled the legislative response. It concerned an episode of the reality television programme, *Big Brother* in 2006. The series was being broadcast on free-to-air television. Something occurred during the episode which was regarded as offensive. The incident was not televised as it was clear that it would have breached the Commercial Television Industry Code of Practice; however, it was streamed via the *Big Brother* website and became widely known, causing public concern. The online content regulatory system, then in place, was unable to deal with the situation because the content was streamed live.[589] Amendments to the BSA were made to regulate content across all delivery platforms, including live content. The ACMA was responsible for the regulation of online content, until the establishment of the Children's eSafety Commissioner under the Enhancing Online Safety for Children Act 2015 (Cth) (OSA 2015). The OSA 2015 has been replaced by the Online Safety Act 2021 (Cth) (OSA 2021), and the Children's eSafety Commissioner has been replaced by the eSafety Commissioner. The Commissioner is an independent statutory office holder within the ACMA, and ACMA staff assist the Commissioner in the performance of their functions and exercise of powers. The OSA 2021 expands online safety protections for children and adults. The online content regulatory scheme is now under the OSA 2021 (Part 9), rather than the BSA. In 2019, following the Christchurch, New Zealand terror attack, the Australian Government rushed through legislation to criminalize the hosting and streaming of 'abhorrent violent material': Criminal Code Amendment (Sharing of Abhorrent Violent Material) Act 2019.[590] 'Abhorrent violent material' is the recording or streaming of 'Abhorrent violent conduct' which is conduct that relates to a terrorist act, murder or attempted murder, torture, rape, or, kidnapping.[591] The law applies to a 'content service' or a 'hosting service'. A content service is either a social media service or a designated internet service. The application picks up definitions from the OSA 2021.[592] News and current affairs reporting in the public interest by professional journalists is a defence.[593] The law requires the eSafety Commissioner to issue a notice to the effect

588. Department of Communications, Information Technology and the Arts, *Review of the Regulation of Content Delivered Over Convergent Devices*, April 2006.
589. B. Jaggers, M.A. Neilsen & R. Jolly, Communications Legislation Amendment (Content Services) Bill 2007 *Bills Digest No. 158*, 23 May 2007, http://www.aph.gov.au/binaries/library/pubs/bd/2006-07/07bd158.pdf (accessed 30 May 2019), 6.
590. The legislation was passed in one day and came into effect two days later. There was minimal consultation.
591. Criminal Code (Cth), ss 474.31–32.
592. Criminal Code (Cth), s. 474.30.
593. Criminal Code (Cth), s. 474.37.

that a specified content or hosting service could be used to access abhorrent violent material. Notice may only be issued where the Commissioner is satisfied on reasonable grounds that the service could be used to access the material.[594]

268. The online content regulatory scheme uses the classification categories under the National Classification Scheme. As with broadcasting, online content regulation uses a co-regulatory model. An industry body, the Communications Alliance (CA) is responsible for the development of codes of practices, and like the broadcasting sector, complaints can be made to the service provider with scope for the eSafety Commissioner to become involved if the complainant is not satisfied with the outcome.

I. Regulation of Illegal and Restricted Content

269. Under the previous regulatory scheme, there were two regulatory regimes for online content: one, which regulated content services with an Australian connection; and, one which regulated content hosted outside Australia. Under the OSA 2021, the eSafety Commissioner has powers to act regardless of where the content is hosted. Content to be regulated is defined as material which is categorized as 'class 1' or 'class 2'. Material can be text, data, speech, music, sound, visual images, or any combination.[595] Class 1 material is material that has been, or would likely be, refused classification under the National Classification Scheme.[596] Class 2 material means material that has been, or would likely be, classified as X18+ or R18+.[597] Class 2 material is divided into two categories which the Commissioner refers to as Class 2A and Class 2B. Class 2A material is material that has or would have been classified as X18+,[598] whilst material that would be considered R18+ falls into the Class 2B category.[599] The Commissioner can take action if they believe that end-users in Australia can access Class 1 or Class 2 material. The Commissioner can act on their own initiative or in response to a complaint.[600]

270. In the event the eSafety Commissioner is satisfied that Class 1 material is available to end-users in Australia, the Commissioner can issue a removal notice requiring the provider to take all reasonable steps to remove the material within 24 hours or such period as the Commissioner allows. [601] The Commissioner has similar powers in relation to Class 2 material, although in this case the service must be provided from Australia.[602] A removal notice may be issued to a provider of Class

594. Criminal Code (Cth), ss 474.35–36.
595. Online Safety Act 2021 (Cth), s. 5.
596. Online Safety Act 2021 (Cth), s. 106.
597. Online Safety Act 2021 (Cth), s. 107.
598. Online Safety Act 2021 (Cth), s. 107(1)(a)–(e).
599. Online Safety Act 2021 (Cth), s. 107(1)(f)–(l).
600. Online Safety Act 2021 (Cth), ss 38 and 42.
601. Online Safety Act 2021 (Cth), ss 109 and 110.
602. Online Safety Act 2021 (Cth), ss 114 and 115.

2A material.[603] The Commissioner may initially make an informal request to a provider to remove the content. In relation to Class 2B material, the Commissioner can issue a remedial notice requiring the provider to take all reasonable steps either to remove the material or ensure the material is subject to a restricted access system.[604] A restricted access system is designed to prevent access to children under 18 years.[605] Failure to comply with a notice may result in civil penalties.

271. In circumstances where a provider offers an app distribution service, an app removal notice may be issued if users in Australia can download an app that facilitates the posting, sharing, or sending of Class 1 material. The notice can only be issued if the eSafety Commissioner is satisfied that the service has been used for such a purpose two or more times in the previous twelve months and during that period one or more removal notices were not complied with. The app removal notice will require the provider to remove the app.[606]

272. The eSafety Commissioner also has powers to issue a link deletion notice to a provider of an internet search engine to cease providing a link to Class 1 material. The notice can only be issued if the material has been subject to a removal notice in the last twelve months and the link could have been accessed two or more times in that twelve-month period by end-users in Australia.[607]

273. The OSA 2021 requires the minister to ensure a statutory review of the legislation is undertaken within three years of its commencement.[608] The legislation is currently under review, the minister having brought forward the review given the growing risks of harm and the implications of emerging technologies.[609]

II. Regulation of Misinformation and Disinformation Content

274. Increasing concerns about the spread of misinformation and disinformation and the role of digital platforms have led the Australian Government to take action. The Australian Competition and Consumer Commission (ACCC), as part of its digital platforms inquiry, recommended that a digital platforms code of conduct should be implemented to address complaints about disinformation, overseen by a regulator such as the ACMA.[610] As part of its response to the digital platforms inquiry, the

603. Online Safety Act 2021 (Cth), ss 114(1)(b) and 115(1)(b).
604. Online Safety Act 2021 (Cth), ss 119 and 120.
605. Online Safety Act 2021 (Cth), s. 108. The Online Safety (Restricted Access Systems) Declaration 2022 sets out minimum requirements for such systems.
606. Online Safety Act 2021 (Cth), s. 128.
607. Online Safety Act 2021 (Cth), s. 124.
608. Online Safety Act 2021 (Cth), s. 239A.
609. Department of Infrastructure, Transport, Regional Development, Communications and the Arts, *Statutory Review of the Online Safety Act 2021: Issues Paper* April 2024), https://www.infrastructure.gov.au/department/media/publications/statutory-review-online-safety-act-2021-issues-paper (accessed 11 Jul. 2024).
610. Australian Competition and Consumer Commission, *Digital Platforms Inquiry, Final Report* (June 2019), recommendations 14 and 15.

Government requested digital platforms to develop a code. Accordingly, the Digital Industry Group Inc. (DIGI), overseen by the ACMA, developed the Australian Code of Practice for Disinformation and Misinformation (Information Code).[611] The Information Code is voluntary and thus only applies to signatories to the Code. In recognition of the differences in business models that might occur amongst the digital platforms, only two objectives are mandatory; other objectives in the Information Code are opt-in covering matters such as fake bots and accounts, disinformation in paid content, political advertising, and promotion of media literacy. The mandatory commitments are:

- Objective 1 requires a signatory to provide safeguards against harms that might arise from disinformation and misinformation.
- Objective 7 requires a signatory to report on the measures they take to combat disinformation and misinformation. These are referred to as 'transparency reports'.

The major digital platforms, such as Meta, Google, Microsoft, Apple, and TikTok, are members of DIGI and signatories of the Information Code. There are currently eight signatories to the Code. Other platform members include Ebay, Discord, and Snap Inc. DIGI manages a complaints process, and whilst the ACMA has an ongoing role in overseeing the operation of the Information Code, it has no authority to deal with complaints relating to the Code. X (aka 'Twitter') is a member of DIGI, but no longer a signatory to the Code. A complaint was made that X had failed to provide a mechanism to the public to report misinformation and disinformation during a national referendum on the Australian Constitution in 2023). DIGI found that a serious breach of the Code had occurred and that X had failed to respond to requests for information or engage in the process. As such X's status as a signatory to the Code was removed.[612]

275. As part of the Government's response to the digital platforms inquiry, the ACMA has to report on the adequacy of the digital platforms' measures to manage disinformation and misinformation. The ACMA has expressed concern about the small number of signatories to the Information Code, lack of awareness of the complaints process, inconsistency of reporting by signatories (as part of the transparency reports), lack of development of key performance indicators, and the failure to address large-scale group messaging, and developments such as generative artificial

---

611. The Code was published on 22 Feb. 2021: https://digi.org.au/wp-content/uploads/2022/12/Australian-Code-of-Practice-on-Disinformation-and-Misinformation-FINAL-_-December-22-2022.docx.pdf (accessed 11 Jul. 2024).
612. DIGI, Complaint by Reset Australia against X (F.k.a Twitter) Upheld by Australian Code of Practice on Disinformation and Misinformation Independent Complaints Sub-Committee (19 Nov. 2023), https://digi.org.au/in-the-media/complaint-by-reset-australia-against-x-f-k-a-twitter-upheld-by-australian-code-of-practice-on-disinformation-and-misinformation-independent-complaints-sub-committee/ (accessed 11 Jul. 2024).

intelligence.[613] In June 2023, the Government published an exposure draft of a bill, the Combatting Misinformation and Disinformation Bill, and introduced a bill into the Australian Parliament in September 2024. The intention of the Bill would be to provide the ACMA with reserve powers if there are concerns that industry self-regulatory measures are inadequate. The ACMA would be able to gather information from digital platform providers, request the development of a code of practice for registration, and develop an industry standard if a code of practice was not considered effective in combatting disinformation and misinformation. The scope to register a code of practice or to develop an industry standard would ensure that the ACMA had enforcement powers over all digital platform providers offering services accessible in Australia.

613. *See* Australian Communications and Media Authority, *A report to the government on the adequacy of digital platforms' disinformation and news quality measures* (June 2021) and *Digital platforms' efforts under the Australian Code of Practice on Disinformation and Misinformation, second report to government* (July 2023).

Chapter 4. Political Broadcasting

§1. Rules on Political Independence of Broadcasters

276. Express maintenance of political independence is not a special concern for the organization of Australian broadcasting. The Boards of the ABC and the SBS are required to maintain the independence of their respective organizations.[614] There is power for the Federal Minister to direct the ABC and the SBS to broadcast matters if it considers that it is in the national interest.[615] The ABC Act and the SBS Act both make clear that, save for this power, or as otherwise expressly required by the legislation, the broadcasters are not subject to direction by the Federal Government.[616]

277. In relation to the private media sector, there are no provisions designed expressly to preserve the political independence of broadcasting services. Only in relation to community broadcasting services is there any recognition of this principle, and even here there is no absolute bar. In allocating a community broadcasting service, the ACMA is required to have regard to the 'undesirability of the Commonwealth, a State or a Territory or a political party being in a position to exercise control of a community broadcasting service licence'.[617]

§2. Fair Representation in Election Periods

278. During an election period, if a private broadcasting sector licensee broadcasts an election matter, the licensee must provide reasonable opportunities for the broadcasting of the election matter to all political parties contesting the election, being parties represented in the preceding parliament.[618] This condition applies to elections being held at federal, state, and territory parliamentary levels and at the local government level. An election matter is defined as a matter which comments on or solicits votes for a candidate, comments on or advocates support for a political party, comments on matters before the electors, or refers to any meeting held in connection with the election.[619] The licence condition does not require the licensee to broadcast the election matter free of charge.[620] As will be noted, the obligation is

614. Australian Broadcasting Corporation Act 1983 (Cth), s. 8(1)(b) and Special Broadcasting Service Act 1991 (Cth), s. 10(1)(a).
615. Australian Broadcasting Corporation Act 1983 (Cth), s. 78 and Special Broadcasting Service Act 1991 (Cth), s. 12.
616. Australian Broadcasting Corporation Act 1983 (Cth), s. 78(6) and Special Broadcasting Service Act 1991 (Cth), s. 13.
617. Broadcasting Services Act 1992 (Cth), s. 84(2)(f). This reservation applies only in relation to licences allocated in the broadcasting services bands.
618. Broadcasting Services Act 1992 (Cth), Sch. 2, cl. 3.
619. Broadcasting Services Act 1992 (Cth), Sch. 2, cl. 1.
620. Broadcasting Services Act 1992 (Cth), Sch. 2, cl. 3(3).

to provide 'reasonable opportunities' not 'equal opportunities', and even this obligation, which has been held by the ABA (the predecessor of the ACMA) does not impose any positive obligation on a licensee to:

> ensure balance, or to broadcast a range of competing opinions. … The obligation to provide reasonable opportunity does not require a broadcaster to actively solicit material from political parties in the interests of canvassing a range of views or providing a balanced report.[621]

279. There are no rules in place to manage the cost of election advertising. The private broadcasting sector's industry codes of practice do not make any special provision for fairness during an election period. It needs to be also remembered that no impartiality obligations, in the sense of no-editorializing, are imposed upon the private broadcasting sector (*see* Chapter 3, section 1 *supra*).

280. Two further licence conditions are relevant to how political and election broadcasting is conducted. There is a prohibition on election advertisements being broadcast from the end of the Wednesday before the polling day until after the close of the poll on the polling day.[622] A broadcaster who broadcasts political matters at the request of another person (which could be a political party) must provide identification details of the person making the request.[623]

281. The public broadcasters are not required to comply with the reasonable opportunities obligation. Instead, they have the authority to determine 'to what extent and in what manner political matter or controversial matter will be broadcast'.[624] Pursuant to this discretion, the ABC allocates free broadcast time to political parties during an election.[625] This allocation applies only to general elections. The allocation is independent of any coverage that may be given to the political parties or to election matters generally in the course of the ABC's news and current affairs coverage. Of course, unlike the private broadcasting sector, the ABC is bound by impartiality obligations. The ABC allocates time to political parties to enable them to make policy announcements and additional time to the Government and Official Opposition to make final pitches in the last week of the election period. Whilst the Government and Official Opposition are automatically allocated time,

---

621. Australian Broadcasting Authority, *Investigation Summary: Malbend Pty Limited, Station 3MP* (Investigation No. 763), 2 Aug. 2001, 31.
622. Broadcasting Services Act 1992 (Cth), Sch. 2, cl. 3A. The SBS is also subject to this prohibition: Special Broadcasting Services Act 1991 (Cth), s. 70C. As the ABC does not broadcast advertisements, it is not subject to this obligation, but it voluntarily observes the blackout in relation to its policy of allocation of free time to political parties: Editorial Policies, Elections, https://www.abc.net.au/edpols/elections/13644770 (accessed 5 Jul. 2024).
623. Broadcasting Services Act 1992 (Cth), Sch. 2, cl. 4. The ABC and SBS are also subject to this prohibition: Australian Broadcasting Corporation Act 1983 (Cth), s. 79A(2) and Special Broadcasting Services Act 1991 (Cth), s. 70A(2).
624. Australian Broadcasting Corporation Act 1983 (Cth), s. 79A(1) and Special Broadcasting Services Act 1991 (Cth), s. 70A(1).
625. Australian Broadcasting Corporation, Editorial Policies, Elections, https://www.abc.net.au/edpols/elections/13644770 (accessed 5 Jul. 2024).

allocation to other parties will be determined by a set of criteria which include matters such as the number of candidates being fielded, demonstrated electoral support, or, in the case of new parties, public support. The Government and Official Opposition are allocated equal time and given the greatest allocation in comparison with the other parties.

282. Unlike the ABC, the SBS is able to broadcast advertising, but like the ABC, it also offers allocation of free airtime to political parties.[626] Its approach to allocation is similar. Any additional time sought by political parties will be treated as advertising and charged accordingly.

§3. News and Current Affairs Programmes

283. No special obligations are imposed on news and current affairs programming in relation to political broadcasting, and, thus, the general rules applicable to news and current affairs (discussed in Chapter 3, section 1 *supra*) will apply. Because there is no requirement of impartiality (save for news coverage), it is open to private broadcasters to take an editorial line.

§4. Political Advertising

284. Save for the ABC which does not broadcast advertisements, there is no prohibition on political advertising, and as seen in the discussion *supra* (section 2), there is minimal regulation of the manner in which such advertising occurs, although, of course, these advertisements will be subject to the general law and any laws dealing specifically with conduct during elections, such as the Commonwealth Electoral Act 1918 (Cth).

626. Special Broadcasting Service, Guidelines on Allocation & Use of Free Airtime (Endorsed 2021), https://drupal.prod.sbs.com.au/sites/sbs.com.au.aboutus/files/sbs_guidelines_on_allocation_and_use_of_free_airtime_-_federal_-_endorsed_2021_updated_26.04.21.pdf (accessed 5 Jul. 2024).

Chapter 5. Advertising Rules

§1. Forms of Commercial Communications

285. The regulation of commercial communications is derived from a combination of the statute, licence conditions, standards, and the industry codes of practice. The ABC Act prohibits the public broadcaster, the ABC, broadcasting advertisements.[627] It is a condition of the licence of community broadcasting services that they do not broadcast advertisements, although they are permitted to broadcast sponsorship announcements.[628] Other private sector broadcasting services and the public broadcaster, the SBS, are permitted to broadcast advertisements. The SBS Act and the editorial practices of the SBS govern commercial communications for the public broadcaster. The BSA, through the means of licence conditions, imposes some restrictions on what licensed broadcasters may advertise (*see infra)*, but the industry codes of practice have the main carriage of the regulation of commercial communications. Thus, commercial communications are another matter that falls within the co-regulatory scheme.[629]

286. In general, the broadcasting regulatory scheme has been very tolerant of the various forms of commercial communications and, save for where there are specific restrictions, has not sought to distinguish between the various forms of commercial communications, or even to define them. Thus, save for specific restrictions (as discussed *infra*), all forms of commercial communications, including sponsorship and product placement, have been acceptable and common. Attention to commercial communication practices did not really arise until the late 1990s when concerns arose about undisclosed paid-for comment practices that seemed to be widespread across the commercial radio industry. Known as the 'Cash for Comment' investigation, it led the ACMA to impose standards on the commercial radio sector whilst the commercial television sector developed new code provisions covering commercial disclosure (*see* section 4 and section 5 *infra*).

§2. Restrictions on Content

287. All broadcasting licensees are subject to a licence condition that prohibits the advertising of tobacco or e-cigarettes.[630] Licensees advertising therapeutic goods must comply with the Therapeutic Goods Administration's Therapeutic Goods (Therapeutic Goods Advertising Code) Instrument 2021. Interactive gambling

627. Australian Broadcasting Corporation Act 1983 (Cth), s. 31. 'Advertising' is not defined.
628. Broadcasting Services Act 1992 (Cth), Sch. 2, cl. 9(1)(b).
629. Broadcasting Services Act 1992 (Cth), s. 123.
630. Broadcasting Services Act 1992 (Cth), Sch. 2, cl. 7(1)(a) (commercial television); cl. 8(1)(a) (commercial radio); cl. 9(1)(a) (community broadcasting); cl. 10(1)(a) (subscription television broadcasting); and, cl. 11(1)(a) (all services regulated by class licences).

services are not to be advertised on broadcasting services.[631] Alcohol advertising on television is permitted but only during certain time periods, whilst no time limits apply to radio.

288. There are specific restrictions in place in relation to advertising directed to children. The restrictions concern the content of the advertising as well as scheduling and quantity (*see* section 3 *infra*). The restrictions are concerned with the periods known as the 'C' (children) period and the 'P' (pre-school) period. No advertising is permitted during the 'P' period.[632] The Australian Content and Children's Television Standards 2020 set out a range of requirements designed to protect children in relation to advertisements directed at them during the 'C' period, which include:

- Advertisements (as well as any other material broadcast) must not demean any person on the basis of race, disability, gender, religion, and so forth; unduly distress or frighten children; encourage unsafe or dangerous use of products; or, advertise products which have officially been declared unsafe or dangerous.
- Advertisements must be 'G' classified.
- Advertisements and sponsorship announcements must be clearly distinguishable as such to a child.
- Advertisements should not mislead or deceive children.
- Advertisements should not put undue pressure on children to ask their parents or other persons to purchase the advertised product or service.
- Advertisements should not create an impression that the product or service will make a child superior to his/her peers or that the person who buys the product or service is more generous than someone who does not.[633]

289. Other restrictions or rules about the form of certain advertisements are to be found in the industry codes of practice. The most detailed of these is the Commercial Television Industry Code of Practice. As a general matter, all advertisements must be given a classification and shown only in the time period suitable for that classification (*see* Chapter 3, section 3 *supra*).[634] It is the responsibility of licensees to ensure compliance.[635] Television advertisers are also expected to comply with the Australian Association of National Advertisers (AANA) codes: the Code of Ethics and the Children's Advertising Code (in addition, of course, to the Australian Content and Children's Television Standards).[636] The AANA is an industry-based organization representing those in the advertising, marketing, and media industry. As part of a self-regulatory scheme, it develops codes for the industry. The

631. Interactive Gambling Act 2001, s. 61DA.
632. Australian Communications and Media Authority, Australian Content and Children's Television Standards 2020, s. 24.
633. Australian Communications and Media Authority, Australian Content and Children's Television Standards 2020, Part 4, divs 1 and 2.
634. FTV, Commercial Television Industry Code of Practice (2015), cl. 2.1.1. *See also* cl. 2.4.
635. *Ibid.*, cl. 1.1.4.
636. *Ibid.*, cl. 5.7.1.

industry-established Ad Standards manages the complaints and determination process for potential code breaches.[637] Other codes will also be relevant including those developed by the AANA: Food and Beverages Advertising Code, Wagering Advertising Code, and the Environmental Claims Code.

290. The Commercial Television Industry Code of Practice also covers industry-specific advertising. Hence, there are rules about the time zones in which advertising for alcoholic drinks can be broadcast. These time zones equate with the classification time zones, although there is an exception for live sporting events broadcast at weekends and public holidays.[638] A similar approach is taken for advertisements for betting or gambling and for intimate products such as condoms or telephone sex-lines.[639] Rules are also in place to reduce and control the promotion of odds and commercials relating to betting or gambling during live sporting events.[640]

291. By contrast, the Commercial Radio Code of Practice contains minimal restrictions on content. It is a provision of the Code that advertisements must be presented in a way that makes clear that they are advertising material.[641] Rules, similar to television, are in place to address concerns about the promotion of gambling and betting odds in sports coverage.[642]

292. The Subscription Broadcast Television Codes of Practice cover similar matters to commercial television, although the specific rules reflect the different nature of subscription broadcasting compared to free-to-air services. Thus, although all advertisements must receive a classification, in relation to scheduling the licensee is simply expected to take into account the maturity of the audience when broadcasting advertisements in certain categories, such as alcoholic beverages, betting and gambling, and, so forth.[643] Only commercial television broadcasting licensees are bound by the Children's Television Standards, but the Subscription Broadcast Television Codes of Practice includes rules relating to advertising directed at children. For services operating under a class licence, the rules in the respective codes of practice address similar content concerns, although with varying degrees of detail.

293. In addition to its Code of Practice which makes some reference to the management of advertising and sponsorship,[644] SBS is also guided by its Commercial, Funding and External Relationships Guidelines.[645] The Guidelines state that the

637. For further information *see* http://www.adstandards.com.au.
638. FTV, Commercial Television Industry Code of Practice (2015), cl. 6.2.
639. *Ibid.,* cl. 6.3.
640. *Ibid.,* app. 3.
641. CRA, Commercial Radio Code of Practice (2017), cl. 4.1.
642. *Ibid.,* cl. 9.
643. ASTA, Subscription Broadcast Television Codes of Practice (2013), cls 6.2 & 6.5.
644. SBS, Code of Practice (2021), s. 4.2.
645. (April 2022), https://www.sbs.com.au/aboutus/wp-content/uploads/2023/04/sbs_commercial_funding_and_external_relationships_guidelines_2022.pdf (accessed 5 Jul. 2024).

SBS content will '... be driven by editorial decisions made in the service of its Charter, not the availability of external funds or other commercial activities' (section 2). In relation to television, SBS also takes account of the Commercial Television Industry Code of Practice rules on timing and placement of advertising, especially in relation to certain product categories. [646]

§3. Time and Frequency Restrictions

294. Unlike other jurisdictions, Australia has a fairly relaxed approach to the regulation of the amount of advertising broadcast. The BSA Act does not specify any quantitative restrictions for commercial broadcasting services, although it does require the codes of practice to include rules regarding the amount of time to be devoted to advertising. Community broadcasting services are subject to a licence condition that restricts sponsorship announcements to no more than seven minutes in an hour (in the case of television) and no more than five minutes (in the case of radio).[647] Subscription television broadcasting services and all subscription services operating under a class licence are subject to a licence condition requiring licence fees to be the predominant source of revenue.[648]

295. The Commercial Television Industry Code of Practice restricts advertising as follows:

(a) On any day, in each hour, a licensee may schedule on average no more than:
  - Thirteen minutes, between 6.00 pm and midnight (outside election periods).
  - Fourteen minutes, between 6.00 pm and midnight (in election periods), provided that no more than thirteen minutes of the commercial communication comprises non-political matter.
  - Fifteen minutes at all other times (sixteen minutes during an election period if the hour includes a news programme, provided that no more than fifteen minutes of the commercial communication comprises non-political matter).

(b) Provided that the averages above are complied with, in an hour, a licensee may schedule the following:
  - Up to fifteen minutes per hour, between 6.00 pm and midnight (outside election periods), but with no more than fourteen minutes scheduled in any four of those hours.
  - Up to fifteen minutes per hour, between 6.00 pm and midnight (in election periods), plus one minute per hour of commercial communication that is a political matter.

646. SBS, Code of Practice (2021), s. 4.2.
647. Broadcasting Services Act 1992 (Cth), Sch. 2, cl. 9(3).
648. Broadcasting Services Act 1992 (Cth), Sch. 2, cl. 10(2)(b) (subscription television broadcasting) and cl. 11(2) (subscription class licence services).

- Up to sixteen minutes per hour at all other times (outside election periods).
- Up to sixteen minutes per hour at all other times (in election periods), plus one minute per hour of commercial communication that is a political matter and scheduled in a news programme.[649]

These provisions apply only to the commercial television primary service. Slightly more relaxed restrictions apply to the service's multichannel channels.[650]

296. These allowances are also subject to compliance with the quantitative restrictions imposed by the Children's Television Standards. No advertising is permitted during a 'P' period, and during a C period advertising is limited to no more than five minutes during every thirty minutes of a C period, unless an Australian 'C' drama is being broadcast, in which case the limit is six minutes and thirty seconds per thirty minutes.[651] During any thirty minutes of a C period, the same advertisement may not be broadcast more than twice.[652]

297. Quantitative restrictions no longer apply to commercial radio.

298. SBS is permitted to broadcast five minutes of advertisements and sponsorship announcements within an hour of broadcast. They may only be broadcast before programmes commence after they end, or during natural programme breaks.[653]

§4. Sponsorship

299. Community broadcasting services are prohibited from advertising but are permitted to broadcast sponsorship announcements. As a not-for-profit sector, sponsorship revenue is intended to support the broadcasting services and their programming. A sponsorship announcement may include the name and address details of the sponsor, as well as a description of the general nature of the business or undertaking, and they may promote the activities of the sponsor. Sponsorship may be of the licensee or a particular programme.[654] Section 123(j) of the BSA requires the community broadcasting sector to include in its code of practice rules about the kinds of sponsorship announcements that may be broadcast by licensees and the kinds of sponsorship announcements that particular kinds of programmes may carry. The

649. FTV, Commercial Television Industry Code of Practice (2015), cl. 5.3. The Code uses the term 'non-program matter' to refer to commercial communications; 'non-program matter' is defined in cl. 5.1.1.
650. *Ibid.*, cl. 5.4.
651. Australian Content and Children's Television Standards 2020, s. 33.
652. *Ibid.*, s. 35.
653. Special Broadcasting Service Act 1991 (Cth), s. 45(2).
654. Broadcasting Services Act 1992 (Cth), Sch. 2, cls 9(1)(b), (3)-(5).

Community Radio Broadcasting Codes of Practice contains some general statements of principle about the relationship between sponsorship and editorial independence. Thus:

- 6.2 Sponsorship will not be a factor in deciding who can access broadcasting time.
- 6.3 We will ensure editorial decisions affecting the content and style of individual programs are not influenced by program or station sponsors.
- 6.4 We will ensure that editorial decisions affecting the content and style of overall station programming are not influenced by program or station sponsors.[655]

300. The Codes of Practice also includes an appendix (Appendix 7) that provides a sample sponsorship policy for the adoption by a licensee. Some of the matters addressed in the sample policy are:

- If accepting sponsorship from a company to promote alcohol, the sponsorship announcement should not promote the misuse of alcohol or be directed to minors.
- Sponsorship announcements should be produced in a manner consistent with the programme in which they are to be placed.
- Individual presenters should not seek sponsorship on behalf of the station, without the written consent of the station management.
- Presenters are not entitled to accept any reward in return for promotion of a product, business, etc.

301. The ACMA developed a set of advisory guidelines to assist community broadcasters in understanding their responsibilities and the distinction between advertising and sponsorship.[656] It is, however, a somewhat fine line between what will be regarded as advertising and what will be regarded as sponsorship, especially because the sponsorship announcements broadcast on community services generally have the 'look and feel' of a traditional spot announcement, although they carry a tag line which makes clear they are providing financial support to the station and/or programme. The ACMA relies on an HCA definition of 'advertising':

> It would seem to be used in a broad general sense which would encompass any broadcast or telecast of material 'designed or calculated to draw public attention' to something … regardless of whether the broadcast or telecast 'serves a purpose other than that of advertising'.[657]

655. CBAA, Community Radio Broadcasting Codes of Practice (2008), cls 6.2–6.4.
656. Australian Communications and Media Authority, *Community Broadcasting Sponsorship Guidelines 2008* (June 2008), https://www.acma.gov.au/sites/default/files/2019-06/Community-Broadcasting-Sponsorship-Guidelines-2008.pdf (accessed 9 Jul. 2024).
657. *Australian Capital Television Pty Ltd and the State of New South Wales v. The Commonwealth* (1992) 177 CLR 106, 166 quoted in Australian Communications and Media Authority, *Community Broadcasting Sponsorship Guidelines 2008* (June 2008), https://www.acma.gov.au/sites/default/files/2019-06/Community-Broadcasting-Sponsorship-Guidelines-2008.pdf (accessed 9 Jul. 2024), 3.

302. Given that the BSA permits the promotion of the sponsor's activities, it is difficult to see where the line is drawn. The ACMA draws the distinction in the following manner:

> The key feature of a sponsorship announcement is its acknowledgment of the financial or in-kind support given by a sponsor to a community broadcasting licensee or a program provided under the service.
>
> The announcement may also promote the activities, events, products, services or programs of the sponsor, provided that it contains an acknowledgment of financial or in-kind support by the sponsor of the licensee or a program.
>
> Sponsorship announcements must be genuine. A licensee must be able to demonstrate (if asked) that the sponsors featured in announcements are actually financial supporters (in cash or in kind) of the licensee or a program provided under the service.[658]

303. The Community Television Broadcasting Codes of Practice adopts a similar approach to community radio, especially in relation to the preservation of editorial independence.[659]

304. Until the 'Cash for Comment' investigation,[660] sponsorship, aside from the particular requirements of community broadcasting, received very little regulatory attention. In relation to commercial broadcasting, there was no specific regulation, save for requirements to keep advertising separate from programming. The 'Cash for Comment' affair concerned a number of prominent radio presenters, who specialized in talk-back programmes, on several CRB stations located across Australia. The programmes of several of the presenters were syndicated which gave them a substantial national reach. The presenters had in place valuable personal and commercial arrangements with sponsors that required them to give on-air exposure to commercial interests. In some cases, the sponsors were industry lobby groups. In general, the arrangements meant that the presenter would provide favourable publicity, informed commentary, or editorial comment relevant to the interests of the sponsor, usually based on the material provided. The commentary was often in relation to matters of current public policy. The commercial arrangements were not disclosed to the public. The ABA found breaches of:

> A code of practice requirement to ensure that advertisements are not presented as news programmes.

658. Australian Communications and Media Authority, *Community Broadcasting Sponsorship Guidelines 2008* (June 2008), https://www.acma.gov.au/sites/default/files/2019-06/Community-Broadcasting-Sponsorship-Guidelines-2008.pdf (accessed 9 Jul. 2024), 13–14.
659. ACTA, Community Television Broadcasting Codes of Practice (2011), cl. 6.3.
660. Australian Broadcasting Authority, *Commercial Radio Inquiry: Final Report of the Australian Broadcasting Authority,* August 2000, http://www.acma.gov.au/~/media/Broadcasting%20Standards/Report/pdf/CommercialRadioInquiry/commradinq_fin%20pdf.pdf (accessed 5 Feb. 2014). *See also* L. Hitchens, 'Commercial Broadcasting – Preserving the Public Interest' (2004) 32(1) *Federal Law Review* 79–106.

A code of practice requirement to ensure fairness and accuracy in news and current affairs programmes: in this case, fairness was not achieved because relevant facts (the existence of the commercial arrangements) were omitted (*see* Chapter 3, section 1 *supra*).
A breach of a licence condition requiring identification of 'political matter' (*see* Chapter 4 *supra*).

305. As a result of the investigation, the ABA held that there had been a systemic failure across the commercial radio industry to ensure effective self-regulation, especially in relation to current affairs programming. The ABA took a range of remedial action remedies, including the imposition of three industry standards:[661]

A standard to require a clear separation of programming from advertising.[662]
A standard to ensure that licensees put in place internal processes to ensure compliance with regulatory obligations.[663]
A standard to ensure disclosure of commercial arrangements between presenters and sponsors.[664]

306. Following a review of the commercial-radio-standards, the ACMA revoked the compliance standard in 2012 and the advertising standard in 2013. The disclosure standard remains in place, with a new standard determined in 2022.[665] Pursuant to the Broadcasting Services (Commercial Radio Current Affairs Disclosure) Standard 2022 (the disclosure standard), licensees must disclose on-air the existence of commercial arrangements (whether with the licensee or the presenter) if the commercial arrangement has the potential to affect the content of a current affairs programme. The intention is that the disclosure standard will make licensees responsive to the need to ensure fair and accurate coverage of matters of public interest. Where a commercial arrangement is in place, the disclosure will be required if the material is broadcast that:

- promotes the name, products or services of the sponsor; or
- includes an interview with an agent, employee or officer of the sponsor in relation to a matter that concerns the sponsor, its products, services or interests; or
- is requested by the sponsor, or which is based on, or similar to, material provided by the sponsor; or
- directly promotes an issue which is directly favourable to the sponsor.[666]

307. The Commercial Television Industry Code of Practice includes rules relating to the disclosure of commercial arrangements in relation to factual programmes. Factual programmes are defined as current affairs, documentary, or infotainment

661. *See* introduction to Ch. 3 *supra* for an explanation of a 'standard'. *See also* Part V *infra*.
662. Broadcasting Services (Commercial Radio Advertising) Standard 2000.
663. Broadcasting Services (Commercial Radio Compliance Program) Standard 2000.
664. Broadcasting Services (Commercial Radio Current Affairs Disclosure) Standard 2000.
665. Broadcasting Services (Commercial Radio Current Affairs Disclosure) Standard 2022.
666. Broadcasting Services (Commercial Radio Current Affairs Disclosure) Standard 2022, s. 10(1)(b).

programmes. The rules cover commercial arrangements made with third parties whether the licensee or a presenter makes them. A commercial arrangement is an arrangement whereby a third party's products or services will be featured in exchange for consideration. Essentially, the facts of the commercial arrangement must be disclosed if the third party's products or services are featured or endorsed in a factual programme. Disclosure can be made either during the programme, in the credits, on the program's official website, or in any way that 'adequately brings the arrangement to the attention of viewers'.[667] It should be noted that neither the disclosure standard for commercial radio nor the code of practice disclosure rules for commercial television preserves the principle of editorial independence. The regulatory model is one based on disclosure, not editorial independence.[668]

§5. Product Placement

308. As with sponsorship, product placement has received very little regulatory attention in Australia. With digital technology, product placement is becoming much easier to undertake at the post-production stage, opening up the commercial possibilities for licensees. The code of practice disclosure rules for commercial television, discussed in section 4, might be seen as also encompassing product placement situations, at least in relation to factual programmes. However, outside of factual programmes, product placement on commercial television is not regulated. Clause 5.2.1(c) of the Commercial Television Industry Code of Practice expressly exempts 'product placement and commercial integration within a Program … ' from the definition of 'non-Program matter' which covers commercials and programme promotions (clause 5.1.1).

309. As with sponsorship, the preferred regulatory principle, at least so far as factual programmes are concerned, is disclosure rather than editorial independence. Despite the exclusion of product placement from the regulation of commercial communications for other programmes, it is apparent that audiences are not necessarily comfortable with the extent and nature of product placement.[669]

667. FTV, Commercial Television Industry Code of Practice (2015), cl. 4.

668. *See* Australian Communications and Media Authority, *Review of Commercial Radio Standards Report* (November 2011), http://www.acma.gov.au/Industry/Broadcast/Radio/Commercial-radio-standards/review-of-commercial-radio-standards-radio-i-acma (accessed 5 Feb. 2014).

669. *See* Australian Broadcasting Corporation' *Media Watch*, Episode 2 Sep. 2019, https://www.abc.net.au/education/media-watch-product-placement-in-television/13938882 (accessed 9 Jul. 2024).

Chapter 6. Right to Information

§1. Access to Major Events

310. Access to major events protection is in place, although the provisions relate to sporting events only. In common with other jurisdictions, these rules were put in place when subscription television was introduced, in 1992, because of the concern that major sporting events would be accessible only through subscription services. There has been criticism of the breadth of the list of protected sporting events (which was once so extensive that it would not have been possible for free-to-air broadcasters to air all of the events on its schedule) and its anti-competitive nature.[670] Over time the list of events has been narrowed and provisions have been introduced to reduce the scope for hoarding of events and provide for the automatic delisting of events. The access legislation was introduced at a time when options for media viewing were much more limited. With the development of television multichannels, streaming services, and mobile and digital platforms, the current scheme has seemed increasingly inconsistent with the media environment. Following a review by the Government, the Communications Legislation Amendment (and Anti-siphoning) Act 2024 (Cth) (PAS Act) was passed in July 2024. As a result, and when this part (Schedule 2) of the PAS Act comes into force, the anti-siphoning scheme will now apply to online services, including streaming and mobile services, referred to as 'media content service' in the legislation (section 146U). Schedule 2 of the PAS Act will introduce a new Part 10B into the BSA. Where relevant the new section references (when in force) are noted in brackets in the following paragraphs.

311. Under section 115(1) (section 146V(1), PAS Act) of the BSA, the Minister can nominate events, which, in the Minister's opinion, should be available free to the general public. These nominated events are included in what is known as 'the anti-siphoning list'. Events on this list are available for broadcasting on free-to-air television services.[671] Subscription television broadcasting licensees are also subject to a licence condition prohibiting them from acquiring the right to televise a listed event unless a national broadcaster or commercial television broadcasting licensees (that broadcast to more than 50% of the Australian population) also have the right to broadcast the event.[672] When the new anti-siphoning scheme comes into force, this licence condition will be repealed and a new provision will apply to the media content service providers (section 146W, PAS Act). The anti-siphoning list operates to give free-to-air broadcasters a first right of refusal on the acquisition of

670. Productivity Commission, *Broadcasting*, Report No. 11 (Canberra: AusInfo, 2000), 434–435.

671. A new list was introduced in 2023: Broadcasting Services (Events) Notice 2023. As part of the 2024 reforms to the anti-siphoning regime, a new list will be developed which will also ensure greater recognition of women's sport and sports played by athletes with disabilities: *see* Department of Infrastructure, Transport, Regional Development, Communications and the Arts, *Anti-Siphoning Review, Proposal Paper* (August 2023), https://www.infrastructure.gov.au/sites/default/files/documents/anti-siphoning-review-proposals-paper.pdf (accessed 11 Jul. 2024).

672. Broadcasting Services Act 1992 (Cth), Sch. 2, cl. 10(1)(e).

sporting broadcast rights. The Minister can decide to remove an event from the anti-siphoning list, and the legislation provides examples of when that discretion might be exercised:

- When the national broadcasters and the commercial television broadcasting licensees have had a real opportunity to acquire an event but have not done so.
- A commercial television broadcasting licensee has acquired the right to televise an event but has not done so, or has broadcast an unreasonably small proportion of the event.[673]

312. Automatic removal from the anti-siphoning list can also occur. If the rights to a listed event have not been acquired, an event will be removed from the list 4,368 hours (twenty-six weeks) before the event commences.[674] The twenty-six-week period is designed to allow subscription services sufficient opportunity to acquire the rights as well as schedule and publicize the event.[675] None of these provisions ensures that sporting events on the anti-siphoning list will actually be broadcast free to the general public. Free-to-air broadcasters who acquire rights to listed events are not actually required to show the events, although this could lead to the Minister exercising discretion under section 115(2). Nor does it mean that significant sporting events will be shown live as broadcasters may not want to interfere with their prime-time schedules.

313. To address some of the limitations of the listed events provisions, rules, known as 'the anti-hoarding rules', were introduced. Under the anti-hoarding regime, free-to-air broadcasters are discouraged from hoarding rights to provide live coverage of listed events. If a commercial television broadcasting licensee has acquired exclusive rights to live coverage of a listed event but does not intend to televise the whole or part of the event or series, the licensee must offer, to either the ABC or SBS, the right to televise the whole or part of the event, or series for a nominal consideration.[676] If the ABC or the SBS have acquired rights that they do not intend to use, then the public broadcaster who has the rights must offer them to the other public broadcaster.[677] Although the anti-hoarding rules are an attempt to encourage the free-to-air broadcasters to use the rights they have acquired, the provisions are still limited in addressing the public's access to significant sporting events. As a practical matter, the public broadcasters may not be in a position to

673. Broadcasting Services Act 1992 (Cth), s. 115(2) (s. 146V(5), PAS Act).

674. Broadcasting Services Act 1992 (Cth), s. 115(1AA) (s. 146V(2), PAS Act). The Minister can prevent the automatic removal if the Minister is satisfied that a national broadcaster or a commercial television broadcasting licensee has not had a reasonable opportunity to acquire the right to televise: s. 115(1AB) (s. 146V(3), PAS Act).

675. The delisting period was originally six weeks, and then twelve weeks. The current period recognizes that the rights to major sports events are likely to be negotiated six months or more before the actual event. It was intended that the period of 4,368 hours would be extended to 8,760 hours under the proposals for the PAS Act, but this was dropped during the legislative process as there were concerns that the extended period might provide a risk of circumvention of the scheme: Supplementary Explanatory Memorandum (2024), 6.

676. Broadcasting Services Act 1992 (Cth), ss 146E & 146H.

677. Broadcasting Services Act 1992 (Cth), ss 146L–146M.

schedule the events. More crucially, the anti-hoarding rules do not apply to the whole of the anti-siphoning list; the anti-hoarding rules apply only to events the Minister has designated.[678]

§2. Short News Reporting

314. There are no regulatory arrangements in place that provide for access to short news reporting. In 2010, a voluntary code was introduced following an agreement between sports administrations and news organizations to ensure that news organizations were able to access sporting events in Australia to report sporting news.[679]

678. Broadcasting Services Act 1992 (Cth), s. 146C. The power to designate under section 146C has only been used on two occasions: Department of Infrastructure, Transport, Regional Development, Communications and the Arts, *Review of the anti-siphoning scheme, consultation paper* (October 2022), https://www.infrastructure.gov.au/sites/default/files/documents/anti-siphoning-consultation-paper-oct-2022.pdf (accessed 11 Jul. 2024), 13.

679. Code of Practice for Sports News Reporting, 2010, https://www.infrastructure.gov.au/media-technology-communications/media-laws-regulation/sports-reporting-australia (accessed 11 Jul. 2024).

Chapter 7. Access to Networks and Platforms

§1. Must-Carry Rules

315. Until 2024, must-carry obligations have not applied in Australia. It has been left to commercial negotiation. There is a retransmission of free-to-air programmes scheme that, in essence, enables the retransmission of free-to-air broadcasts, without the need to seek permission or remuneration of the broadcaster. The provisions only apply if the retransmission meets the statutory definition of 'retransmission', which requires the content of the broadcast to be unaltered, and broadcast simultaneously with the original transmission (or delayed until the equivalent local time).[680] Such retransmission does not require the permission of the original broadcast and does not infringe the copyright of the broadcaster,[681] although the scheme does not cover the underlying rights which are covered under a statutory licensing scheme.[682] The Communications Legislation Amendment (Prominence and Anti-Siphoning) Act 2024 (PAS Act) creates a must-carry (termed 'prominence') framework which will be phased in. The new framework is a recognition that free-to-air television broadcasting services and broadcasting video-on-demand services (BVOD services) are one of the many content options available on connected television devices, and are often difficult for the public to find, whilst prominence may be given to services paying for such positioning. The PAS Act introduces a new part 9E to the BSA. Once implemented, the framework:

- will require manufacturers of 'regulated television devices' to adhere to a set of prominence requirements. A 'regulated television device' is domestic reception equipment capable of connecting to the internet and receiving BVOD services.[683] It must also be a device that is primarily designed for the viewing of audiovisual material, excluding devices such as computers, tablets, and so forth.
- will enable 'regulated television services' to be guaranteed prominence on the device. A regulated television service is a linear broadcast service provided by national broadcasters, the commercial and community television broadcasting licensees. [684]Certain BVOD services provided by the free-to-air television services will also be included in the framework.
- will also prescribe minimum prominence requirements with which a regulated television device manufacturer must comply. These will be developed through regulations made under the PAS Act and will include matters such as the display or positioning of a service, installation of applications to provide access, and any electronic programme guides that may be used.[685]

680. Copyright Act 1968 (Cth), s. 10.
681. Broadcasting Services Act 1992 (Cth), s. 212. The retransmission must be within the licence area of the broadcaster, unless the ACMA has otherwise permitted.
682. Copyright Act 1968 (Cth), s. 135ZZK.
683. Communications Legislation Amendment (Prominence and Anti-Siphoning) Act 2024, s. 130ZZI.
684. Communications Legislation Amendment (Prominence and Anti-Siphoning) Act 2024, s. 130ZZJ.
685. Communications Legislation Amendment (Prominence and Anti-Siphoning) Act 2024, s. 130ZZO.

– will prohibit any devices being supplied that do not comply with the minimum prominence requirements.[686]

§2. Other Access Obligations for Networks

316. Access to networks is the responsibility of the generic Australian competition regulator, the Australian Competition and Consumer Commission (ACCC). The CCA provides for an industry-specific access regime for communications: Part XIC.[687] The access regime, introduced in 1997, was initially designed to promote access agreement through commercial negotiation so that the regulatory regime would only come into operation if negotiations failed. However, negotiated outcomes proved difficult to achieve, given the dominance of the vertically integrated telecommunications operator, Telstra. Thus, a series of legislative reforms have occurred that have given the ACCC more power to set the terms for negotiation.[688]

317. The access regime operates through the declaration of service so that once a service is declared by the ACCC, the service provider is obliged to provide access pursuant to the standard access obligations. Services under the access regime are listed carriage services or services that facilitate the supply of a listed carriage service.[689] One of the first services to be declared (although no longer a declared service) was subscription broadcasting services, including the carriage of analogue signals and the use of conditional access services, including set-top units and subscriber management services. Because of vertical integration in the subscription television market, it was difficult for other service providers to gain access to cable networks.

318. A service can be declared by the ACCC or by a service provider who has given a special access undertaking.[690] A special access undertaking contains the price and conditions upon which the provider is willing to provide access to its services. Standard access obligations are a basic set of obligations requiring the service provider to supply the declared service so that the person seeking access can provide their carriage or content services; take all reasonable steps to ensure that technical and operational quality of the declared service is equivalent to those which the access provider provides to itself; and, take all reasonable steps to ensure that services in relation to fault detection, handling and rectification of technical and operational quality will be equivalent to those which the access provider provides

686. Communications Legislation Amendment (Prominence and Anti-Siphoning) Act 2024, s. 130ZZN.
687. The Competition and Consumer Act 2010 (Cth) also includes a telecommunications industry-specific competition regime: Part XIB.
688. A. Grant & D. Howarth, 'Access and Structural Regulation' in A. Grant & D. Howarth (eds), *Australian Telecommunications Regulation* (Sydney: CCH Australia Ltd, 2012, 4th ed.), 195, 202–204.
689. Competition and Consumer Act 2010 (Cth), s. 152AL.
690. Competition and Consumer Act 2010 (Cth), s. 152AL. There are also specific provisions in relation to the NBN.

to itself.[691] The standard access obligations form the basis for negotiations between the parties to agree on the terms and conditions for access, referred to as an 'access agreement'.[692] If an agreement cannot be reached, the terms and conditions to apply will be:

– The special access undertaking, if one has been provided.
– The binding rules of conduct, if the ACCC has made such rules. The ACCC has the power to make such rules where it considers that there is an urgent need to address access problems. The binding rules of conduct will specify the terms and conditions based on the standard access obligations.[693]
– The terms and conditions specified in an access determination made by the ACCC. The ACCC has the power to make access determinations in relation to each declared service.[694]

691. Competition and Consumer Act 2010 (Cth), s. 152AR.
692. Competition and Consumer Act 2010 (Cth), s. 152BE.
693. Competition and Consumer Act 2010 (Cth), s. 152BD.
694. Competition and Consumer Act 2010 (Cth), s. 152BC.

Chapter 8. Standards and Interoperability

319. The Radiocommunications Act 1992 (Cth) regulates the spectrum planning, allocation, and use which must be undertaken in a manner which promotes the long-term public interest.[695]

320. Any-to-any connectivity is considered an important principle in the organization of communications and the Telecommunications Act 1997 (Cth) has a key role to play here in the maintenance of technical and operational standards.

695. Section 3. The BSA also has some role in spectrum planning in relation to broadcasting.

Part IV. Ownership Regulation

§1. Introduction

321. Sector-specific regulation of media ownership and control in Australia has been and continues to be, centred on traditional media platforms, broadcasting services and, for the purposes of cross-media regulation, newspapers. The regulation applies only to commercial services. Competition law also has a role to play encompassing the broader media market, including online services. As the media environment changed and new business models emerged, there was increasing pressure for reform – in the sense of relaxation – of the sector-specific ownership and control rules. There were substantial media ownership reforms in 2006 that removed many of the rules then in place, including foreign ownership restrictions. The Government at the time had wanted to remove all cross-media regulation, but to secure the passage of the legislation through Parliament agreed to retain some form of cross-media regulation. However, in 2017 the Federal Government secured substantial relaxation of the media ownership and control rules, including cross-media regulation.

322. With the changing media market and audience news consumption, there have been concerns about the impact on local news and public interest journalism. In addition, there has been a recognition that media diversity needs to be better understood and more nuanced. In December 2020, the ACMA published a research paper examining how diversity in news and opinion and the availability of local news could be measured.[696] The paper proposed a framework that would seek to measure diversity, in relation to news, across print, television, radio, and online. The framework proposed key measures of diversity such as source, content, and consumption, and for localism, connection, originality, and civic journalism, and a set of indicators to support the measures. Following a request from the Federal Government to update the framework, the ACMA led a consultation.[697] As a consequence, the ACMA developed a revised Media Diversity Measurement Framework. The revised framework no longer includes localism as a stand-alone component but

696. Australian Communications and Media Authority, *News in Australia: diversity and localism, News Measurement Framework* (December 2020), https://www.acma.gov.au/publications/2020-12/report/news-australia-diversity-and-localism (accessed 16 Jul. 2024).

697. Australian Communications and Media Authority, *A new framework for measuring media diversity in Australia: consultation paper* (January 2023), https://www.acma.gov.au/sites/default/files/2023-01/Consultation%20paper_A%20new%20framework%20for%20measuring%20media%20diversity%20in%20Australia.pdf (accessed 16 Jul. 2024).

incorporates localism within each of the diversity elements, whilst the indicators were simplified and reduced in number.[698] The Government accepted the ACMA's advice and has provided funding to the ACMA to develop, or take carriage of, the key datasets and to establish a regular reporting series.[699] From the Government's perspective, the Framework aligns with its News Media Assistance Program which is designed to provide an evidence base to inform policy and reform in relation to news, public interest journalism, and media diversity.[700]

§2. Monomedia Ownership Restrictions

323. The only remaining monomedia restriction in operation are the rules limiting control of the media. These rules apply only to commercial television and radio services. Under the limitation on control rules, a person must not be in a position to exercise control of:

- More than one commercial television broadcasting licence in the same licence area.[701]
- More than two commercial radio broadcasting licences in the same licence area.[702]

Similar restrictions apply to the holding of directorships.[703] A rule which limited control according to the size of audience reach was repealed as part of the 2017 reform. However, a new provision requiring local content from regional commercial television licensees if they fall under the control of a network that covers more than 75% of Australia's population was introduced (*see* Part III, Chapter 3, section 2, IV *supra*.[704]

324. Determining whether the rules apply to a certain situation will depend upon the application of the phrase 'in a position to exercise control'. This phrase governs all the ownership and control rules, including the cross-media framework, and hence will apply to newspapers as well as broadcasting licensees. The concept of

698. Australian Communications and Media Authority, *A new framework for measuring media diversity in Australia: Advice to government on the outcomes of public consultation and implementation* (August 2023, published December 2023), https://www.acma.gov.au/sites/default/files/2023-12/A%20new%20framework%20for%20measuring%20media%20diversity%20in%20Australia.pdf (accessed 16 Jul. 2024).
699. The Hon. Michelle Rowland MP, Minister for Communications, *Mapping a new approach for media diversity in the digital era* (media release) (12 Dec. 2023), https://minister.infrastructure.gov.au/rowland/media-release/mapping-new-approach-media-diversity-digital-era (accessed 16 Jul. 2024).
700. *See* Department of Infrastructure, Transport, Regional Development, Communications and the Arts, *News Media Assistance Program: Consultation Paper* (December 2023), https://www.infrastructure.gov.au/department/media/publications/consultation-paper-news-media-assistance-program-december-2023 (accessed 16 Jul. 2023).
701. Broadcasting Services Act 1992 (Cth), s. 53.
702. Broadcasting Services Act 1992 (Cth), s. 54.
703. Broadcasting Services Act 1992 (Cth), s. 55 (television) & s. 56 (radio).
704. Broadcasting Services Act 1992 (Cth), Pt 5, Div. 5D.

'control' is broad with the intention to cover de facto control and to avoid potential statutory loopholes. Control is defined to include a control that arises by reason of 'trusts, agreements, arrangements, understandings and practices, whether or not having legal or equitable force and whether or not based on legal or equitable rights'.[705] Essential to the determination of whether a person is in a position to exercise control is Schedule 1 to the BSA.[706] Schedule 1 is in the form of a legislative essay. It covers the factors that may be relevant to a determination of control, sets out rules for deciding who is in a position to exercise control, and describes a method for tracing company interests. A person who has company interests that exceed 15% will be deemed to be a person who is in a position to exercise control of the company.[707]

325. However, company interests are not the only way in which control may arise and Schedule 1 illustrates other means. Thus, for example, a person may be in a position to exercise control, because the person:

- Can control the selection or provision of a significant proportion of programmes broadcast by the licensee or of the material to be published in a newspaper.
- Can control a significant proportion of the operations of the company.
- Can appoint or secure the appointment or veto the appointment of at least half of the board of directors.
- Can exercise direction over any substantial issue affecting the management or affairs of the licensee or company.[708]

§3. Cross-Media Ownership Restrictions

326. The cross-media rules, now referred to as media diversity rules, apply to ownership and control situations across commercial radio, television, and associated newspapers. Newspapers covered by the media diversity rules are those newspapers that are published in English, at least four days per week, and, at least 50% of the circulation is by means of sale.[709] A newspaper will be an associated newspaper if at least 50% of its circulation occurs within the licence area of a commercial television broadcasting licence.[710] The same basis for association applies to radio if it reaches at least 2% of the licence area's population.[711]

705. Broadcasting Services Act 1992 (Cth), s. 6.
706. Broadcasting Services Act 1992 (Cth), s. 7.
707. Broadcasting Services Act 1992 (Cth), Sch. 1, cl. 6. The 15% company interests can be determined by tracing interests through a chain of companies: Broadcasting Services Act 1992 (Cth), Sch. 1, cl. 7. Interests can also be determined through a tracing formula: Broadcasting Services Act 1992 (Cth), Sch. 1, cl. 8.
708. Broadcasting Services Act 1992 (Cth), Sch. 1, cls 2 & 3.
709. Broadcasting Services Act 1992 (Cth), s. 6.
710. Broadcasting Services Act 1992 (Cth), s. 59(3).
711. Broadcasting Services Act 1992 (Cth), s. 59(4A).

327. The media diversity rules prohibit transactions that will constitute an 'unacceptable media diversity situation'. An unacceptable media diversity situation is determined using a points system, whereby points are allocated according to the number of independent and separately controlled media operations and groups present within the relevant licence area.[712] An independently controlled media operation will count as one point as will a media group that controls two or more media operations. An unacceptable media diversity situation exists if, in the case of:

- A metropolitan licence area, the number of points in the licence area, is less than five.
- A regional licence area, the number of points in the licence area, is less than four.[713]

328. This element of the media diversity rules is usually referred to as 'the 4/5 rule'. The 4/5 rule does not distinguish between the influence and audience of services available within a licence area. However, the rules use the radio licence area for the determination of points as a radio licence area is more likely to reflect the influence of radio services and newspapers in a community, whereas a television licence area will usually cover a larger geographical area. The media diversity rules are not intended to capture other media operations such as online platforms.

§4. Foreign Investment

329. Until the media reforms in 2006, the BSA included restrictions on the foreign ownership of commercial television broadcasting services and STB services. Following the repeal of those controls, the Federal Government's Foreign Investment Policy now governs foreign investment in media.[714] Australian Government policy encourages foreign investment, and the general approach is to review foreign investment on a case-by-case basis, where they come within the terms of the policy. Media businesses are considered one of the sensitive sectors, and as such foreign investment proposals will require approval. Australian media business means publishing daily newspapers, broadcasting television or radio (including websites on which the newspapers or broadcasts may be accessed), or operating an electronic service (designed to capture traditional media businesses as well as businesses that exclusively publish or broadcast online) that meets the threshold and content

712. Broadcasting Services Act 1992 (Cth), s. 61AC. A media operation is a commercial television broadcasting licence, a commercial radio broadcasting licence, or an associated newspaper. A media group is a group of two or more media operations: Broadcasting Services Act 1992 (Cth), ss 61AA.
713. Broadcasting Services Act 1992 (Cth), s. 61AB.
714. The Treasury, *Australia's Foreign Investment Policy* (May 2024), https://foreigninvestment.gov.au/sites/foreigninvestment.gov.au/files/2024-04/australias-foreign-investment-policy.pdf (accessed 14 Jul. 2024).

tests.[715] The content test for an electronic service is focused on news and content that is concerned with issues or events engaging Australians in public debate. As a sensitive sector, all direct investment in the media sector requires prior approval, regardless of the value of the investment. In reviewing foreign ownership proposals, the transaction will be considered on the basis of whether it would be contrary to the national interest. In determining the national interest, the Government will take into account factors such as national security; competition; other government policies, such as tax; the impact of the investment on the economy and community; and, the character of the investor.[716] As part of the media ownership and control reforms, a new requirement was introduced, requiring foreign persons with media interests to disclose details of their interests.[717] The public electronic register is maintained by the ACMA. Disclosure is required for company interests (defined by the BSA) of 2.5% or more.

§5. Competition and Mergers

330. In addition to the specific ownership and control regime provided by the BSA, the CCA also has a role to play in media mergers and general competition regulation. Section 77 of the BSA makes clear that the ownership and control regime applies notwithstanding the CCA. Equally, it has been held that the ownership and control regime is not an exclusive regime.[718] As such a transaction must satisfy both the BSA ownership and control rules and the CCA competition and merger provisions and may fail because of one or other of the regimes. The competition aspects of the CCA deal with mergers and anti-competitive conduct and the ACCC is responsible for the administration of the CCA regime.

331. Pursuant to section 50 of the CCA, an acquisition of shares or assets that would have, or is likely to have, the effect of substantially lessening competition in the market is prohibited. Prior approval for a merger is not required, although approval can be obtained prior to the merger taking place, and seeking it would be sensible, to ensure that the transaction does not breach the merger rules. Approval can be given through two processes: informal merger review; or, authorization. Enforceable undertakings that address concerns about the merger may be offered as a condition of achieving clearance or authorization for a merger.[719] If clearance is not sought, the ACCC can apply to the Federal Court for an injunction to prevent a

715. The Treasury, Guidance Note: 7, Business Investments (January 2024) https://foreigninvestment.gov.au/sites/foreigninvestment.gov.au/files/2023-12/guidance-note-7-business-investments-january-2024.pdf (accessed 14 Jul. 2024).
716. The Treasury, *Australia's Foreign Investment Policy* (May 2024), https://foreigninvestment.gov.au/sites/foreigninvestment.gov.au/files/2024-04/australias-foreign-investment-policy.pdf (accessed 14 Jul. 2024).
717. Broadcasting Services Act 1992 (Cth), Pt 5, Div. 10A.
718. *Austereo Ltd v. Trade Practices Commission* (1993) 41 FCR 1 (FCA).
719. Competition and Consumer Act 2010 (Cth), s. 87B.

merger proceeding. If the merger has taken place, the ACCC can apply to the Federal Court for orders for financial penalties or divestiture.[720]

332. Unlike the media ownership and control regime that is concerned with public interest objectives such as diversity of opinion, the section 50 merger provisions are concerned with the impact of a merger on economic competition within a market. However, the ACCC will consider non-price matters such as a reduction in quality, for example, in the range of content.[721] A market is defined to mean a market for goods or services in Australia, a state, territory, or region of Australia.[722] The market identified for the purposes of applying the merger provisions may not be the same as what might be seen as the relevant market for the diversity of ideas. In defining a market to examine a merger transaction under the CCA, the ACCC will consider the product, geographic and functional markets, and will determine the boundaries of the market by testing for substitution. The ACCC's *Media Merger Guidelines* outlines the complexity of media markets in the current environment: 'Media refers to the means of mass communication, and the term can be used to cover the message (which may be content or advertising), the medium (mode of delivery), or the messenger (media outlet). Media outlets typically generate revenue from advertising and/or subscription fees, although the concept of what constitutes a media business is likely to evolve over time.'[723] In testing for substitution, the ACCC may also consider modes of delivery of content, and this may bring into consideration media platforms beyond the traditional forms of media. The ACCC acknowledges that convergence means that some media services may now be closer substitutes despite different platforms.[724]

333. The general provisions of the CCA dealing with anti-competitive conduct such as misuse of market power, anti-competitive agreements, and, exclusive dealing will apply to the media, like any other industry.[725] As well as the Part IV general provisions, there is a specific anti-competitive conduct regime under the CCA, administered by the ACCC, applying to networks and service providers.[726] There is also a specific regime for access to networks and service providers (*see* Part III, Chapter 7 *supra*).

334. The Digital Platforms Inquiry recommended that certain designated digital platforms should be required to develop codes of conduct to govern the relationships between the platforms and media businesses. The likely platforms for designation

720. Competition and Consumer Act 2010 (Cth), ss 76, 80 & 81.
721. Australian Competition and Consumer Commission, *Media Merger Guidelines,* 2017, https://www.accc.gov.au/about-us/publications/media-merger-guidelines-2017 (accessed 15 Jul. 2024), para. 43, and, *see generally* paras 36–43.
722. Competition and Consumer Act 2010 (Cth), s. 50(6).
723. Australian Competition and Consumer Commission, *Media Merger Guidelines,* 2017, https://www.accc.gov.au/about-us/publications/media-merger-guidelines-2017 (accessed 15 Jul. 2024), para. 12, and, *see generally* paras 11–19.
724. *Ibid.*, paras 16–17.
725. *See* Competition and Consumer Act 2010 (Cth), Pt IV.
726. Competition and Consumer Act 2010 (Cth), Pt XIB.

were Google and Meta. The ACCC recognized that both digital platforms and media businesses benefited when platforms carried news, whether via links, extracts, or reproduction, from media businesses. However, the Commission concluded that there was an imbalance in bargaining power because the media businesses were unable to negotiate individually terms for the use of their content.[727] The recommendation led to the enactment of the Treasury Laws Amendment (News Media and Digital Platforms Mandatory Bargaining Code) Act 2021 which provides for a mandatory code of conduct (developed by the ACCC, and informally referred to as the news media bargaining code) governing commercial relationships between news media businesses and 'designated' digital platforms. The code will apply to a platform which has been designated by the Treasurer. The legislation inserts a new Part IVBA into the CCA. Under Part IVBA, a platform may be designated if the Treasurer is satisfied that there is a significant bargaining power imbalance, and the platform has made a significant contribution to the sustainability of the Australian news industry (through agreements to remunerate those businesses for their news content).[728]

335. To date, no platforms have been designated. However, the fact of the code and the potential for designation appears to have had the intended effect as both Google and Meta reached voluntary agreements with more than thirty news media businesses. It has been estimated that more than AUD 200,000,000 has flowed to news media businesses because of the voluntary agreements.[729] There was also some evidence that the funds had contributed to creating more journalist positions.[730] However, the future impact of the code now seems doubtful. In early 2024, Meta announced that it would not be renewing its agreements, having decided to withdraw its Facebook news tab. It argued that flow to the tab was negligible and did not justify the agreements it had made.[731] Although the Government could designate Meta under Part IVBA, if it satisfies the tests under section 58E, it has given no indication that this is under consideration. The withdrawal of Meta seems to have had a significant impact with redundancies announced across the major commercial media companies.[732]

727. Australian Competition and Consumer Commission, *Digital Platforms Inquiry: Final Report* (June 2019), Ch. 5.
728. Competition and Consumer Act 2010 (Cth), s. 52E.
729. *See* The Treasury, *News Media and Digital Platforms Mandatory Bargaining Code: The Code's first year of operation* (November 2022), https://treasury.gov.au/sites/default/files/2022-11/p2022-343549.pdf (accessed 16 Jul. 2024), 8, n. 24.
730. *Ibid.*, 8–9.
731. Centre for Media Transition, *Meta – going, going ... .gone* (15 Mar. 2024), https://www.uts.edu.au/research/centre-media-transition/news/meta-going-going-...gone (accessed 16 Jul. 2024). It has been suggested that one reason for the reduced flow was because Meta didn't make its news tab visible on its menu page or app.
732. Australian Broadcasting Corporation, *Nine Entertainment's job cuts are the latest in a line of commercial media outlets feeling the economic chill* (28 Jun. 2024), https://www.abc.net.au/news/2024-06-28/nine-entertainment-job-cuts-commercial-media-slowing-economy/104036502 (accessed 28 Jul. 2024).

Part V. Supervision: Media Regulator

Chapter 1. Organization

§1. Australian Communications and Media Authority

336. The ACMA is the regulatory authority for the broadcasting sector. It also has some regulatory responsibility for the ABC and the Special Broadcasting Service (SBS). The ACMA was formed in 2005, the product of two former regulatory authorities, the Australian Broadcasting Authority and the Australian Communications Authority.[733] The former had responsibility for the regulation of the broadcasting sector, and the latter, for telecommunications and radiocommunications. As a result of the merger, the ACMA has regulatory responsibility for broadcasting, telecommunications, radiocommunications, and the Internet. The impetus for the merger was the convergence of media and the increasing difficulty of coherent regulation, for example, as audiovisual content became available on other digital platforms such as mobile telephones, where there were two regulatory authorities.[734] However, the establishment of the ACMA was not accompanied by any substantive change in the regulatory frameworks for broadcasting, telecommunications, and radiocommunications, a situation that has largely continued. The ACMA is primarily funded through parliamentary appropriations.

337. The Authority is comprised of a full-time Chair and a full-time Deputy Chair, and not more than seven members.[735] A member of the Authority may be a full-time or part-time member.[736] A member is appointed to the office for not more than five years. A member may be appointed more than once but not serve more than a total of ten years.[737] A commissioner of the ACCC is an associate member of the Authority, and the Chair of the ACMA is an associate member of the ACCC.[738] This is to ensure that there is input from both relevant authorities on competition issues

733. The ACMA was established under the Australian Communications and Media Authority Act 2005 (Cth).
734. Explanatory Memorandum, Australian Communications and Media Authority Bill 2004 (Cth).
735. Australian Communications and Media Authority Act 2005 (Cth), s. 19.
736. Australian Communications and Media Authority Act 2005 (Cth), s. 20.
737. Australian Communications and Media Authority Act 2005 (Cth), s. 21.
738. The Australian Communications and Media Authority Act 2005 (Cth) empowers the Minister to appoint an associate member to the ACMA for specific purposes: s. 24. *See also* Competition and Consumer Act 2010 (Cth), s. 8A.

(*see* Part IV *supra*). The Authority also works through a number of committees. These committees include in their membership representatives from industry, government, the community, and academia.

338. The Deputy Chair of the ACMA is also the Chief Executive Officer and the full-time members are supported by five general managers and eleven executive managers. The ACMA employs around five hundred staff. The general managers are responsible for the following areas: communications infrastructure; content; consumer; corporate and research; and, legal services. The ACMA also provides support to the eSafety Commissioner, established in 2015 and responsible for the online content scheme (*see* Part III, Chapter 3, section 8 *infra*).[739]

§2. Other Regulation

339. The two public broadcasters, the ABC and the SBS, manage complaints about their editorial policies internally, although the ACMA has the power to investigate complaints if the public broadcasters fail to deal with the complaints adequately (*see* Chapter 3 *infra*).[740]

739. More information about the structure of the ACMA can be found at www.acma.gov.au.
740. Broadcasting Services Act 1992 (Cth), s. 150.

Chapter 2. Tasks

§1. Australian Communications and Media Authority

340. The Australian Communications and Media Authority Act 2005 (Cth) sets out in detail the statutory functions of the ACMA. The three main statutory functions are in relation to telecommunications (section 8), spectrum management (section 9), and broadcasting, content, and datacasting (section 10).

341. In relation to the telecommunications and spectrum management functions, the statutory responsibilities are expressed in similar terms and include:

- In the case of telecommunications, to regulate telecommunications in accordance with the Telecommunications Act 1997 and the Telecommunications (Consumer Protection and Service Standards) Act 1999.
- In the case of radiocommunications, to manage the radiofrequency spectrum in accordance with the Radiocommunications Act 1992.
- To advise and assist the relevant industry.
- To report to and advise the Minister in relation to the relevant industry.
- In the case of telecommunications, to report to and advise the Minister in relation to matters affecting consumers, or proposed consumers, of carriage services.
- In the case of telecommunications, to monitor, and report to the Minister on, all significant matters relating to the licensing of carriers under the Telecommunications Act 1997.
- To manage Australia's input into the setting of international standards for the relevant industry.
- To make available to the public information, to conduct public educational programmes, and to give advice to the public about matters relating to the relevant industry.[741]

342. In relation to the broadcasting, content, and datacasting functions, the statutory responsibilities include:

- To regulate broadcasting services and datacasting services in accordance with the BSA 1992.
- To plan the availability of segments of the broadcasting services bands on an area basis.
- To allocate, renew, suspend and cancel licences and to take other enforcement action under the BSA 1992.
- To conduct investigations or hearings relating to the allocating of licences for community radio and community television services.
- To conduct investigations as directed by the Minister under the BSA 1992.
- To design and administer price-based systems for the allocation of commercial television broadcasting licences and CRB licences.

741. Australian Communications and Media Authority Act 2005 (Cth), ss 8–9.

- To collect any fees payable in respect of licences.
- To conduct or commission research into community attitudes on issues relating to programmes and datacasting content.
- To assist broadcasting service providers and datacasting service providers in developing codes of practice that, as far as possible, are in accordance with community standards, and to monitor compliance with those codes of practice.
- To develop programme standards relating to broadcasting in Australia, and to monitor compliance with those standards.
- To monitor and investigate complaints concerning broadcasting services (including national broadcasting services) and datacasting services.
- To inform itself and advise the Minister on technological advances and service trends in the broadcasting industry, internet industry and datacasting industry.[742]

343. In undertaking its statutory functions in relation to broadcasting, the ACMA must also be mindful of the regulatory policy of the BSA.[743] Section 4 of the BSA sets out the regulatory policy:

(1) The Parliament intends that different levels of regulatory control be applied across the range of broadcasting services, datacasting services and online content services according to the degree of influence that different types of broadcasting services, datacasting services and online content services are able to exert in shaping community views in Australia.

(2) The Parliament also intends that broadcasting services and datacasting services in Australia be regulated in a manner that, in the opinion of the ACMA:
   (a) enables public interest considerations to be addressed in a way that does not impose unnecessary financial and administrative burdens on providers of broadcasting services and datacasting services;
   (b) will readily accommodate technological change; and
   (c) encourages:
   - the development of broadcasting technologies and datacasting technologies, and their application; and
   - the provision of services made practicable by those technologies to the Australian community.

344. In light of this regulatory policy, the ACMA is charged with exercising its functions and powers, using them in a manner that will:

(1) … .
   - produce regulatory arrangements that are stable and predictable; and
   - deal effectively with breaches of the rules established by [… the BSA].

742. Australian Communications and Media Authority Act 2005 (Cth), s. 10.

743. The Telecommunications Act 1997 (Cth) also includes a statement of regulatory policy which requires the use of self-regulation where possible and regulation to be carried out in a way that does not unduly burden industry, provided the objectives of the legislation are not compromised: s. 4.

(2) Where it is necessary for the ACMA to use any of the powers conferred on it by [.... the BSA] ..., the Parliament intends that the ACMA use its powers .... In a manner .... commensurate with the seriousness of the breach concerned.[744]

345. Pursuant to the BSA,[745] the ACMA has a range of statutory powers that may be called in aid of its enforcement powers, and its statutory powers more generally. It can gather information to inform itself on any matter relevant to its statutory functions, although the process it undertakes must be the quickest and most economical in the circumstances and one that will promote the due administration of the BSA.[746] The ACMA may also conduct investigations for the purpose of exercising its functions, including for the purpose of gathering information.[747] It may also be directed by the Minister to conduct an investigation.[748] Investigations can include involvement by the public through written submissions, and persons can be called to provide documents or answer questions.[749] The ACMA also has the power to hold hearings in the exercise of its statutory functions, or the Minister may direct it.[750] Hearings are to be conducted quickly and economically, and with a minimum of technicality and formality, provided that the requirements of the BSA and the proper consideration of matters before the hearing are not compromised.[751] Hearings will usually be in public.[752]

346. Despite the presence of the investigation and hearings powers, the co-regulatory scheme that operates for broadcasting tends to mean that the ACMA does not generally initiate these powers in relation to its enforcement role. In general, the ACMA does not undertake compliance monitoring but relies on receiving complaints.

§2. Other Regulation

347. The functions of the ABC and the SBS are set out in their respective statutes and statutory charters. *See* Part III, Chapter 1 *supra* for information about the structure and tasks of the public broadcasters.

744. Broadcasting Services Act 1992 (Cth), s. 5.
745. The remainder of Part V will deal with broadcasting and the Broadcasting Services Act 1992 (Cth) only. Enforcement of the online content regime is considered in Pt III, Ch. 3, §8 *supra.*
746. Broadcasting Services Act 1992 (Cth), s. 168.
747. Broadcasting Services Act 1992 (Cth), s. 168(1)(b) & s. 170. It can also hold hearings for the purpose of gathering information: s. 168(1)(b). Pt 13, Div. 2 sets out more detailed provisions regarding the conduct of investigations.
748. Broadcasting Services Act 1992 (Cth), s. 171.
749. Broadcasting Services Act 1992 (Cth), ss 172–173.
750. Broadcasting Services Act 1992 (Cth), ss 182–183. Pt 13, Div. 3 sets out more detailed provisions regarding the conduct of hearings.
751. Broadcasting Services Act 1992 (Cth), s. 186.
752. Broadcasting Services Act 1992 (Cth), s. 187.

Chapter 3. Sanctioning Powers

§1. Australian Communications and Media Authority

348. Sanctions available will depend upon whether a breach of a licence condition, a standard or an industry code of practice rule has occurred. Prior to 2006, the enforcement powers available to the ACMA were limited. Some breaches could only result in criminal sanctions, or suspension or cancellation of a licence, which limited the scope for the ACMA to act because such sanctions might have been overly punitive in the circumstances. Further, there was the difficulty of discharging the criminal standard of proof for criminal proceedings. The ACMA was also limited in relation to industry codes of practice and had no direct enforcement powers where breaches had been found.[753] As a result of these concerns, a range of enforcement powers was conferred on the ACMA:

- Civil penalty provisions
- Injunctions
- Enforceable undertakings
- Infringement notices.[754]

349. The ACMA also has the power to impose a sanction if a broadcasting service is operating without a licence. The services affected by this are: commercial radio and television broadcasting services; STB services; and, community radio and television broadcasting services. Providing service without a licence can be a criminal offence or subject to a civil penalty.[755] For criminal prosecutions, the ACMA must refer the matter to the Commonwealth Director of Public Prosecutions. The ACMA can initiate civil penalty proceedings in the Federal Court. Civil penalty liability is determined on the matter having been proved on the balance of probabilities, rather than on the criminal standard of 'beyond reasonable doubt'. The ACMA also has the power to impose remedial directions on a person who is in breach of the provisions requiring a broadcasting service to be licensed. A remedial direction directs the person to take action to ensure that the person does not breach the provisions.[756] Breach of a remedial direction can constitute a criminal or civil penalty breach.[757] The ACMA may also seek an injunction in relation to the provision of unlicensed services.[758]

---

753. Explanatory Memorandum, Communications Legislation Amendment (Enforcement Powers) Bill 2006 (Cth).
754. Communications Legislation Amendment (Enforcement Powers) Act 2006 (Cth). *See also* Broadcasting Services Act 1992: Enforcement Guidelines of the ACMA (2011).
755. Broadcasting Services Act 1992 (Cth), Pt 10, Div. 1 & Div. 1A. Penalties are imposed according to penalty units. Thus offering a commercial television service without a licence is subject to a maximum criminal penalty of 20,000 penalty units. A penalty unit is currently set at AUD 275: Crimes Act 1914 (Cth), s. 4AA(1). The penalty for a civil penalty breach will be within the discretion of the court but must not exceed the criminal penalty: s. 205F(4).
756. Broadcasting Services Act 1992 (Cth), s. 137. The remedial direction is directed at breach of the civil penalty provisions prohibiting the operation of a service without a licence.
757. Broadcasting Services Act 1992 (Cth), ss 138–138A.
758. Broadcasting Services Act 1992 (Cth), s. 205Q.

350. The sanctions open to the ACMA in relation to licence conditions will depend upon the type of licence condition. A set of licence conditions is imposed upon licensees under Schedule 2 of the BSA (*see* Part III, Chapter 2, section 2, VIII and Chapter 3 *supra*). Compliance with programme standards imposed under Part 9 of the BSA is a Schedule 2 licence condition. Breach of these licence conditions is a criminal offence and civil penalty contravention.[759] The ACMA may also impose licence conditions on licensees, for example, to comply with an industry code of practice.[760] Breach of these and other licence conditions in the BSA are not criminal or civil penalty breaches. However, the ACMA may give remedial directions for action to be taken to ensure that the condition is not breached or will not be breached in the future.[761] Remedial directions might require the licensee to implement effective systems for monitoring compliance and ensuring that the licensee's employees and contractors understand the licence condition obligations.[762] Breach of a licence condition or remedial direction can lead to suspension, for up to three months, or cancellation of a licence.[763]

351. Where it is believed that the provision of a broadcasting service may have resulted in an offence or civil penalty contravention under the BSA or a breach of a licence condition, a person may complain to the ACMA.[764] The ACMA may investigate the complaint if it considers it desirable to do so.[765]

352. The process is different for industry codes of practice because these form part of the co-regulatory scheme. If a person makes a complaint to the ACMA in relation to a breach of a code of practice, the ACMA will not investigate the complaint unless the person has first made the complaint to the relevant broadcasting service provider. The ACMA will investigate a complaint if the person has made the complaint in compliance with the relevant industry code of practice, and has not received a response within sixty days after making the complaint or the person has received a response that s/he considers inadequate.[766] Under the co-regulatory scheme, the industry codes of practice do not provide for any sanctions where the broadcasting service provider finds a code breach. If the matter is investigated by the ACMA, its options for enforcement are relatively limited. It can impose a

759. Broadcasting Services Act 1992 (Cth), ss 139 & 140A. These provisions will also apply to the obligations imposed upon subscription television broadcasting services in relation to expenditure on Australian drama: s. 139(2)(c).
760. Broadcasting Services Act 1992 (Cth), ss 4–44 (commercial broadcasting services), ss 87–88 (community broadcasting services), ss 99–100 (subscription television broadcasting services), ss 118–119 (class licences).
761. Broadcasting Services Act 1992 (Cth), s. 141(1) (in relation to individual licences) and s. 141(4) (in relation to class licences).
762. Broadcasting Services Act 1992 (Cth), s. 141(2) & s. 141(4).
763. Broadcasting Services Act 1992 (Cth), s. 143. In relation to a class licence, the ACMA may apply to the Federal Court for an order that a person cease to provide the service covered by the class licence where it considers that service is being provided otherwise than in accordance with the relevant class licence: s. 144.
764. Broadcasting Services Act 1992 (Cth), s. 147.
765. Broadcasting Services Act 1992 (Cth), s. 149.
766. Broadcasting Services Act 1992 (Cth), s. 148. If a complaint is made in accordance with s. 148, then the ACMA may investigate the complaint in accordance with s. 149.

licence condition requiring the licensee to comply with a code of practice.[767] Further, a breach will then constitute a breach of licence condition. If the ACMA believes that the relevant broadcasting service sector is not operating its code of practice in a manner that provides appropriate community safeguards, it may determine that a standard should apply in relation to that aspect of the code.[768] Following the 'Cash for Comment' investigation, the predecessor of the ACMA imposed three standards on the commercial radio industry. Compliance with standards is a condition of a broadcasting service licence.

353. The ACMA can accept enforceable undertakings to secure compliance with the BSA or industry codes of practice.[769] A person giving an undertaking will agree to take action to ensure compliance with the Act or a code of practice or to avoid action that would contravene the Act or an industry code of practice. If the ACMA considers that an undertaking has been breached, it can apply to the Federal Court for an order directing the person to comply with the undertaking. The court has a wide discretion as to the orders it can make but, specifically, it can also order that the person in breach accounts to the ACMA for the financial benefit it has received directly or indirectly as a result of the breach or compensates anyone who has incurred loss or damage as a result of the breach.[770]

§2. Other Regulation

354. Complaints that the ABC or SBS have breached their codes of practice must first be directed to the broadcasters. Complaints are managed internally. The ABC Ombudsman deals with content complaints within the ABC.[771] Where a complaint is upheld, an acknowledgement of the error is made and published. A range of actions is taken, including corrections and remedial action.

355. The Office of the SBS Ombudsman deals with complaints about breaches of the SBS Code of Practice. If a breach is upheld, the SBS has discretion as to the action it may take including:

– acknowledging that a breach has occurred;
– apologizing for the breach;
– issuing a correction, retraction, or apology; or
– publishing the correct information.[772]

767. Broadcasting Services Act 1992 (Cth), ss 43–44 (commercial broadcasting services), ss 87–88 (community broadcasting services), ss 99–100 (subscription television broadcasting services), ss 118–119 (class licences).
768. Broadcasting Services Act 1992 (Cth), s. 125.
769. Broadcasting Services Act 1992 (Cth), s. 205W.
770. Broadcasting Services Act 1992 (Cth), s. 205X.
771. Australian Broadcasting Corporation, *Complaints Handling Process* (May 2023) https://about.abc.net.au/wp-content/uploads/2023/05/Complaints-Handling-Process-external-08052023.pdf.
772. Special Broadcasting Service, Codes of Practice (July 2021, amended April 2022), code 6.2.3.

356. A person may complain to the ACMA about a breach of a code of practice by one of the public broadcasters if the person has received no response sixty days after making the complaint or considers that the response received is inadequate.[773] As with private broadcasting, the ACMA may investigate the complaint if it considers it desirable to do so.[774] If after investigation the ACMA considers that there has been a breach by the ABC or the SBS of their codes of practice and that it should take action '... to encourage the ABC or the SBS to comply with the relevant code of practice', then it may by notice recommend that the relevant public broadcaster complies with the relevant code of practice and, if appropriate, publish an apology or retraction.[775] The ACMA has the power to give a report to the Minister if it considers that the relevant broadcaster has not taken action (within thirty days of the recommendation under section 152) that the ACMA considers appropriate.[776]

773. Broadcasting Services Act 1992 (Cth), s. 150.
774. Broadcasting Services Act 1992 (Cth), s. 151.
775. Broadcasting Services Act 1992 (Cth), s. 152.
776. Broadcasting Services Act 1992 (Cth), s. 153.

Selected Bibliography

Molitorisz, S. *Net Privacy: How We Can Be Free in an Age of Surveillance*. Sydney: NewSouth Publishing, 2020.

Pearson, M. *The Communicator's Guide to Media Law and Ethics*. Abingdon: Routledge, 2024.

Rodrick S., B. Clift, J. Ireland & L. Power. *Australian Media Law*. 6th edn. Sydney: Thomson Lawbook Co, 2021.

Rolph, D. *Rolph on Defamation*. 2nd edn. Pyrmont: Thomson Reuters, 2024.

Rolph, D. *Contempt*. Alexandria: Federation Press, 2023.

Rolph, D., et al. *Media Law: Cases, Materials and Commentary*. 3rd edn. Oxford: Oxford University Press, 2022.

Useful Websites

Australian Classification, https://www.classification.gov.au.

Australian Communications and Media Authority, http://www.acma.gov.au.

Australian Competition and Consumer Commission, https://www.accc.gov.au.

Australian Government, Department of Infrastructure, Transport, Regional Development,

Communications and the Arts, https://www.infrastructure.gov.au.

Australian Press Council, http://www.presscouncil.org

Australasian Legal Information Institute (a comprehensive resource for Commonwealth, state, and territory legislation, and case law), www.austlii.edu.au.

Centre for Media Transition (UTS), https://www.uts.edu.au/research/centre-media-transition

Communications Alliance, https://www.commsalliance.com.au.

Digital Industry Group Inc., https://digi.org.au.

eSafety Commissioner, https://www.esafety.gov.au.

Media, Entertainment and Arts Alliance, https://www.meaa.org.

Office of the Australian Information Commissioner, http://www.oaic.gov.au.

Public Interest Journalism Initiative, https://piji.com.au.

Selected Bibliography

Index

The numbers here refer to paragraph numbers.

Index

www.ingramcontent.com/pod-product-compliance
Lightning Source LLC
Chambersburg PA
CBHW071342230926
51846CB00002B/422
* 9 7 8 9 4 0 3 5 1 4 4 9 9 *